Hand Planes
in the Modern Shop

Kerry Pierce

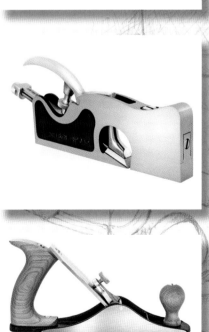

Schiffer Publishing Ltd

4880 Lower Valley Road, Atglen, PA 19310

Schiffer Books are available at special discounts for bulk purchases for sales promotions or premiums. Special editions, including personalized covers, corporate imprints, and excerpts can be created in large quantities for special needs. For more information contact the publisher:

Published by Schiffer Publishing Ltd.
4880 Lower Valley Road
Atglen, PA 19310
Phone: (610) 593-1777; Fax: (610) 593-2002
E-mail: Info@schifferbooks.com

For the largest selection of fine reference books on this and related subjects, please visit our web site at
www.schifferbooks.com
We are always looking for people to write books on new and related subjects. If you have an idea for a book please contact us at the above address.

This book may be purchased from the publisher.
Include $5.00 for shipping.
Please try your bookstore first.
You may write for a free catalog.

In Europe, Schiffer books are distributed by
Bushwood Books
6 Marksbury Ave.
Kew Gardens
Surrey TW9 4JF England
Phone: 44 (0) 20 8392 8585; Fax: 44 (0) 20 8392 9876
E-mail: info@bushwoodbooks.co.uk
Website: www.bushwoodbooks.co.uk

Dedication

Elaine, Emily, and Andy—more good fortune
than I ever could have imagined.

Acknowledgments

Some woodworking books can be written in relative isolation, relying on personal experience and shop photos. Others require the contributions of many individuals, and this book is one of those. I'm deeply grateful to each of the following people:

Lee Richmond of The Best Things, who shared photos of planes he has handled, as well as an example the only Clifton plane I have ever used

Joel Moskowitz of Tools for Working Wood, who shared photos of some of the magnificent planes in his collection

Jim Leamy, who allowed me to use again the story about his work that I originally wrote for *Woodcraft* magazine (and of course, the editors of *Woodcraft*)

Gary Roberts of Toolemera.com, who not only scanned pages from some of the historically important books and paper ephemera in his collection, but also shared his insights in regard to the interpretation of those materials

Charles Murray, who demonstrated the use of his Stanley #51 and #52

Wally Wilson of Lee Valley Tools, who allowed me to use many of the magnificent planes manufactured by his company, as well as providing photos of their entire line of planes for my Illustrated Glossary

Tom Lie-Nielsen of Lie-Nielsen Toolworks, who also shared tools and images of his company's entire line of planes.

Larry Williams of Clark and Williams, for sharing images of his company's wooden planes.

Max Stebelton, who repeatedly gave me access to the tools in his incredible collection.

My brother Kevin, who generously agreed to review the manuscript before I submitted it to the publisher, and who also cleaned up and re-lettered my drawings.

And in particular Pete Schiffer, who took a chance on an idea other publishers saw as too narrowly focused. I'm very grateful.

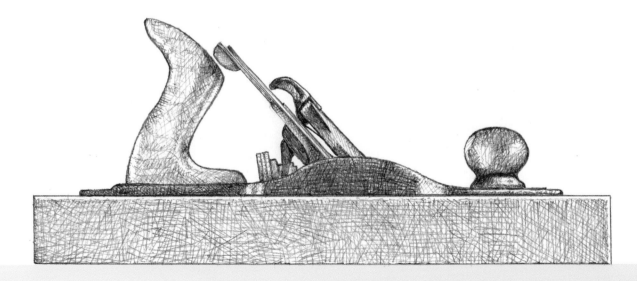

Contents

Introduction
There's No Zealot Like a Reformed Sinner

I'm a fairly recent convert to the doctrine of hand plane use. Six years ago, I was pushed into it by an oncologist who wanted me to reduce my exposure to woodshop dust in order to improve my health after a bout of non-Hodgkins lymphoma.

Prior to that, my collection of hand planes had included a metal smoother and a metal jack, as well as a couple of block planes. Also, tucked into a pile of woodshop miscellanea on the bottom shelf of a storage cabinet, I had a matched pair of tongue-and-groove planes my father-in-law had given me years before, but those were—at least for me—planes only in theory because I'd never managed to take a shaving with either one.

I think I was like a lot of furniture makers who grew up in the 1950s and 1960s. I knew what hand planes were. I owned several, and I used them on a fairly regular basis. But I had come of age at a time when hand plane use was confined to touch-up work. While I might use one to take a bit of width from the edge of a door, I would never use one to surface that door.

There were reasons for this near-sighted perspective. The last-surviving manufacturers of wooden planes had gone out of business long before I was born, and a few years later, Stanley Tools dropped all but the most basic forms from their once richly diverse line of metal planes. As a result, when you surveyed the hand plane stock in a hardware store of the period, all you saw were block planes and smoothers and maybe a jack plane or two. Naturally, then, you thought that represented the whole range of the hand plane universe. But if you moved on to the machine tool department, you discovered a

much larger universe, one including machine jointers and planers, belt sanders of all kinds, and shapers small enough for the home shop—all machines designed to fill holes in a woodworking shop's tool inventory once occupied by hand planes.

With every passing year, American furniture makers of the 20th century moved farther from a comprehensive use of hand planes. When we wanted to surface a glued-up panel, we pulled out power sanders. When we wanted to make a molding, we used a shaper, a molding head on the tablesaw, and later, a machine router. We knew intellectually that earlier generations had performed this work with hand planes, but we saw those tools as the woodshop equivalents of flint-tipped arrows. Surfacing and molding planes were tools for the primitive savages of woodworking's past. In this newer, nobler age, we ground away at our wood only with those cutting edges that could be strapped to an electric motor.

Of course, in the process, we lost our hearing, we drew decades of dust into our lungs, and we confined our molding choices to those miserly few profiles that could be produced with machinery, not realizing that tens of thousands of wider, richer, more appealing profiles were moldering away in abandoned tool collections tucked into barns and garages and basements all around us.

Then, somewhere in the last few decades, I became aware that some furniture makers were once again interested in hand planes. I began to see magazine articles about these tools and ads for companies determined to make high-quality hand planes once again available to American craftsmen. Of course, I didn't pay much attention. I didn't think I needed the illumination of that particular candle. But then a brush with Stage 4 cancer shifted the ground on which I stood.

Reduce my exposure to dust? Well, I could buy a monster dust collection system. I could buy a bigger respirator. I could even get one of those deals that pumped cleansed air into a head-sized hood.

Or—I finally realized—I could simply turn off the machinery.

Part 1: The sounds of silence

I'm not an extremist. I don't mean turn off all the machinery all the time. A tablesaw, a thickness planer, a jointer, and a radial arm saw can allow a craftsman—protected by a dust mask and hearing muffs—to speed through so much of the drudgery of stock preparation. But if you turn off the machinery for just two of a woodshop's most time-consuming operations—creating smooth, blemish-free surfaces and profiling moldings and molded edges—you can significantly improve the quality of your woodshop life without sacrificing efficiency.

Before I discovered the capacities of hand planes, so many of my "woodworking" hours were spent with a belt sander rumbling in my hands. It was monstrously dull work. Plus the sander threw off clouds of dust so dense that sometimes I could hardly see the surface I was working. I had considered a downdraft table and a better air-cleaning system, but my shop is so small I hate to give away space to things that don't actually help me do my work, so I continued my reliance on a small air cleaner and on fans and open windows, even in January in Ohio. But still, when I left the shop after a bout of machine sanding, I looked like someone had cracked a five-pound sack of flour over my head.

Noise is the worst part of machine sanding. That's true if you're using a hand-held belt sander or a stationary belt sander or even an oscillating sander. They're all powered by electric motors that throw off much of the energy they consume in the form of noxious sound. You can pack foam into your ear canals and strap muffs to your head, but machine sanders still find ways to drive their urgent knives of sound deep into your brain.

The noise a router makes is even worse. They don't generate as much dust as machine sanders, and I'm not sure they generate a greater *volume* of sound, but there is something unsettling about the shrill frequencies a router can produce.

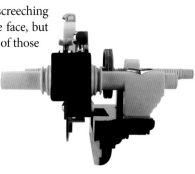

When I was younger, I worked for almost a year in a foundry that made intake and exhaust manifolds, and I worked two more in a factory that machined enormous crankshafts for stationary diesel engines. When you opened the door to either place, a sonic wall of pounding, screeching steel smacked you in the face, but nothing I heard in either of those places could raise the hair on the back of my neck quite like a router winding up to attack a stick of wood.

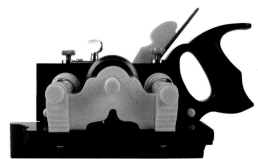

Opposite:
These boys are working in the woodshop of the Henry Street Settlement of New York City in 1910. The tools in the cabinet on the right indicate the importance of hand planes in woodcraft of that era. Nine transitional jack planes are lined up in the left hand side of the cabinet, with five metal smoothers and four block planes on the right. The boy on the right is checking an edge with a square, an edge he'd probably just planed with the jack plane on the bench before him. *Courtesy of the Library of Congress.*

Right:
In the past 20 years, several craftsmen in the United States, Canada, and England have established themselves as some of the finest planemakers in history. This reproduction of an ebony and ivory Sandusky presentation plane was made by one such craftsman, Jim Leamy of the United States, who specializes in meticulous recreations of 19th century plow planes. *Courtesy of* Woodcraft *magazine.*

Part 2: On the other hand

When I imagine an 18th century shop owned by a master craftsman like John Goddard or John Townsend, my mind conjures up a room in which work is accomplished in relative quiet and in the absence of airborne dust. The 18th century workman surfacing a wide panel at one of the benches in that shop had no need of a dust mask, even if one had been available. That's because the material he was removing from the panel was bound up in the shavings curled around his feet instead of drifting, pulverized, through the air of the shop. The ambient noise level was so low he could hear the rhythmic whoosh, woosh, woosh of his plane's passage along the work. He could hear the sound of saw teeth dragging in a kerf at an adjacent bench, as well as the modest clatter produced by an apprentice who dropped a tool on the room's wooden floor, and when the shop door opened, everyone heard and everyone looked up at the sound.

But ten years ago, when I was running a belt sander in my 20th century shop, I couldn't hear the door opening. Sometimes I didn't even hear when one of my kids stood behind me and yelled because I was so deeply buried in the isolation of sander noise, hearing muffs, and respirator.

Obviously, turning off surfacing and molding machinery will make our work environments less hazardous to our health by making those environments cleaner and quieter, but I think there's another, perhaps even more important, reason for choosing hand planes over power tools.

Woodworking is about more than the fabrication of useful goods. Certainly, the end product is important. We like to see our work valued by the people to whom we sell it or the people to whom we give it. We like being able to point to a well crafted piece and say (if only to ourselves): "I built that." But just as important is the shop experience. We desire those hours at our benches when we can demonstrate (if only to ourselves) that we have mastered one of the skills associated with our craft.

When you learn to cut dovetails by hand, that process is intrinsically satisfying in a way that exceeds the value of the dovetailed end product. When you learn to plane with a wood-turning skew, that process is intrinsically satisfying, even if you throw away the spindle on which you first

In the latter part of the 19th century and early 20th century, some European tool makers were producing infill planes of extraordinary quality. A metal shell, often dovetailed together, was stuffed with tropical hardwood, like the rosewood of this Norris smoother. *Joel Moskowitz photo.*

demonstrated the skill. But it doesn't take any skill to plug a router into the wall, to turn it on, or even to run a bit of material past the fence on a router table. Anybody can do that. But if you're going to create that same molding profile with a hand plane, you need to possess the skill to sharpen the iron, to set the iron, and to move the plane along the work in a meaningful way. Skills like these are fundamental to our craft. These are skills which—once mastered—we can acknowledge with pride, but they're not difficult skills to acquire. This book will tell you how. But the skills are real. They aren't just fodder for the ad copy under a catalog photo of some new electric-powered widget, designed primarily to extract money from your wallet.

Most 19th century American planes were made of wood, like this panel raiser from the Shaker community at Pleasant Hill, Kentucky.

Part 3: What machinery sellers don't tell you

If you're going to surface 100 cherry table tops 36" on a side, you don't want to tackle the job with bench planes. What you want is a wide belt sander. That machine might cost $15,000-$20,000, but it's the only efficient way to surface 100 table tops. If you're going to run 20,000 lineal feet of oak crown molding, you don't want to do the job with a molding plane. You need a multiple head molder. This machine will probably cost even more than the wide belt sander, but when you're facing such a daunting project, you need the efficiency of high-powered equipment.

But in my 40 years in the shop, I've never faced either situation or any remotely like either one. When I make tables, I make one, and when I make molding, I make just enough for the piece I currently have under construction. Sometimes that means 10 feet, sometimes a little more, sometimes a little less. And for jobs like these, the efficiency of hand planes is competitive with the efficiencies of machine tools. If you set one table top in front of a machine tool enthusiast equipped with a hand-held belt sander and another table in front of a hand plane enthusiast equipped with three good bench planes, the hand plane enthusiast is quite likely to finish first, and the surface he produces will be superior to the sanded surface because it won't be scratched into flatness by abrasive particles. You would probably see a similar outcome if you put a hand plane enthusiast face to face with a power tool enthusiast in a race to make six feet of molding. That's because it takes time to install a router bit into a table-mounted router, to set the depth of cut, and to set the fence. But the hand plane enthusiast doesn't have to set anything. A molding plane's fence and depth of cut are preset, integrated into the sole of the plane. All he has to do is apply it to the work.

Of course, the people who sell woodworking machinery won't tell you this. They probably don't know because they were raised in a 20th century woodworking culture, which taught that—for the sake of accuracy, efficiency, and the quality of the woodshop end product—the only proper way to work wood is through the use of good-quality power tools.

I believe they're wrong. For a woodworking hobbyist or a woodworking professional making pieces one at a time, I believe the hand plane approach is the most accurate, the most efficient, and the most likely to produce a quality end product. In addition, the hand plane approach allows that end product to be produced in a quieter, cleaner shop, one in which the woodworking craftsman can enjoy the process as well as the finished work.

In the 21st century, some individual planemakers are still producing infills on a par with any made in the 19th century. In addition, there are several companies manufacturing metal planes of a quality I believe has never been equalled by earlier manufacturers. This Veritas low-angle, bevel-up jointer is an example of such a plane.

Lie-Nielsen Toolworks— another contemporary manufacturer of high quality metal planes— offers a line of bench planes, loosely based on, but superior to, the classic Stanley bench planes. This #8 is the largest example in the company's line of bench planes.

Chapter 1
A Brief History of Planemaking

This page from Diderot's 18th century book series *Encyclopedie* shows a group of sashmakers at work in a well lit shop. The only plane visible is the long bench plane disappearing out the right-hand margin. Oddly, there are no sash planes present, although we do see what appears to be a pile of shavings in the lower right corner of the engraving. *Courtesy of Gary Roberts, Toolemera.com*

The earliest known hand plane is one found in the ash at Pompeii where it had been buried by the eruption of Mt. Vesuvius in 79 A.D. Other planes dating to the Roman Empire have been found in other locations, and some of those planes look remarkably similar to planes being used today.

But there are few antique planes that can be dated to the period between the fall of the Roman Empire and the rise of the Renaissance. Plane craft—like other crafts in that dark era—seems to have stagnated because when the record once again reveals the use of hand planes—for example in Renaissance-era illuminated manuscripts—the sophisticated iron-clad planes used by Roman joiners seem to have disappeared, leaving only those planes made entirely of wood.

But the planemaking picture changes in the 17th and 18th centuries. In Joseph Moxon's "Mechanik Exercises or the Doctrine of Handy-Works," published in 1678, and Denis Diderot's "Encyclopedie," published serially during the latter half of the 18th century, we see drawings that indicate a wide variety of planes for jointing, leveling, smoothing, rabbeting, plowing, etc.

We also have actual planes from that rich period in the craft's history, planes which demonstrate an accelerating pace of innovation. In the late 18th century, the first planes fitted with double irons (cutting iron and cap iron) make their appearance. By the end of the 18th century planemakers were once again making metal-clad planes. In addition, there are wooden planes from this period which exhibit extraordinary complexity. For example, a coachmaker's plow built by Christopher Gabriel (1746-1809) could cut grooves that were simultaneously compassed and radiused.

Part 1: Planemaking becomes a profession

The use of a maker's mark is an important sign of professionalism in the planemaking field. Among the earliest marked planes are those made by Jan Ardentz of the Netherlands. In the late-17th century, he began marking his planes with the initials I. A., the "I" being the letter then used for today's "J." This practice quickly crossed the English channel, where, by 1700, the London planemaker Thomas Granford had begun the now-familiar practice of embossing his name on the end-grain of the plane's nose. His apprentice Robert Wooding, who worked in London from 1710-1728, also marked his planes in this way.

During the first centuries of the European settlement of America, most of the hand planes used in the Colonies were either English imports or craftsman made, but as the Colonies matured, American planemakers began offering professionally made tools produced by local craftsmen. The earliest known American maker was Francis Nicholson, who began marking his planes soon after his English predecessors began marking theirs. In 1716, at age 34, Nicholson was living in Rehoboth, Massachusetts, where he was listed as a joiner (carpenter). He moved to Wrentham, Massachusetts, in 1728 where he lived until his death in 1753. Only three of the six known Francis Nicholson marks include a reference to Wrentham, a fact which—along with stylistic details on marked planes—suggests that the other three marks might identify earlier tools, perhaps made as early as his time in Rehoboth.

The Revolutionary War disrupted American life not only during the war itself; but also for years afterwards, leaving the American economy in shambles, with the government buried in debt, American currency inflated almost to worthlessness, and British-controlled markets closed to American merchants. Almost a decade passed before the economy had improved enough to offer widespread support for trades as specialized as planemaking.

During the closing decades of the 18th century and the opening decades of the 19th century, English design books were exerting a powerful influence on American furniture and architecture and on the tools with which they were made. The first of these was Thomas Chippendale's *The Gentleman and Cabinet Maker's Director* which was published in England in 1754, making its appearance on this side of the Atlantic soon

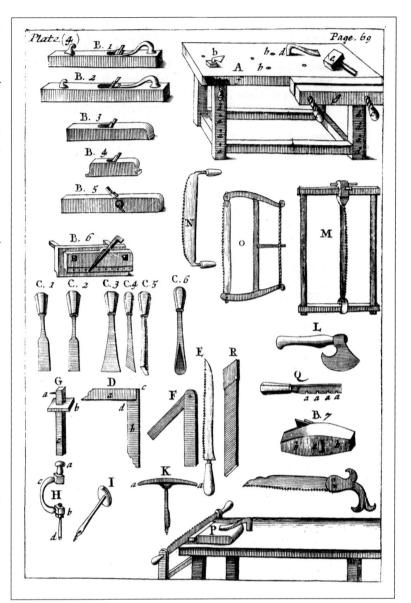

This page from Joseph Moxon's *Mechanik Exercises or the Doctrine of Handy-Works*, published in 1678 shows seven different planes: six in the upper left quadrant and one more in the lower right quadrant. According to the Moxon text, B1 is a Fore plain (sic), B2 a Joynter (sic), B3 a Strike Block, a plane designed for miter and bevel work, B4 a smoothing plane, B5 a rabbet plane, and B6 the plow (not identified as a plane) B7, the lone plane in the lower right quadrant is presented, according to the text, to show what the sole of a plane looks like. *Courtesy of Gary Roberts, Toolemera.com.*

after. Chippendale's book was followed by the design books of Robert Adam, Thomas Sheraton, and George Hepplewhite. Each of these books included furniture and/or architectural designs requiring different and—and in some cases—more elaborate moldings than those which could be cut by planes then on hand in American cabinet shops.

By the beginning of the 19th century, the American population had risen to almost 4 million. Some among that number were people of means who desired architecture and furniture like that seen in the English design books. In post-Revolutionary-War America, the only way that desire could be expressed was through the efforts of woodworking craftsmen equipped with planes profiled to cut these exciting new molding forms. This was an age of opportunity for American planemakers.

Part 2: The Big Picture: Copeland/Chapin/Union

In the 19th century, American planemakers sometimes changed professional alliances with other planemakers at a bewildering rate. For example, the D. & M. Copeland planemaking firm of Hartford, Connecticut, united planemaking brothers Daniel and Melvin Copeland for a period of three years, from 1822 to 1825. Then in 1825, that partnership ended and Melvin went into business with another brother, Alfred, in a firm identified as M. & A. Copeland, also located in Hartford. Meanwhile, in 1826, Melvin's brother Daniel created the firm of Copeland and Chapin with former Copeland apprentice Hermon Chapin near New Hartford, Connecticut.

19th century American craft apprenticeships were most often entered into by teenaged boys; however, when Chapin apprenticed with D. & M. Copeland in 1822, he was already 23 years old, and he already knew one trade, having worked as a sawyer in his family's business. Chapin's relative age and experience makes Daniel Copeland's decision, at age 31, to leave a partnership with his brother to join in one with a mere apprentice, less surprising. Chapin was, in fact, the same age Daniel's brother Melvin had been when D. & M. Copeland was formed.

The Copeland and Chapin partnership, too, was short-lived. In 1828, Chapin bought out Copeland's interest and created the Union Factory, which, in short order, became one of the most important planemaking firms in New England, employing 40 men by the time of the 1850 census.

Many of the men who worked in Chapin's shop had the details of their duties spelled out in a written agreement signed by employee and employer, with one copy of that agreement remaining in the possession of the worker and the other copy remaining in Chapin's possession. Between 1830 and 1865, Chapin's copies of these agreements were kept in a Work Agreement Ledger, which has survived to this day, and sample agreements were published in Kenneth Roberts 1983 book *Wooden Planes in 19th Century America, Vol. II.*

The four-year agreement Chapin signed with Henry D. Bolles in January of 1830 states that Bolles would be paid $230 per year as payment for 312 work days. In addition, Chapin agrees to board Bolles during that term and to provide him with "such articles of goods as he may from time to time be in want of at… low prices." In a three-year agreement with William Winship signed on March 9, 1830, Chapin spells out piece rates for various planes and plane parts. The agreement states that Winship would be paid $1.00 each for screw arm plows, $.08 for boxing a plow fence, and a rate of $.75 per hundred for "grinding plow plates."

The Chapin business continued its periodic reorganizing in the latter half of the 19th century. In 1860, H. Chapin/Union Factory became H. Chapin and Sons, bringing to the business Chapin's sons Edward, George, and Phillip. In 1865, the business became H. Chapin's Sons under the leadership of Edward and George. Then in 1868, George sold out to Edward.

The most important planemaker to work in the Chapin business was Solon Rust who—at age 17 in 1850—went to work for Chapin as a rule maker. He quickly changed jobs in the Chapin business, focusing on planemaking. Then in 1857, he left Chapin to work for another planemaker, Linson Deforest.

Deforest offered 51 types of plow planes, including the #494 ivory plow that came equipped with solid gold nuts and washers for the extraordinary price of $1000. It may have been Rust's familiarity

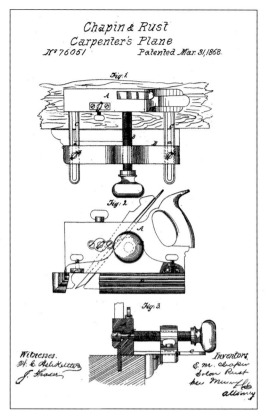

This drawing is part of the patent issued to E.M. Chapin and Solon Rust in 1868 for a self-regulating plow plane. It wasn't the first patent issued for such a plane. In 1834, a patent for a different style of self-regulating plow was issued to Israel White of Philadelphia. In the eyes of Chapin and Rust, their self-regulator was different than any other because, on the right hand side of the plane, its arms never moved beyond the plane's body. *Courtesy of U.S. Patent & Trademark Office*

This letterhead for H. Chapin's Son Company identifies the company's 1826 founding. The notation about this company, in 1897, having succeeded an earlier one indicates that this letterhead was used during the last years of the company's existence. *Courtesy of Gary Roberts, Toolemera.com.*

with the Deforest line of plows that encouraged H. Chapin & Sons to rehire Rust in 1864, with the possible intent of reinvigorating their line of plow planes. At that time, H. Chapin's Sons offered only beech, rosewood, and boxwood plows. In any case, four years later, E. M. Chapin and Solon Rust were jointly issued a patent for a brand new self-regulating plow that could be operated without the necessity of clearing the bench of tools and parts from the right side of the plow because none of the plow arms extended beyond the right side of the plow body.

When Edward Chapin died in 1897, two of his sons—Hermon Mills Chapin and Frank Mills Chapin—reorganized the company yet again as H. Chapin's Son & Co. Four years later, that company united with L. C. Stephens & Co. to become Chapin-Stephens.

The opening decades of the 20th century marked the end of American wooden-plane making on a commercial scale, as buyers expressed preferences for the metal planes being manufactured by Stanley and its many competitors. Chapin-Stephens lasted longer than most, but in 1929, the company's assets were acquired by Stanley which kept the line of rules and dropped the wooden planes.

Part 3: The Little Picture: Planemaking in Small Towns

While Chapin/Union Factory produced tens of thousands of planes, many 19th century craftsmen purchased their surfacing and molding tools from local makers who made only hundreds or perhaps, in some cases, only dozens of planes. The output of John Strode of Fairfield County, Ohio, and his son George Strode, also of Fairfield County, is typical of this small-scale production.

John was born May 30, 1796, in Berkeley County, Virginia (now West Virginia) to Edward and Elizabeth Strode and the family then traveled to Ohio in 1803. There is no documentary evidence regarding John's life between the move to Ohio—when John was just 7—and his 1823 marriage in Fairfield County, Ohio, to Hannah Davis. But the quality and sophistication of many of the planes bearing his name suggest at least a casual planemaking apprenticeship, and this period of his life—age 7-27—would have been the likely time for such an education.

The output of John Strode, a planemaker from Fairfield County, Ohio (1796-1865), was typical of the thousands of men (and occasionally women) working at this trade far from the urban centers in the Northeast. Instead of thousands of planes, it's likely that Strode made only hundreds, but as you see here, those planes represented a wide range of profiles. On the right, you see several simple profiles, and on the left, two handsome complex profiles. *Collection of Max Stebelton.*

John could have learned the trade in Fairfield County. There were cabinetmakers advertising in the Lancaster (Fairfield County) newspaper, *The Ohio Eagle*, in the years leading up to John's 1823 marriage, and any of these craftsmen might have also served as planemakers. Or he could have traveled to a larger city in Ohio. According to the U.S. Bureau of the Census, by 1820, Cincinnati, Ohio—just 100 miles from Fairfield County—had grown to become the 14th largest city in the nation with almost 10,000 residents.

In the 1850 census, John is listed as a planemaker with landholdings valued at $3250, but family tradition says he also worked as a cabinetmaker and a chairmaker. Two pieces of furniture attributed to John exist today in Lancaster, the county seat of Fairfield County: a double rocker in a cabin at the Fairfield County Fairgrounds and a sideboard in the Georgian, a restored 1832 home in Lancaster.

Max Stebelton, a contemporary tool collector in Fairfield County, Ohio, has spent years assembling a group of planes made by the Strode family of planemakers. His collection currently includes 21 specimens, four of which are the work of George, the son (1824-1898). The remaining 17 are the work of the father John Strode (1796-1865).

A large bench plane is probably the least well executed example in Stebelton's

The Strode collection of Max Stebelton includes this pair of crisp—but refinished—table planes.

collection of John Strode planes. The eyes and chamfers, in particular, are crudely formed when compared to the sure-handed execution found of the molding planes bearing his mark. This suggests that the bench plane might be the earliest example of John's work among the planes in Stebelton's collection. In fact, it might even date to the period before he served his apprenticeship. It is a plane on which it's possible to see him striving to emulate the look of planes produced by professional planemakers.

The bodies of nearly all of the planes bearing John Strode's mark are made of beech which was—and still is—common in the forested hills of Appalachian Southern Ohio. This is typical of planemaking practice all across the Eastern United States in the 19th century. Less typical is his use of lignum as a boxing material, in place of the boxwood used almost everywhere else. Turned nuts on John's sash, plank, and plow planes are often what appears to be apple burl or root. In this case, too, boxwood was the preferred material for most planemakers.

Turning seems to have been the weakest element in John's planemaking repertoire. The coves and beads on his screw-arm nuts are less gracefully executed than those on similar planes made elsewhere, showing some uncertainty at the lathe. But his molding planes are as crisply delineated as those produced in the shops of large planemaking firms of the time.

The John Strode molding planes in Stebelton's collection include a typical selection of the time. There is a round, a side bead, as well as several complex molders. In addition, there is a matched pair of table planes in crisp—if refinished—condition.

But the centerpiece of Stebelton's collection is a presentation plow made by John's son, George. The structure of this plow is reminiscent of the three-arm self-regulating plows made by Israel White in Philadelphia and patented by him in 1834. The two outside arms are unthreaded and slide in mortises cut through the body of the plane, while the center arm is threaded in order to move the fence back and forth. All three arms are attached to a bridle mounted on the top of the fence, and while the threaded center arm moves the fence back and forth, the unthreaded outside arms keep that fence properly aligned.

The George Strode plow is a masterpiece of country craftsmanship, rich with appealing detail. On the top front of the plane body there is large inlaid ivory heart surrounded by a larger inlaid ebony heart, as well as a sunburst rosette inlaid on the outside of the bridle centered on the end of the screw-arm. But it is the handling of the three arms on the side of the plane opposite the bridle that makes this example so unusual and so compelling. Each of the three arms tapers toward an ivory finial—not a simple ivory cap like those on presentation planes made by the Sandusky Tool Company or the Ohio Tool Company—but a full-blown finial.

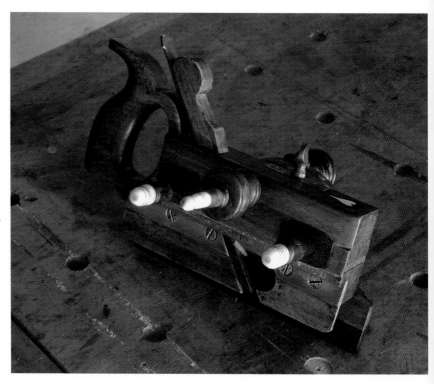

The centerpiece of Stebelton's Strode collection is this magnificent, self-regulating presentation plow, which features an ivory heart, an inlaid sunburst, and three unusually long ivory finials. (A modern Jim Leary reproduction of this plow can be seen on the title page of this book.)

Part 4: The English Infill Plane

The infill form—a metal plane shell stuffed with fitted wood— can be traced as far back as the Roman Empire, but for the purposes of infill connoisseurship, the form's earliest incarnations occurred in Britain in the final years of the 18th century.

Robert Towell, born in 1787, is generally regarded as the first great maker of infill-style planes, but Towell was preceded by at least one other maker of note: Christopher Gabriel, whose work in the field is documented not only in a fair number of signed planes but also in an account book in which he recorded the progress of his toolmaking business between the years 1771 and 1794. But it was neither Towell nor Gabriel who put these planes on the map. That distinction belongs to Stewart Spiers, a craftsman from Ayr, Scotland.

Spiers was born on October 22, 1820, to a family of cabinetmakers, and it is likely that he practiced that trade as a young man. According to family lore, he got his start as a planemaker by accident. He had purchased a rough casting from a local foundry and fashioned from it a plane intended for his own use. He then sold the plane to another cabinetmaker at a handsome profit, and—again, according to family lore—that initial sale was the genesis for the Stewart Spiers firm of planemakers.

The plane in the front is a panel plane built by Robert Towell (1787-???), an early maker of infill planes. The plane in the rear is a much later infill jointer, an A1 made by T. Norris and Sons early in the 20th century. *Joel Moskowitz photo.*

Opposite:
This is the first patent granted Leonard Bailey for a transitional bench plane with a wood body and a metal adjustment mechanism. Despite the widely held perception that these planes occupied a middle period between the eras dominated by wood and then metal planes, metal planes and transitional planes existed concurrently in the final quarter of the 19th century. Courtesy of U.S. Patent & Trademark office

This large panel plane with dovetailed, rosewood-filled shell is typical of the offerings of the Stewart Spiers company.

This Knowles-type cast-iron bench plane, based on the Hazard Knowles 1827 patent, is one of the earliest cast iron planes. Notice that the iron (cutter) of this plane, like the iron in the Towell plane, is secured by a wedge, a method typical of early metal planes, instead of the lever cap found on later metal planes. *Collection of Max Stebelton.*

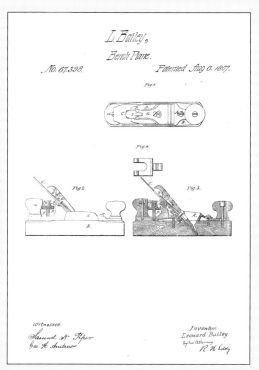

According to tool historian Kenneth Roberts, Spiers began his career in the early 1840s, shortly before the publication of the 1845-46 Ayr Directory which presents the first published reference to his place of business at No. 10 River Street in Ayr, a location at which his shop remained throughout Spiers' life.

Thomas Norris' appearance in the field came along at a later date, although it's difficult to know exactly when. His first appearance in the London Directory as a maker of metal planes occurred in 1873, although the 1914 T. Norris and Son catalog identifies 1860 as the year of the company's founding.

In any case, Norris started after Spiers, and it seems clear that his planes were modeled after those offered by the Scottish planemaker, and by the turn of the century, these two craftsmen had codified the many infill forms contemporary tool collectors have come to prize and contemporary toolmakers have come to emulate.

Part 5: American metal planes

In 1827, Hazard Knowles was awarded the first American patent for a cast-iron plane, but his idea was met with a shrug. American craftsmen had a centuries-old familiarity with wooden bench planes that was hard to overcome. Plus, at that time, there were technical problems confronting anyone who wished to make cast iron planes in sufficient numbers and at low-enough prices to make inroads into the bench plane market. But by the second half of the 19th century, the situation had changed. Metallurgical technology had advanced enough to make it possible to manufacture cast iron planes that could compete in the market place. Plus, at that same time, inventors like Benjamin Blandin, John Gage, Justus Traut, and Leonard Bailey were patenting a blizzard of ideas for new metal planes, as well as for improvements on existing metal planes. While some of those patented ideas are mere historical curiosities, others are important additions to the field of hand plane design. In fact, the Leonard Bailey patents for adjustable metal bench planes dating to that period are the foundation on which most of the metal bench planes of the 20th and now 21st centuries are based. The combination of improved metallurgy and innovative plane design set the stage for the most important event in the history of modern planemaking: the birth of the Stanley line of metal planes.

In 1869, the Stanley Rule and Level Company acquired a small firm of plane and spokeshave makers: Bailey, Chany, and Company (along with the existing Leonard Bailey's patents). Then, scant months later, in January of the following year, the Stanley Rule and Level Company published a catalog offering an entire line of metal planes. This was a remarkably confident step because at that moment in history there was no established market for these tools. The market was created in the next few decades, in large part, through the efforts of that one company. In the words of Alvin Sellens, Stanley historian, the success of the Stanley line of metal planes occurred as a result of "Aggressive advertising through the use of pocket catalogs, testimonials, trade magazines, and exhibition at industrial fairs…." Simultaneously, Stanley's control over the market they were creating was solidified by their acquisition of one firm of competing planemakers after another.

Stanley's success at popularizing its brand is one of the most important stories in the history of American planemaking. Unfortunately, the company's triumph inevitably contributed to the demise of wooden planes. I say "unfortunate" because—while metal bench planes are perfectly suitable replacements for wooden bench planes— the same can't be said for the molding-making planes Stanley offered. At best, the company's combination planes are poor substitutes for the shelf of wooden molders Stanley claimed these combination planes replaced. At worst, the complexity and weak performance of Stanley's combination planes caused craftsmen of the time to give up the idea of making their own moldings, turning instead to the bland offerings of millwork shops.

Chapter 2
Bench Planes

An exquisite bench plane, like this late 19th century Spiers smoother, is more than a functional tool. It is also a man-made artifact with a powerful aesthetic and historical presence.

Assembling a Collection of Users

I have over a hundred ready-to-use planes in my shop (and more packed away in boxes), which is, of course, ridiculous.

The majority of those planes are molders, each cutting a different profile. Others are joinery planes: plows, dado planes, shoulder planes, moving filletsters, miter planes, etc. Nevertheless my 20 or so bench planes see far more use than the 75+ molding and joinery planes in my collection. In fact, while I sometimes go a week or more without picking up any of my molders, I doubt that I've ever gone a single day in the shop without using one or more of my bench planes; and on some days, it seems like one or another of these planes—the workhorses of any traditional shop—is constantly in my hands.

Part 1: Bench plane sizes: small, medium, large

The term bench plane identifies a class of tools used to level, smooth, thickness and joint individual boards, as well as to level, smooth, and thickness glued up panels. Although power-tool enthusiasts may disagree, I believe bench planes should always be close at hand, near the bench (hence the name) because the creation of almost any wooden part requires that stock must be leveled or smoothed or fit—and at each of these tasks, planes excel, allowing a craftsman to remove a few thousandths of thickness from a part in an easy but highly controlled manner.

The bench plane class includes Stanley's famed Bailey-style planes designated #1 through #8, as well as the similar offerings of other manufacturers of bench planes, like Clifton, Record, and

Millers Falls (and other brands of less repute). It also includes Stanley's revered Bedrock series, as well as the undervalued transitional planes offered by Stanley and other makers at the turn of the last century. In addition, this group includes the many different types of wooden planes used to level, smooth, and joint during that era before planes with metal bodies or metal adjustment mechanisms became widely available. It also includes the modern Lie-Nielsen planes numbered like the Stanley Bailey-style #1 through #8 (but designed to resemble the Bedrock series), as well as the Lie-Nielsen bevel-up smoother, jack (and the Stanley #62), and jointer. Plus, it includes the Veritas line of planes numbered 4-6, as well as that company's bevel-up smoother, jack, and jointer. And finally, it includes those wood-stuffed metal-encased infill smoothers, panel planes, and jointers made by English companies during the last half of the 19ᵗʰ century and the first half of the 20ᵗʰ.

If you're just now beginning to investigate the field of hand planes, the size of that list may seem overwhelming, but it's possible to simplify this picture by thinking of each bench plane as falling into one of three functionally different size classes: small, medium and large.

The "small" class is made up of planes designed to smooth surfaces already leveled by longer planes. Smoothers are short—usually between 7" and 10" in length—with the redoubtable Stanley #4 being the most well known example of this class.

Also, there are planes outside those length parameters that are sometimes identified as smoothers. The Stanley #1s and #2s theoretically fall into this class, but—at least in my eyes—they are more toy than tool because neither is designed to be used with

Although technically smoothers, I believe the #1s and #2s are a bit too small for effective two-handed operation. The plane in the foreground is a Stanley #1. The plane in the rear is a Lie-Nielsen #1.

one hand and both are too small to be wielded in a meaningful fashion by two hands—at least by my two hands. The smoother group also includes some larger tools, like the English panel plane. I have, for example, a Spiers panel plane that measures 16-1/4" in length, over two inches longer than a Stanley #5, which belongs in the medium group. This panel plane, like all English planes of this type, was built to do smoothing work on large glued up panels.

The "medium" class is made up of planes of intermediate length, say 12-18". These are planes that might be used to level a small glued-up panel or to joint an edge short enough to make handling a conventional jointer awkward. This group includes the wooden

jack, as well as the Stanley #5. These tools are the most versatile in the bench plane field because they can be used to smooth, as well as to level and joint.

Traditionally, the medium class of planes included one other important tool: the fore or try plane, which is a couple of inches longer than the jack. While the manner in which stock is worked by planes is remarkably consistent from the time of Joseph Moxon (the author of *Mechanick Exercises* published in 1703) to today, the planes with which that work is accomplished have changed. In earlier centuries, a craftsman might first begin the leveling process through the use of a fore or try plane, which was about the length of a Stanley #6. That plane, equipped with a cambered iron, was used to lower the high spots on a board that manifested twist or bow or cupping, lowering those areas quickly by removing heavy shavings. This is work that we today might accomplish with a shorter plane, a jack, a Stanley #5 or in some cases, an even shorter plane, a scrub plane, something like the Stanley #40.

The "large" group is made up of long planes, those a minimum 20" or more in length. In the 19ᵗʰ century, this group was further divided into three parts: trying planes 20-22", long planes 24-26", and jointers 28-30". Today, however, at least in the United States, these more specialized terms have given way to the term "jointer," which encompasses all three.

Part 2: The characteristics of a good bench plane?

1. A good bench plane has a flat sole. By "flat" I mean a sole that is flat and in the same plane all around the mouth and at both ends. "Flat" is important, but perfection isn't necessary. A plane that has, for example, a small area that's a few thousandths of an inch low somewhere between these critical locations, will function just as well as a plane with a sole that is perfectly flat from end to end. In fact, I think excessive flattening in the quest for perfection is more of a problem than insufficient flattening. While there's no question that a sole with a significant arc along its length can make useful planing

The plane in the foreground is a #606, one of the planes in Stanley's premium Bedrock line. The plane behind it is a #6, from Stanley's line of conventional bench planes. The #606 in this condition commands a price of $100-$125, while the #6—virtually the same plane dating from the same era and in very similar condition—can be picked up for less than half that amount.

17

The key difference between the Bedrock #606 (bottom plane) and the #6 (the plane in the middle of the image) is in the manner by which the frog mates with the plane body. The #606 has a much larger machined interface, one that brings these two elements together so "… they are practically one solid piece of metal," according to the 1926 Stanley Tools catalog (the #606 frog, top right, the #6 frog, top left). There is also a difference in the manner of frog attachment. While the frogs in the #1-#8 line of bench planes are attached with a pair of machine screws that pass through the frog and are then turned into tapped holes in the plane body, the frogs of Bedrock planes are attached by a pair of "frog pins." A pair of "frog attachment screws" is turned through tapped holes running parallel to the plane's sole, ending in a pair of vertical holes in which the "frog pins" terminate. The tapered tips of these screws fit into cone-shaped holes on one side of the pins "… drawing the pins downward and clamping the frog absolutely rigid in its place," according to the 1926 catalog.

difficult or impossible, a plane is a remarkably forgiving tool that can be made to perform with a sole that has a couple of moderately low spots.

Unfortunately, some craftsmen, in the quest for perfection, remove so much material during the flattening process that the plane's performance is compromised. In the case of a wooden-bodied plane, this is because the front and back surfaces of the throat are cut at angles which move apart as they rise, and the flattening process inevitably widens the mouth as the sole is raised into this ever-widening throat. In such a case, a mouth grown large can be fixed by means of a patch (discussed in the chapter on wooden plane restoration, page 34). In the case of an infill plane, however, the damage caused by excessive flattening is more significant.

The throat of an infill plane is also made up of front and back surfaces that angle toward the plane's toe and heel as they rise, and here, too, the mouth is widened when the material is removed from the sole around the throat. Unfortunately, the enlarged mouth of an infill plane is essentially unfixable.

Excessive flattening isn't a problem in the case of Bailey-style planes because these planes have movable frogs which can be repositioned to shrink a mouth grown too wide.

2. A good bench plane has an iron bedded solidly enough to resist chatter, which is a stuttering vibration of the cutting edge that occurs when the iron is not well secured. Instead of a smooth surface, a chattering iron leaves behind a pattern of corrugations perpendicular to the plane's direction of travel.

Resistance to chatter can be achieved in several different ways. Wooden planes typically have irons which are quite thick on the business end. That thickness alone stiffens the iron against vibration. Plus, these planes usually have cap irons which are sprung so that they press on the iron just behind the cutting edge, stabilizing that edge. In addition, a tightly fit wedge stabilizes the iron/cap iron assembly by pushing it

against the bed along the full length of that bed. Infill planes also have very thick irons and cap irons. In addition, the lever cap screw found on infill planes of later manufacture can exert enormous force, pressing the iron/cap iron assembly down tight against the bed, in that manner further stiffening the cutting edge. More commonly seen planes—like the Stanley bench plane series #1-#8—employ remarkably thin irons, and these planes, too, have cap irons with sprung ends to stabilize the cutting edge. But because of the thinness of the material used for Stanley-type irons and cap irons, these planes are more likely to produce chatter than wooden and infill bench planes, at least when the irons in these more traditional planes are bedded correctly. For that reason, many modern users purchase after-market irons and cap irons cut from thicker steel to reduce the tendency to chatter in their Bailey-style tools.

3. A good bench plane has a reasonably tight mouth. Any bench plane with a mouth more than 1/16" wide is capable of leaving behind areas of tearout because the surface of the wood ahead of the iron isn't held down by the leading edge of the mouth. This allows a chip to be lifted from the surface being smoothed. The lifting begins in that space between the cutting edge—which lifts a shaving from the surface being worked—and the leading edge of the mouth. Smoothers, in particular, should have tight mouths, none wider than 1/32". In fact, smoothers used for finishing—those designed to take gossamer shavings—should have even tighter mouths, open just enough to accept the shaving lifted by the plane's minute depth of cut.

4. A good bench plane is comfortable in the hands. If you're taking only a few shavings, a comfortable knob and tote are of only minor importance, but if you're spending a day leveling and smoothing a group of hardwood panels, you want a tool that doesn't bite the hands that move it.

Part 3: The characteristics of a superior bench plane?

1. A superior bench plane has considerable mass. It's quite possible to do good work with light Stanley-type planes, but craftsmen accustomed to such tools are often amazed at the performance of—for example—a well-tuned infill. Such a plane will have several advantages over their Stanley-type counterparts, the most important of which is the presence of mass, because mass does two very important things for plane users. First, mass produces momentum. Once a user gets a heavier plane moving across the work, the plane's mass will assist him/her in keeping it moving, often right through difficult patches on the surface being worked. Second, mass helps a user keep a plane's sole in constant contact with the surface being worked because a heavy plane is less likely to rock—minutely—from side to side as it is pushed through a stroke.

There is a tradeoff, however. A really heavy plane is more tiring to operate during a long work session. I have a 23" infill jointer that weighs almost 11 pounds, and while I love using it to take a couple of shavings from the edge of a board, if I have to joint a large number of edges, I'm much more likely to reach for a lighter plane than I am for my infill monster.

2. A superior bench plane has a low center of gravity. While I enjoy my Stanley #7s, the upright posture of the frog/iron/cap iron assembly—as well as the plane's relatively thin sole—gives the tool a high center of gravity. By contrast, a plane like the Veritas low-angle bevel-up jointer has all its weight packed way down low just above the surface being worked. That might not seem like much of a difference when you read about it in a book, but if you get a chance to use these two planes side by side, I think you'll find that it's easier to keep the Veritas jointer flat on the surface being worked than it is to keep the #7 in such an alignment, particularly when you're working an uneven surface.

3. A superior bench plane has an adjustable mouth. Most of the bench planes I've described have adjustable mouths, although this end is achieved in different ways. The mouths on Stanley-style planes—even those lacking the frog adjustment screw—can be changed by loosening the frog attachment screws and repositioning the frog. The low-angle, bevel-up planes all have adjustable mouth plates that can be positioned to change the width of the mouth.

Part 4: The characteristics of an exquisite bench plane?

1. An exquisite bench plane has history. My bench plane collection includes a pair of Spiers infill smoothers and a Spiers panel plane, made probably somewhere in the very early years of the 20th century, as well as a Norris A-5 made a few years later. These planes were likely used in the shops of English craftsmen in the first half of the 20th century, and every time I take one of these tools in my hands and apply it to my work, I'm connected to those earlier furniture makers in a way that's tangible enough for me to feel in my hands (at least that's what I believe). In addition, I have a Shepherd panel plane and a Shepherd smoother (built from kits) made by Chris Schwartz, the editor of *Popular Woodworking* magazine. Chris is a craftsman and hand tool enthusiast for whom I have great respect, and every time I use one of the tools he built, I am connected to Chris and his own work.

This trio of wooden bench planes might have graced the shop of almost any 19th century craftsman. The jointer in the rear is long enough to flatten just about any edge or surface. The jack plane is in the middle is appropriate for a variety of tasks: jointing short edges, leveling small panels, and general bench plane work. The smoother in the foreground is called a razee-style plane which identifies the step at the rear into which the tote of this smoother is integrated.

In addition to the company's standard line of cast-iron planes, Stanley also experimented with steel-bodied planes and with aluminum-bodied planes like the A6 you see here. According to the 1926 catalog, this plane weighed only 3-1/2 pounds, much less than the conventional #6 which weighed in at 6-1/4 pounds. Neither experiment with alternative metal was a success.

2. An exquisite bench plane has powerful aesthetic presence. A well-made plane gets me in the gut in much the same way as a piece of sculpture. In fact, I would argue that a well made plane *is* a piece of sculpture, an artifact that induces pleasure as easily when it is viewed and touched as when it is used. All of my infill planes strike me in this way. So, too, do the Lie-Nielsen planes I own. It doesn't surprise me that people collect such planes with no intention of ever putting them to use, purchasing them simply as objects to be displayed and enjoyed in much the same way others display more conventional works of art.

3. Finally, an exquisite bench plane may have significant financial worth. My brain recognizes the fact of financial value, but this is the one characteristic of good bench planes for which I have little feel. The collecting literature is filled with the stories of bench planes of significant historical value that fetched thousands of dollars at auction, and while I appreciate this fact intellectually, I don't feel it in the same way I feel the other characteristics of exquisite planes.

In an English shop in the 19th century, panel planes were used primarily as smoothers of large panels, although these two panel planes are as long as many jacks. The plane in the rear is a Spiers. The plane in the foreground is a Shepherd reproduction of a smaller Spiers panel plane.

Part 5: Bench plane brands

If money is no object, you can't do better than the metal bench planes sold by Lie-Nielsen Tools and the Lee Valley Veritas line. Both companies manufacture metal-bodied planes built to exacting standards, and both ship planes ready to go from the box directly to the bench. I'm the proud owner of a dozen planes made by each company, and I've never been disappointed by the performance or the beauty of anything made by these two firms. In fact, if I knew

I was about to be stranded on some desert isle stacked with rough lumber and if I was told I could take only one plane onto that isle, my choice would be the Lie-Nielsen #62—which can be made to do just about anything. (Of course that low-angle, bevel-up Veritas has a lot to recommend it also.)

The bench planes offered by the American maker Clark and Williams are also built to exacting standards. The first time I held one of their planes in my hands and experienced its carefully articulated beech surfaces, I realized what it would have been like for an 18th or 19th century cabinetmaker when he first put his hands on the work of a master period planemaker. If you like the lightness of wooden planes, you can't do better than the planes offered by this three-man firm.

And if money *really* is no object, you might consider custom-made bench planes produced one at a time by craftsmen like Konrad Sauer and Jim Leamy.

But for most of us, money is an object, and fortunately, there are low-cost options that make it possible to build collections of perfectly usable bench planes for very little money, while saving up for the Lie-Nielsen or Veritas or Sauer or Leamy.

eBay is one good source of antique tools, but that company's decision to limit sales only to those buyers willing to surrender access to their checking accounts or credit cards removes it as an option

The arc of Stanleys beginning on the left is my collection of Stanley users. They range in size from the #8—the big plane on the left—to the #3—the plane closest to the Lie-Nielsen planes. Although it's technically a bench plane, I've never actually used the Lie-Nielsen #1 (second from right), but the Lie-Nielsen #4-1/2 is one of my favorite smoothers.

for many. But there are other sources. Garage sales and yard sales sometimes offer tools, but if you go looking for planes, you may need to visit a lot of yards and garages before you find anything to purchase. In our area, antique malls and antique shows are the best choices. Some, in fact, have booths devoted exclusively to tools, many of which are planes.

Planes from premium antique lines, like the Stanley Bedrock series, will nearly always be offered at prices out of proportion to their intrinsic worth. A Stanley #604 (Bedrock) in good condition may be listed for $100 or more, while a Stanley #4 in similar condition might sell for $15, and the differences in performance are too slight to matter. Yes, the Bedrock planes have a larger contact surface between the bottom of the frog and that section of the plane body with which the frog mates, but that fact isn't likely to demonstrably skew the performance between well-tuned planes in these two different classes. In other words, if you only have $50 to spend on your first smoother, don't buy a Bedrock plane (unless you're buying from a seller who doesn't recognize the Bedrock name) because your $50 will purchase only a badly rusted and battered #604 while that same $50 will be more than enough to buy a WWII era or earlier #4 in excellent condition. It might even buy a #4-1/2, which is better yet because of that plane's superior width and weight.

Part 6: Buying quality antique planes

Once you've found a used tool to consider, take a few minutes to look it over.

In the case of metal-bodied planes, check for casting cracks. These often show up around the mouth. Sometimes the sidewalls, too, may be cracked as a result of having been dropped on a concrete floor. A welder can repair the crack, but the plane will never again have any value as a collectible, and cast-iron welding is an expensive repair.

Check to see that the adjustments—lever cap cam, depth-of-cut adjuster, lateral adjustment lever—work freely. You should have a screwdriver in your pocket so you can determine that the various screws can be turned—those mounting the frog, as well as the frog adjustment screw on planes that have this feature. You should also check the screws used to mount the tote and knob. If any of these screws—for either adjustment or simply attachment—is rust-frozen,

The thickness of the soles beneath the totes reveal the relative amount of wear these two razee smoothers have experienced, making the plane in the rear a better candidate for restoration.

restoration will be more difficult and in some cases impossible.

Check, also to see if the sole is reasonably straight by laying a straightedge against the sole. And, if you want to make a really thorough evaluation, lay a couple of winding sticks across the sole, one at either end, and sight them for evidence of twist.

Finally, check the knob and tote for cracks and breaks. Unrepaired cracks aren't much of an issue, as long as all the wood is still present, but poorly repaired cracks, coated with some kind of adhesive can present problems, because—before you can glue the parts back together—you must remove the old glue. This is possible if the previous fixer used hide glue, but if they used anything else—well, it's often not possible to enact a repair because so many of the adhesives used in the past 75 years are impervious to any solvent you might have in your shop. In such a case, the best option may be to replace the broken knob or tote with wood from a parts plane. Often, the tip of the tote's horn is missing as a result of collisions with concrete floors. If the missing part is quite small, you can fair the tip beyond the line of the break. It's also possible to graft on some new rosewood, if you have access to the material.

In the case of wooden planes, check first for blown cheeks. Cheeks are the thin sidewalls outside of the wedge slots. Often a wooden plane will have cracks showing on the outside of the plane's body at these locations. These cracks are the result of either grain runout or a previous owner's zeal in hammering the wedge into place. (Sometimes, too, blown cheeks are the result of a wedge—tightened during a dry winter—being left in place during a humid summer which causes the wedge to swell.) In my eyes, a blown cheek immediately disqualifies a plane because, although the seller may assure you that such a minor defect can be fixed with a little glue, the truth is a repair is all but impossible, and—even if a repair is made—those repaired cheeks will likely blow out again even if you're careful when setting the wedge.

The cheeks on this smoother were possibly blown out by a combination of an overly tightened wedge and a seasonal humidity change. Although the crack looks minor, it would be very difficult to repair, so this plane is not a good candidate for restoration.

Check to see that the wedge fits its slots from top to bottom. Gaps between the legs of the wedge and the tops of the wedge slots probably result from someone—who was perhaps not skilled—planing away at those legs to make the wedge fit. Unfortunately once an excess of material has been removed from the legs, the wedge will never again secure the iron as well as it should.

Also, in the case of wooden bodied bench planes, check the mouth. If it's gaping, it can be shrunk by making a patch, but if you're not willing to do that fussy work, the plane will never be a good user.

In the case of wooden jacks or jointers, use your straight edge and winding sticks to check for arc or twist. Slight errors can be easily fixed, but a wooden plane with serious sole problems may require more fixing than it's worth. No wooden antique will be perfectly straight, but unless the error is significant, it's fairly simple to straighten the sole of wooden plane with a little arc or twist along its length. Smoothers are so short that they rarely manifest significant sole deviation, although almost every smoother will have to spend a little time on the lapping plate in order to bring about their best performance.

Finally, examine the checks. It seems few 19th century wooden bench planes are completely free of checks, but most have little effect on the plane's performance. The only checks that should reject a plane are those that threaten the structural integrity of the tool.

You're not likely to see an infill plane at an antique mall or show in the U. S. In many years of antiquing in the Midwest, I've only seen three, and those were shoulder and bullnose planes. I have never seen an infill bench plane. Because of an infill's intrinsic worth—both in terms of function and dollar value— I would be willing to consider one that's pretty badly battered. One of my favorite planes (the repair of the plane is documented on pages 40-41) is a Spiers parallel-sided smoother that came to me with a big chunk missing from the bun, as well as a tote broken into pieces, some of which were missing. I spent most of one day fixing the broken parts, and while the repaired plane has little value as a collectible—it's simply a beast as a smoother.

Transitional planes—wood blocks as bodies paired with a metal Bailey-style adjusters—are enigmas. These planes can be made to perform very ably, but they seem to command only junk prices. I've purchased transitional jointers in fine condition for $50. Plus, on his website devoted to Stanley planes, Patrick Leach describes a sect of tool zealots in the Northeastern U.S. that celebrates its meetings with funeral pyres composed of blazing transitional planes, a claim he supports with a photo of burning transitionals. Nevertheless, most of these planes are eminently usable tools—with the exception of a few of extraordinarily cheap design. I'm thinking here about Stanley's Liberty Bell line and the inadequate bedding system appearing on those planes.

One of the benefits of owning transitionals is this: If you want to fasten a fence to a jack or a jointer, it's easier to do so with a wooden-bodied plane than it is with one made of metal.

Finally, when inspecting any antique plane, take a good look at the amount of usable iron left below the cap-iron-screw slot. If the cutting edge is only 3/4" below the bottom of the slot, that iron won't survive many more sessions on the grinding wheel. Fortunately, it's fairly easy to acquire new irons simply by buying parts planes and discarding the plane bodies after you've scavenged the irons and any other usable parts.

It's hard to find an antique wooden bench plane completely free of checks, but rarely do these defects impact a plane's performance. Both the smoother in the foreground and the jointer in the rear have checked soles, but both planes are reliable users. (Both planes have had wide mouths closed with inlaid patches.)

The larger plane in the rear is a normal-sized smoother. The smaller plane in the foreground is a miniature, a variety of plane with great appeal for some collectors.

Opposite, top:
This drawing shows the differences in iron thicknesses in commonly encountered planes. In part, the differences are a reflection of the use to which a specific plane will be put. For example, the plow plane iron at the top needs thickness because the bottom 2" is supported only by the front edge of a thin skate. There is, however, also a great disparity in thickness among irons found in planes intended for the same purpose, a disparity that typically reflects variations in tool quality. The thinnest iron—the Stanley at the bottom—is the plane I would consider to be the weakest (among those represented here) entry in the bench plane field. Those bench planes with irons 3/16" thick—the Veritas bevel-up, the wooden jack, the modern infill jointer, the Spiers panel plane—all come from planes several steps up the quality ladder.

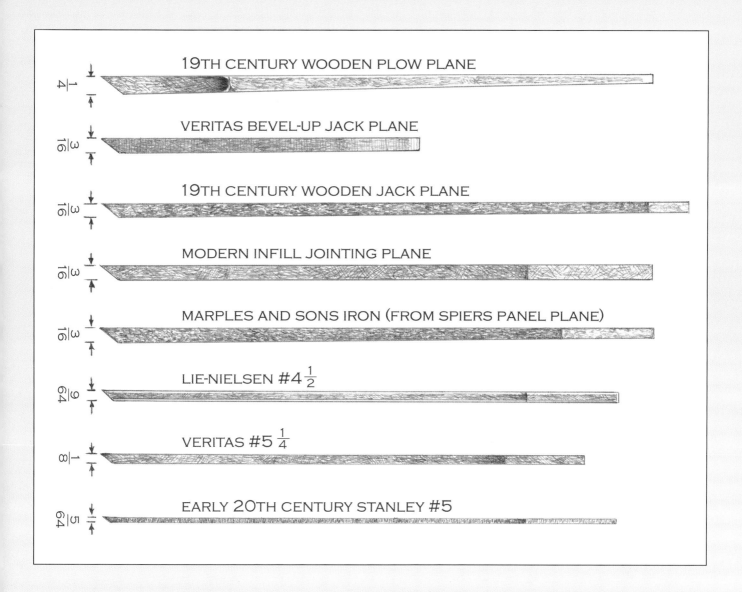

19TH CENTURY WOODEN PLOW PLANE

$\frac{1}{4}$

VERITAS BEVEL-UP JACK PLANE

$\frac{3}{16}$

19TH CENTURY WOODEN JACK PLANE

$\frac{3}{16}$

MODERN INFILL JOINTING PLANE

$\frac{3}{16}$

MARPLES AND SONS IRON (FROM SPIERS PANEL PLANE)

$\frac{3}{16}$

LIE-NIELSEN #4$\frac{1}{2}$

$\frac{9}{64}$

VERITAS #5$\frac{1}{4}$

$\frac{1}{8}$

EARLY 20TH CENTURY STANLEY #5

$\frac{5}{64}$

Part 7: The most important sizes

Probably the most used and most useful plane in anyone's tool collection is a good block plane with an adjustable mouth plate. The Lie-Nielsen #60-1/2 —which is never far from my hand—is a good example of such a plane. But the next plane and the next plane and the next plane should be good bench planes because while a block plane is handy for all kinds of trimming and clean-up jobs, it's simply inadequate for the stock leveling and smoothing that go on daily in any busy shop.

If it's necessary to purchase your bench planes one at a time, a "small" plane, a good smoother, should be your first choice, either a traditional bevel-down smoother like the Lie-Nielsen #4-1/2 or a bevel-up smoother like the Veritas low-angle bevel-up. Either would be an excellent first bench plane. Fortunately, however, there are also low-cost options for craftsmen working on a budget. Those Stanley #4-1/2s manufactured before the end of World War II are excellent smoothers. Plus they're equipped with the Bailey-style adjuster all Americans learn to operate at birth. I should add here that the latter-day Stanleys sold with plastic knobs and totes were manufactured with such indiffer-ence that—although an experienced craftsmen can coax them

into satisfactory results—an inexperienced user would be better served by using the same money to purchase an earlier Stanley, one made prior to—say—the 1950s.

(As I began writing this book, I learned of Stanley's new "pre-mium" line, the planes featuring cherry knobs and totes. However, although I asked several times for samples to test, Stanley declined to send me any.)

Alternatively, if you like the lightness and "feel" of a wooden smoother, such a plane could also make a good first choice, but my experience suggests that novices are more likely to get good results with a plane equipped with an adjuster than they will with a wood plane that requires tapping skill to set the iron.

The next plane on your list should be a "large" plane, a jointer. This plane should be long enough to bridge the valleys on edges you may be jointing and on surfaces you may be flattening. Any-thing in the 20"-24" range will suit the needs of most craftsmen. This is the plane with which you'll level large panels. It is also the plane with which you'll joint edges prior to gluing individual boards into panels.

The third plane on your list should be one from the "medium" sized class: a jack. An Lie-Nielsen #5 or a Veritas #5-1/4 are both excellent choices. Craftsmen working on a budget should once

23

The Clifton #4-1/2 (foreground) is a worthy bench plane that performs much like its cousin, the Lie-Nielsen #4-1/2 on the right, better than its ancestor, the Stanley #4-1/2 in the middle.

again consider an antique Stanley: the #5. In the past 150 years, the company has churned out enough of these to put a jack plane in both hands of every, man, woman, and child in the U.S., so they're easy to find, often in good condition at reasonable prices.

Wooden jacks are nearly as numerous, but here, too, novices might be better served by purchasing a plane with an adjuster.

With these three planes, there is little bench plane work you can't accomplish, but, over time, you'll see reasons to add intermediate sizes to your collection. You may even find reasons to add multiple planes of the same size. This is a particularly useful approach in the smoother category. Having several smoothers set up in different ways can be a real time saver (in addition to providing you with an excuse to buy more planes). For example, I have one smoother set up to take a fairly thick shaving, another set to take a thinner shaving, and several set to take very fine shavings. This may seem redundant, but in actual practice it's very handy.

When I first put a smoother on a panel that's been leveled by longer planes, the surface of that panel will be—although level— still marked by the passage of those longer planes. If—after testing that surface with a smoother set to take a very fine shaving—I find no sign of tearout, I often switch to a smoother taking a heavier shaving. If that plane results in a surface that is smooth in all but a couple of difficult areas where they grain may be switching

directions, I change then to a smoother set to take the thinnest possible shaving, and with that plane I work those last difficult areas until the entire surface is uniformly smooth.

Why not bypass the confusion and start with the smoother set to take the finest shaving? Sometimes, that's necessary. If the surface is really turbulent with swirling grain around pinhole knots or if the panel is curly or bird's eye material, I will use that smoother set to take the finest shaving as my first resort after the leveling plane has finished its work. But that can be a slow process because that particularly smoother takes a shaving only a few thousandths thick. It may then take an hour's work to smooth even a small panel. By contrast, when the panel is straight-grained, I can use intermediate smoothers set to take thicker shavings, and in that manner, quickly finish a panel.

This is the two-part Clifton cap iron, my only complaint about this otherwise excellent plane. The top section of that cap iron has a registration post that fits inside the hole drilled in the bottom section. Also, there's a lip on the underside of the bottom section that fits into the groove on the top side of the upper section to keep the lower part of the cap iron in the correct alignment.

The Clifton Plane

Because I had heard that the English producer of Clifton planes was producing a quality product, I made several attempts early on to get the company to send me a plane to use in my preparation for this book. I never seemed to find the right person to ask and my requests were ignored. However, as the book was nearing completion, I noticed that The Best Things, an internet seller of good quality antique and contemporary planes, was handling the Clifton line, and I knew Lee Richmond of The Best Things, who had earlier sent me planes to review for a magazine article, so I contacted Lee and asked if he could send me a plane to try. He sent me one of his personal Cliftons, a #4-1/2.

Like the Lie-Nielsen line of bench planes, the Clifton line is based on the classic Bailey-style planes made by Stanley. Also like the Lie-Nielsen bench planes, the Clifton planes are better made than their Stanley ancestors, with much heaver irons and cap irons than those found on antique Stanleys and with a generally more refined appearance. In fact, the level of refinement was quite similar to that seen in Lie-Nielsen planes, with the edges of the iron and cap iron slightly relieved and the edges of the body casting highly polished.

And of course, the plane worked as well as you would expect such a plane would work; that is to say, superbly.

I think it's very difficult to identify real differences in performance among the manufactured bench planes I recommend in this book: Lie-Nielsen, Veritas, and now—cautiously—Clifton. The manufacturers of all three lines produce well made planes equipped with enough mass to power through difficult grain, with thick enough irons and cap irons to resist chatter, and with a pleasing overall appearance.

For me the elements which differentiate one from another are in the details, like the two-part cap iron of the Clifton. I don't like it.

After sharpening, when I've positioned the cap iron on the iron, I turn the iron/cap iron assembly over to tighten the cap screw. And of course at that point, the bottom section of the Clifton cap iron falls off, and I have to lean over, pick up the part, and start the cap iron setting process over.

There is a reason for Clifton's two-part cap iron. It allows you to hone the cutting edge without having to loosen the cap screw, thereby losing the cap iron position. You simply lift off the bottom section and hone. That makes sense, but I have to say that this two-part construction felt awkward in my hands, after forty years of honing unattached irons.

The bottom of the cap iron is faintly magnetized. I assume this feature was added to keep the bottom section of the cap iron in place when the cap iron is inverted, and the magnetism is strong enough to hold that bottom in place—if I remember to turn it over very, very slowly. Of course, in my shop I'm always in a hurry, and every time I turned the iron/cap iron assembly over, the bottom of the cap iron landed on the floor. I could probably teach myself to move slowly when I perform this task, but my first impression is that this two-part cap iron is probably a deal breaker for me.

But there are other details about the Clifton I like very much. The depth-of-cut adjustment is the smoothest I can ever remember using. Of course, I have no way to know if that's an idiosyncratic feature of the one Clifton I used or a feature to be found on all of the Clifton planes. I also like the knob and tote, which are bubinga like the wood on the Veritas planes. And the stamped graphic at the top of the iron just looks cool.

The Clifton #4-1/2 is priced at $300, slightly less than the $325 price of a Lie-Nielsen #4-1/2.

Bench Plane Types

I believe power tools are not the answer for every small-shop surfacing problem, even in an age of woodworking machinery of extraordinary sophistication and complexity. Yes, wood panels of almost any size can be leveled and smoothed by a power jointer or a power planer or a wide-belt sander, but the surfaces produced by these machines are marked—however subtly—by flaws inherent in the processes that created them. Power jointers and planers leave behind ripples—the tracks of knives mounted on rotating heads—and wide-belt sanders leave behind surfaces scratched into flatness by the particles embedded on the sanding belts. But even more important is the issue of cost. Machines with the capacity to joint/plane/sand the top of even a modest-sized table are quite expensive, beyond the means of most hobbyists and many owners of one-man shops—to say nothing of the valuable shop space these machines can devour.

Fortunately, in the last 20 years, there has been a renaissance in the fabrication of hand planes, as well as in the discussion of how they might be most effectively used. Manufacturers like Lie-Nielsen Toolworks and Lee Valley Tools, as well as dozens of individual planemakers, are today producing planes of a quality that has probably never been surpassed. At the same time, the woodworking literature is addressing the ways these simple machines can be used to surface panels of any size at a fraction of the cost of similarly capable surfacing machinery.

Part 1: Wooden planes

Although metal-bodied planes have been found in the wreckage left behind by the eruption of Vesuvius in A. D. 79, wooden planes have been the surfacing tools of choice for most of the past 2000 years. According to John Whelan, the author of "The Wooden Plane: It's History, Form, and Function," the known lineage of this simple machine reaches even further back, all the way to the fourth century B.C. in Greece and in Egypt.

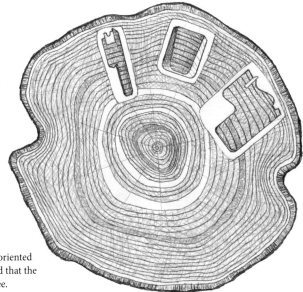

"However" Steel

A knowledgeable Clifton enthusiast recently told me that the "forged high-carbon steel" of the Clifton iron is superior to the A2 steel in a Lie-Nielsen iron because forged high-carbon steel sharpens to a finer edge. However, according to Lie-Nielsen Toolworks, the A2 steel that comes in their bench planes holds an edge extremely well, but the company also offers irons made of O-1 steel which they declare "will take a slightly finer edge when sharpened at 25 degrees or lower." However, the Lee Valley website says that A2 steel "takes a keener edge" than O-1 steel. "O-1" they say 'is a good choice for rapid honing but requires it more often."

This information is confusing, especially for someone like me who doesn't have enough of a science background to interpret steel characteristics in any meaningful way. All I can do is nod my head when I hear this information. I suspect all the claims are true, and that the apparent subtle contradictions are a result more of my faulty understanding of steel making than of any attempt to dissemble by the manufacturers.

But even if I understood the theoretical differences among these steels, how could I decide what those differences might mean in real-world planing?

My shop routine couldn't provide any answers. I've ground and honed hundreds of irons both for new planes and for antiques, and I'm sure every one of those grindings and honings was subtly different, although mine might be more alike than grindings and honings done by a novice. And even if I could find some way to produce a batch of truly consistent edges, how would I measure the longevity of those edges? Maybe you could devise some laboratory experiment in which you had a machine pushing planes equipped with different irons, along boards of the same species, boards identically hard with the grain aligned in identical configurations. But that wouldn't be real world planing.

In my real-world shop, I don't plane the same species every day. Some days I work pine, some days walnut, some days ash, some days hard maple, hickory, butternut. I've also worked with sassafras, cedar, and on and on. I've even asked my planes to clean up the sawn edges of plexiglas. (No, I didn't humiliate a good plane by using it this way. I chose a high-mileage Stanley #3.) The fact that an edge might need touching up after a couple of days use in my shop probably has more to do with the material I've asked it to cut or variations in my honing technique than with the intrinsic qualities of the steel.

At least, that's what I suspect.

The classic wooden bench plane is just a block of wood—often beech—through which a throat is cut, along with housings for the iron/cap iron/wedge assembly. The grain in that block is aligned so that the tree's annular rings pass through the plane from side to side rather than from top to bottom. In addition, the plane is laid out so that the sole is that part of the plane that was, in the living tree, closest to the bark, and ideally the plane is oriented so that the annular rings—when viewed from the side of the plane slant down from toe to heel.

Most wooden bench planes are simply elongated cubes between 2-1/2" and 3-1/2" in width and about the same in height, but often smoothers and miter planes were constructed in a coffin shape, tapering slightly in width toward both ends. Smoothers tend to run between 6-1/2" and 9-1/2" in length, jacks between 14" and 16", fore planes 20" to 22", and jointers from 24" to 30". You may also occasionally run across much longer bench-type planes. Several years ago, I found (and foolishly didn't buy) a jointer over six feet in length. It had no tote and was bored on both sides with round mortises. This was an example of a cooper's jointer which was designed to be used upside down, raised on legs (the round mortises on the example I didn't buy). In use it would have resembled an unfenced power jointer because the user would have moved the stock being worked down the sole across the cutting edge, instead of moving the plane down the stock.

Most wooden smoothers lack totes. Instead, the bodies of the planes are softened with wide chamfers and radii to make them more comfortable to push against. But larger planes are nearly always equipped with totes. Wooden jack planes typically have an open tote, a straight length of hand-sized wood shaped to fit inside the user's closed hand. This is mortised into the top surface of the plane behind the throat. These totes almost always feature a horn at the top designed to rise above the web between the thumb and forefinger on the user's hand. Planes in the large category usually feature closed totes which encircle three fingers of the user's push hand. These, too, are surmounted with a horn. The horn on either an open or a closed tote is the most fragile element of a wooden bench plane. These are often chipped or broken off altogether as a result of the plane falling onto a hard surface.

The sharp edges at the tops of the cheeks—those areas on either side of the

This single iron smoother made by the Eureka Springs, Arkansas firm Clark and Williams represents the best qualities of the 18th century English planes on which their line is based.

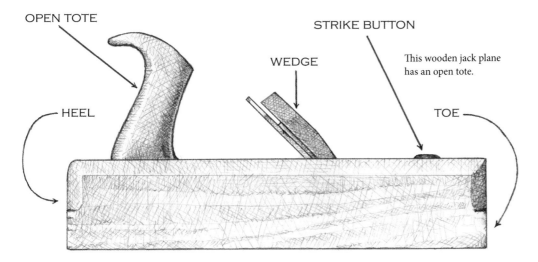

plane just above the wedge slots—are softened with long tapered bevels known as eyes so that the fingers of a user reaching into the throat to remove shavings aren't scuffed by sharp edges.

Many wooden bench planes are also equipped with strike buttons—small round extrusions of hardwood end grain sometimes called "starts"—inlaid either on the top side of the plane ahead of the throat or on the heel. To free the iron, the plane user taps on these buttons with a mallet. Alternatively, a user can free an iron by pinning the plane body against his side with his arm, while the fingers of that hand are wrapped loosely around the iron/cap/iron/wedge assembly and rapping on the heel of the plane with a mallet.

Typically, wooden bench plane irons are bedded at an angle of 45 degrees, which is a good compromise for most woods. Planes with steeper bedding angles were designed for use with harder woods, while planes with shallower bedding angles were often intended for miter work. The performance of a wooden plane is in part determined by the flatness of this bed. High spots anywhere or low spots at either end of the bed can cause the iron to rock in use, even when it's properly wedged, and this movement can produce cutting defects.

The user of a wooden bench plane secures the iron/cap iron assembly by positioning the iron and wedge, then tapping on the top of the wedge with a mallet, pushing the tapered legs of the wedge deeper into the also-tapered wedge slots and causing them to press down on the iron/cap iron assembly. Adjustment is made by tapping on the iron itself or by tapping on the body of the plane in a way that causes the cutting edge of the plane to rise or fall. The alignment is then secured by additional tapping on the wedge.

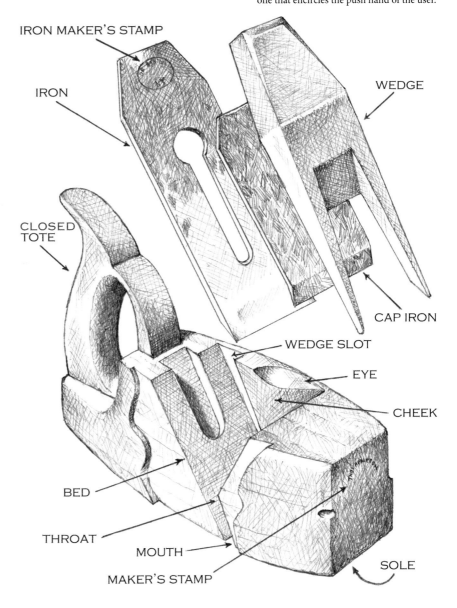

This razee-style smoother has a closed tote, one that encircles the push hand of the user.

IRON MAKER'S STAMP

IRON

WEDGE

CLOSED TOTE

CAP IRON

WEDGE SLOT

EYE

CHEEK

BED

THROAT

MOUTH

MAKER'S STAMP

SOLE

27

The cutting edge of the iron for a wooden plane is made of steel welded onto a large blank of cast iron. In cross-section, the irons are wedge-shaped, tapering from a thickness of about 3/16" at the cutting edge to as little as 1/16" at the top. Typically, in the case of a used plane, the top edge of the iron is bent over or mushroomed from repeated blows of adjustment. Cap irons are attached through the use of a cap screw threaded into a hole in the cap iron. The head of that screw passes through a hole in the iron which is placed above a slot cut through most of the length of the iron, all the way down to the welded steel. The head of the cap screw is inserted through the hole. Then the shaft of that screw is passed up through this slot as the cap iron is moved into the correct position. When the tip of the cap iron has reached a point just above the tip of the cutting edge (on the back of the iron), the cap screw is tightened, bringing the head of the screw tight against the iron. This draws the tip of the cap iron tight against the back side of the iron near the cutting edge. Because the cap iron is arced along its length, the act of tightening the screw flexes the cap iron, placing great pressure on the tip, in this manner stiffening the cutting edge, as well as guiding shavings up into the throat.

It would be difficult to overstate the importance of wooden bench planes in the lives of woodworking craftsmen prior to the rise of metal planes in the late-19th century. While the tool kit of many joiners might have lacked an array of molding planes or joinery planes, bench planes were in the kit of virtually everyone who made a living putting hands to wood, a kit that would have included at least one plane each from the small, medium, and large categories (discussed on page 17). The 1872 catalog of the Greenfield Tool Company offered boxed sets of five wooden bench planes, presumably a typical array for a craftsman of that era. The set consisted of a smoother, a jack, a 22"fore plane, a 26" jointer, as well as a shallow angle miter plane. These planes would have been enough to handle any job of stock preparation.

The preceding description applies to classical European and American wooden bench planes, but there are, of course, other kinds of wooden planes. Japanese planes are typically cut from much shallower blocks of wood, and the irons of these planes are short and quite thick, equipped with a screwless metal cap iron which functions simultaneously as a wedge. This two-layered sandwich of steel is wedged against a steel rod used as a bridge. These planes are designed to be pulled toward the user, rather than pushed in the way of Western planes. A variation of this design with a wood bridge and wood wedge has gained favor in the shops of many contemporary Western craftsmen as well.

Tapping on the heel of the plane with a mallet will cause the iron/cap iron assembly to scoot fractionally up the bed, raising the cutting edge. Tapping on the toe of the plane will cause the iron to scoot fractionally down the bed, lowering the cutting edge.

Check the iron's lateral adjustment by sliding your thumb across the cutting edge on both sides of the iron.

There are also wooden planes to which metal adjusters have been added. These are planes lacking the applied metal framework of the transitionals (which will be discussed later in this chapter). Instead, these are planes for which the wood block provides the structure to which metal adjusters (and sometimes a lever cap) have been added. The Norris firm of infill planemakers marketed planes of this type, equipped with the famed Norris adjuster. Also, the modern German planemaker E. C. Emmerich today markets a complete line of wooden bench planes equipped with metal adjusters. In fact, one of the first American men to experiment with this idea may have been Leonard Bailey, the famed Stanley designer, who in 1858 patented a metal lever cap to be used on wooden planes: a cap almost identical to the lever caps found on metal Bailey-style planes even today.

Adjusting the irons of wooden planes: The irons in wooden planes can be adjusted for use in more than one way. Each of the two methods I'll describe here involve tapping, so first I'd like to talk about tapping instruments. Many hand plane enthusiasts use metal hammers for tapping, and if you look at the heels of planes, as well as at the tops of their irons, you can see the consequences of metal hammers. To avoid adding to the damage, I use only wooden mallets which are much kinder to planes and their irons.

Traditionally, the process works as follows: First, lay the wooden plane, sole down, on a bench. Insert the iron/cap iron assembly (if there is a cap iron) allowing the cutting edge to meet the top of the bench. Add the wedge, pushing it into position with your fingers. If the iron protrudes too far, tap on the heel of the plane (on the strike button there if one is present). This causes the iron to slide fractionally up the bed. Then test the depth of cut, either by sliding a thumb across (NOT ALONG) the edge. If it is not down far enough, tap on the toe of the plane. This slides the iron fractionally down the bed. Test the iron again. If the depth of cut seems to be nearly correct, with either your thumb or your eye—sighting down the sole—check to see that there is an equal amount of cutting edge on each side of the iron. Correct any inequities by tapping the sides of the iron. When the cutting edge is where you want it, tap firmly on the top of the wedge.

But there is also a more direct method, one that doesn't rely on tapping the heel and toe to move the iron. First lay the plane, sole down on a bench. Insert the iron/cap iron assembly until the tip of the iron strikes the bench top. Add the wedge, pushing it gently into position. Wiggle the iron up about 1/8". Give the wedge one light tap. Then tap the top of the iron gently until it descends to the correct depth of cut, proceeding slowly with several gentle taps. Make lateral adjustments as necessary by tapping the sides of the iron. When the cutting edge is the way you want it, tap the wedge more firmly into place. If your tapping causes the iron to descend too far, remove the iron and wedge and start again.

The ultimate test of either method is to take a few shavings. Sometimes very slight problems in depth-of-cut or lateral adjustment won't reveal themselves until you've put the plane to work. For this reason, it's important to take those first shavings from a piece of scrap instead of that 30" x 72" walnut table top you've spent two full days assembling.

At first, both of these methods will seem difficult to master, particularly for craftsmen accustomed to the ease of a Bailey-style adjuster, but you may be surprised at how quickly you can master either of these techniques.

Part 2: Infill planes

The identifying characteristic of an infill plane is the presence of wood stuffing which fills a metal shell. This is in contrast to the more common metal planes in which wood is confined to the knob and tote.

The most common antique infill planes are smoothers (7-1/2" to 8-1/2" in length) which exist in two different forms. One is a coffin-shaped plane, about the same general size and shape as the wooden coffin-shaped smoothers that preceded it. The other is a slightly larger plane with parallel sides. The next step up in size is the panel plane (13-1/2" to 17-1/2" in length). These have parallel sides. The parallel-sided jointers are the largest of the breed, sometimes reaching 28-1/2" in length.

In addition, many makers offered infill planes in other configurations, among them shoulder, rebate, chariot, bullnose, and mitre, with the mitre form preceding the others in the history of the genre.

Some of the early Spiers planes—as well as some of the later Norris planes—consisted of wood stuffing fitted into an iron or gunmetal cast body, and some of the later Norris planes were constructed around a rolled steel channel. But the finest and most highly prized of the infill planes were those with sides dovetailed to the soles. The dovetailed components were cut with small gaps in the joints to allow assembly. These gaps were later filled by peening the metal of the joints with a hammer. Careful examination of these dovetailed bodies usually reveals evidence of this method of construction.

The irons of infill planes are held in place in three different ways. The oldest examples set their irons through the use of wedges like those found in traditional wooden planes. Some of these planes have tapered wedge slots milled into the plane's metal sides. Tapping the wedge deeper into these tapered slots causes the wedge to become fixed tightly in place. In other cases, the wedge is tightened against a decorative metal bridge which extends across the width of the plane. However, the most common method of fixing the iron of an infill plane is through the use of a lever cap held in place by metal pins passing into the sides of the lever cap through the metal cheeks of the plane. Tension is applied by turning a thick bolt that passes vertically through the lever cap, applying pressure on the top of the cap iron.

Traditionally, the irons of infill planes were set the same way irons of wooden-bodied planes were set, through a combination of experienced guesswork and tapping. Then early in the 20th century, T. Norris & Son began to offer infill planes with adjusters that rivaled the convenience of the Bailey-style adjuster. The Norris adjuster is designed around a threaded metal rod housed in a channel cut into the wooden bed that supports the iron. The uppermost end of this rod rises above the top of the iron and terminates in a knurled adjustment knob. Rotating this knob causes the rod to turn. As it turns, it engages a threaded hole in a small steel cup which—depending upon the direction of rotation—either draws that cup toward the top of the bed or pushes it toward the bottom. The large head of the cap-iron screw is fit into this cup, and as a result, the iron/cap iron assembly rises and falls as the cup rises and falls.

This adjuster was a minor revolution in the field of toolmaking, one that brought the T. Norris & Son's company its greatest success. In fact for the last few decades of the company's existence, the adjuster was the focus of their advertising. Unfortunately, this convenience wasn't enough to save the firm, and in the post-War years, T. Norris & Son closed its doors, just as Spiers Planes had in the years leading up to World War II.

Adjusting the irons of infill planes: The irons of infill planes equipped with Norris-style adjusters are simple to set. The knurled knob which rises above the top of the iron controls both vertical and lateral movement. To adjust the iron, simply back off the pressure on the lever cap bolt, make the necessary vertical adjustment by rotating the knob and the lateral adjustment by racking the knob left or right. When the cutting edge is the way you want it, retighten the lever cap bolt.

The concept is simple, but the adjusters don't always work as efficiently as you expect them to. The adjuster on my A5, for example, has a fair amount of slop in it. If I rotate the knurled knob 5 or 6 degrees and check the shaving, I often find that the rotation has caused no perceptible change in shaving thickness. Another 5 degrees of rotation might be similarly non-productive, and then suddenly an additional 5 degrees of rotation causes a significantly different shaving thickness. Newer infill planes, equipped with adjusters made by modern makers, typically demonstrate a much closer relationship between knob rotation and depth of cut.

You set the irons of Spiers-style planes in much the same way as you set the irons in wooden-bodied planes. Begin by backing off the lever cap bolt. Then tap the iron into the correct position, using either the indirect heel-and-toe tapping or the direct tapping-on-the-iron method. When everything looks and feels right, snug up the lever-cap bolt. You should never use a tool to tighten the bolt, and it isn't necessary to draw it down to the maximum possible with unaided hand strength. All that's needed is enough tension to keep the iron from sliding around in use.

Once you have the iron set, take a shaving. If it's too heavy (rank) or not heavy enough, reset the iron.

Both the Norris #A5 on the left and the Jim Leamy smoother on the right have Norris-style adjusters, although the adjuster in the Leamy plane is a modern version made by Ray Iles.

Part 3: Metal planes

The most important selling point for the metal bench plane has always been the adjuster. Professional and amateur craftsmen who found the process of adjusting wooden bench planes to be mysterious and/or frustrating embraced the levers and wheels that could be made to produce incremental adjustments of the cutting edges of their metal planes—without the nuisance and imprecision of tapping. And just as important is the invention of the moveable frog for metal bench planes. When a wooden plane's mouth had grown wider either through repeated resurfacings of the soles or repeated grinding of the iron, a craftsman had to tighten up the mouth with a wood patch in order to restore the plane to its former level of performance. Metal planes with moveable frogs were another matter entirely. The mouths of these planes could be tightened simply by repositioning the frog, a modification that took only a screwdriver and a minute or two. In addition, if the mouth needed to be opened up for some rough work, it could be opened just as easily. It was, therefore, no longer necessary to have a separate plane with a wide mouth.

The use of hand planes had suddenly became much easier, so easy, in fact, that it made sense for an individual who might use a plane only once or twice a year to keep a couple of planes stored in the garage or basement. The planes might then sit in storage until—in many cases—

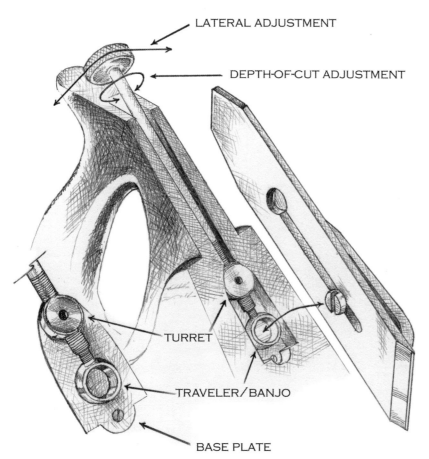

LATERAL ADJUSTMENT

DEPTH-OF-CUT ADJUSTMENT

TURRET

TRAVELER/BANJO

BASE PLATE

The Norris-style adjuster used on many later Norris planes, as well as on many modern infill planes, combines depth-of-cut adjustment and lateral adjustment in the same control. Rotating the knob raises and lowers the cutting edge, while racking the knob changes the lateral adjustment. Notice that the traveler on the bottom of the adjuster engages the iron/cap iron assembly by capturing the cap screw.

they were forgotten, only to be unearthed years later. Antique malls and junk stores are littered with such tools, and while some—very early Stanleys for example—have significant dollar values, most are just tools, which can be restored to usefulness with a little labor.

The depth-of-cut adjuster on the classic Stanley line of bench planes (numbered #1-#8) is a brass wheel mounted on the back of the frog. That wheel engages a metal yoke attached to the frog via a metal pin on which the yoke pivots. This yoke penetrates the frog, engaging the metal wheel on one end—grasping it with a two-tined metal fork—while on the other end engaging the cap iron with a nub, the end of which is housed in a small horizontal slot cut in the cap iron. When rotation on the brass wheel causes the fork on one end of the yoke to rise or to fall, the other end—fit into the cap iron—mirrors this movement in reverse, raising and lowering the cap iron which is itself attached to the iron with the cap screw.

Frog repositioning on Stanley bench planes is achieved in two different ways. For planes numbered #1-#8, repositioning is achieved by removing the lever cap and the blade/cap iron assembly and loosening the two frog attachment screws. These penetrate the frog and are turned into the plane body below. The frog may then be moved forward or backward and the screws retightened. But things changed with the Bedrock line (#602-#608) early in the 20th century. The Bedrock frog was attached through the use of a pair of frog clamping screws turned into the body of the plane just below the back side of the frog. This meant that mouth adjustment could be accomplished without removing the lever cap and the iron/cap iron assembly. When the frog clamping screws are loosened, the frog can be moved by turning the frog/throat/mouth adjustment screw which turns into the body of the plane and has a collar which engages a small metal tab screwed to the back bottom of the frog. The frog is then fixed in the new position by retightening the frog clamping screws.

In addition to the inventions of the adjuster and the moveable frog, metal planes offered other convenient features to attract potential purchasers. In 1885, Stanley introduced the lateral adjustment lever. This thin metal bar, which is attached to the top front of the frog with a pivot pin, has a round metal disk riveted to its bottom end. With the iron in place, that disk fits into the long vertical slot cut into the middle of the iron. When the lateral adjustment lever is pushed to the right, the disk engages with the slot, pushing the top end of the iron to the left. This action pushes the left side of the cutting edge down.

Here too the designers at Stanley have eliminated the tapping process in iron adjustment. With this lateral adjustment lever, a plane user can sight down the sole of the plane to the cutting edge while moving the lever back and forth in order to make the cutting edge perfectly parallel with the width of the sole.

Adjusting the iron on a Bailey-style metal plane: Adjusting the cutting edge of a Bailey-style plane couldn't be simpler. To raise it, turn the depth-of-cut adjuster counter clockwise. To lower it, turn the adjuster clockwise. Lateral adjustment is similarly straightforward. When you rack the lateral adjustment lever to the right, you lower the left side of the cutting edge. To lower the right side, rack the lever to the left

Critics of the Bailey-style adjuster often talk about the problem of backlash, which is rotation of the adjustment knob unaccompanied by any movement of the cutting edge. This occurs because the nub on the end of the yoke in the adjustment linkage doesn't completely fill the small horizontal slot in the cap iron. Therefore, it's necessary to rotate the adjustment knob about one full turn before the nub connects with the opposite side of the slot and the adjustment process can begin.

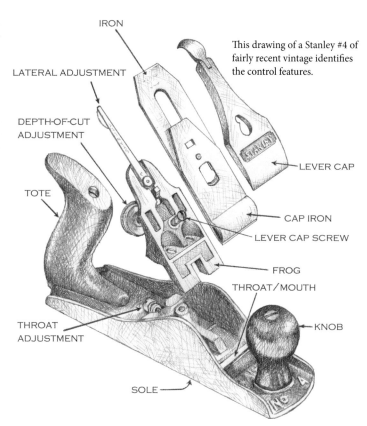

This drawing of a Stanley #4 of fairly recent vintage identifies the control features.

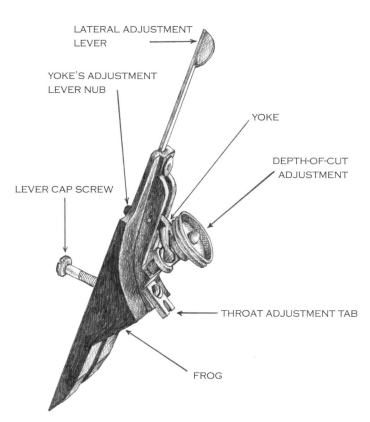

The yoke penetrates the frog with a Y-fork on one end that engages the depth-of-cut adjustment knob and on the other end engages the horizontal cap iron slot with a small nub.

This problem is magnified when Stanley planes are retrofit with heavier irons, sometimes doubling the amount of backlash, and there are websites that demonstrate ways that the cap iron slot might be modified to minimize the problem.

This Lie-Nielsen #4-1/2 is a modern version of the Bailey-style planes that Stanley has manufactured for over a century. This particular model is equipped with a high-angle frog to give it an advantage when used with difficult wood.

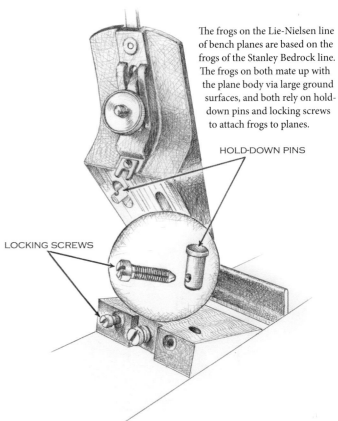

The frogs on the Lie-Nielsen line of bench planes are based on the frogs of the Stanley Bedrock line. The frogs on both mate up with the plane body via large ground surfaces, and both rely on hold-down pins and locking screws to attach frogs to planes.

HOLD-DOWN PINS

LOCKING SCREWS

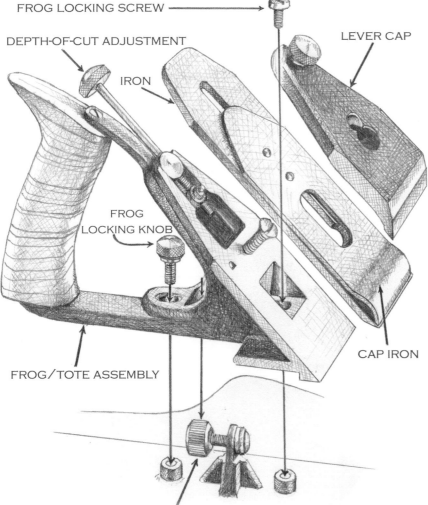

FROG LOCKING SCREW

DEPTH-OF-CUT ADJUSTMENT

IRON

LEVER CAP

FROG LOCKING KNOB

FROG/TOTE ASSEMBLY

CAP IRON

MOUTH ADJUSTMENT KNOB

Although similar to Bailey-style bench planes in general configuration, the Veritas line has several distinctive features not found on the Bailey-style planes. Mouth adjustment on the Veritas bench planes is made by moving a subassembly that includes the frog, tote, and a portion of sole, rather than the frog only. The lever cap is also different, substituting a knurled knob for the Bailey-style cam clamp. Also, the Veritas bench planes incorporate an adjuster used in most of the planes in the Veritas line. Resembling the Norris-style adjuster, it joins depth-of-cut and lateral adjustment control in the same control.

Part 4: Bevel-up metal planes

The metal plane class includes one other style that is recognizably different than the Bailey-style planes. These are the low-angle, bevel up bench planes. Although the design is based on low-angle block planes sized to be used with one hand, these are larger tools intended for two-hand operation. Lie-Nielsen Toolworks and Lee Valley Tools now offer these planes in both smoother and jointer sizes, as well as the original jack plane size of the Stanley #62.

Both Lie-Nielsen Toolworks and Lee Valley Tools offer bench planes based on the Stanley #62. This Veritas smoother is typical of those offerings.

Part 5: Transitional planes

Some plane enthusiasts believe that transitional planes were designed by Stanley to smooth the transition between the wooden planes that preceded them and the metal planes that followed them, but if that's true, these planes must have accomplished that work in short order because their 1869 debut was followed by the 1870 debut of the company's line of metal bench planes. Nevertheless, transitional planes did meet some of the demands of craftsmen reluctant to leave their wooden bench planes behind. Their comparative lightness and their smooth wood soles likely appealed to traditionalists, and transitional planes paired these traits with the ease of adjustment that gave metal planes their marketing advantage.

But in one important regard, the transitional plane is no improvement on its wooden predecessor: Closing up a mouth grown wide due to wear or to resurfacing of the sole means a fairly complicated fix. Although the metal frog is movable in much the same way as the frog on the #1-#8 series, the frog on a transitional plane doesn't support the iron all the way down to the cutting edge as it does in the case of a metal plane. On a transitional plane, the two inches of bed below the frog—that portion of the bed designed to support the cutting edge—can't be moved. It's simply a part of the plane's wood body. And if the frog is moved forward without creating some support for that back side of the cutting edge of the plane, the iron would be unrestrained at that point, a circumstance that leads to chatter.

It is possible to fix the bed problem without surgery. Shims can be added to the wooden bed below the frog, but for that approach to work, it's necessary to find or to make shims of the specific thicknesses required by the amount of sole wear, and that complicates the repair process. While I have heard that the planes of a great craftsman were shimmed with folded paper, it seems an inelegant solution. When I have needed to close the mouths of transitional planes, I just put in a patch, in the same way I do for wooden planes.

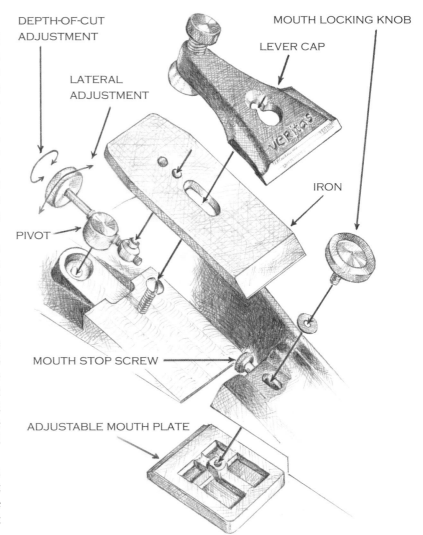

DEPTH-OF-CUT ADJUSTMENT

LATERAL ADJUSTMENT

PIVOT

MOUTH STOP SCREW

ADJUSTABLE MOUTH PLATE

MOUTH LOCKING KNOB

LEVER CAP

IRON

This drawing of the control elements of a Veritas low-angle, bevel-up jointer illustrates the working characteristics of this line of planes.

Bench Planes: Restoring a Wooden Bench Plane

A wooden plane dating to the 19th century or the early 20th century will almost always have some issues that need to be addressed before it can be put to use. This process begins with a cleaning of the wood with a damp rag and a mild detergent. I use a dilute solution of Murphy oil soap.

Next, check the sole with a straight edge and a pair of winding sticks. While the soles of metal planes may exhibit modest amounts of twist or bow, wooden planes are often found with more significant errors in flatness, and although a plane can often produce a shaving with an imperfect sole, the best results will be achieved after the sole has been given some attention.

If you choose to level the sole with another plane, that plane should be long enough to bridge the low spots on the sole you're flattening. If you use a smoother to flatten the sole of a jointer, that smoother may simply ride up and down the high and low spots, removing material without flattening. The sole of a smoother, however, can be flattened with another smoother.

The soles of wooden planes can also be flattened on a lapping table in the same way you might flatten the sole of a metal plane, and if the sole has just one or two significantly high spots, those can be reduced with a short plane before switching to a lapping table.

Although the flattening process eliminates one kind of error, it inevitably causes another: a widening mouth. This is because the front and back walls of the plane's throat angle away from each other as they rise within the body of the plane. The result is that flattening work that removes material near the mouth must be followed with a mouth patch if the plane is to return to its original level of performance.

Fixing a mouth grown too wide begins by cutting out a patch of the appropriate size from a bit of hardwood. Patches should be between 3/16" and 1/4" thick. The grain in the patch should run in the same direction as the grain in the sole. The shape of the patch is largely a matter of taste. The best period patches I've seen are bowtie-shaped, aligned lengthwise on the sole, but I've also seen first-rate period patches done as triangles or simple rectangles. Most of the patches I've installed are triangles, although I can't explain why.

Once the patch is made, you need to establish the desired width of the patched mouth. Begin by setting the iron in the plane being patched to a depth appropriate for the kind of work that the plane will be used to perform. Then with a straightedge, mark the desired location of the front of the mouth. With a pencil, trace the outline of your patch onto the sole with one side of the patch snugged up to the front edge of the mouth. Then, with the patch removed, cut the pencil lines with a marking knife.

Next, deepen the track of the marking knife with a paring chisel and begin working the patch mortise with a router, dropping the iron maybe 1/16" at a time.

When the mortise is deep enough to accept most of the patch's thickness, glue it and clamp it in place under a wood block protected with a bit of waxed paper. When the glue has cured, carefully level the patch with a small plane.

You should also check the fit of the wedge legs in the wedge slots. This fit should be near perfect along the full length of the slots on both sides of the plane. If it isn't, remove the wedge and the iron/cap iron assembly and inspect the bed. Sometimes crud will become impacted

When I'm shopping for planes, I don't take along a straight edge long enough to check the sole of a jointer, but before I buy such a plane, I sight along the sole to get a general idea. Then, when I get the plane home, I lay a straightedge along the sole.

Two pieces of straight material longer than the width of a plane can be used as winding sticks. (The longer the sticks, the easier it is to identify twist.) Lay one across each end of the plane's sole. Then lower your eye enough to sight the top of one stick against the top of the other. Any side-to-side discrepancy is evidence of twist. Sometimes to further refine my understanding of the sole, I'll position the winding sticks at different locations along the length of the sole.

on the bed under the iron. This can cause a poor fit. Fortunately, it's easy to scrape out.

If it isn't a crud buildup that's causing the misalignment, sight down the bed from the top, comparing the back side of the mouth to the top edge of the bed in much the same way you sighted the tops of the winding sticks when checking the flatness of the sole. Any disagreement between these lines could indicate a bedding error that could impact the fit of the wedge legs in the wedge slots.

Identifying an error here is one thing; fixing it is another, more difficult, matter, so please be cautious about making adjustments of the bed. The 19th century planemakers who leveled the beds of bench planes had enormous skill and experience. I've often been unsuccessful in my efforts to level beds with wide paring chisels in the way of those 19th century craftsmen. I have better luck with a wide planemaker's float, a cross between a rasp and a scraper. It's also possible that the wedge legs themselves may require a tune-up with a block plane, but this, too, is something that requires skill and experience to do well, so proceed cautiously.

Most of your restoration time will be spent re-establishing a cutting edge on the iron, which is covered in the sharpening chapter.

1

This particular plane was crowned at the mouth, so before I worked the full length of the sole, I took out most of that crown with a smoothing plane. I then finished leveling the sole on my lapping table.

2

My lapping table is a marble windowsill, siliconed to a 2 x 6. I attach sandpaper to the top of the marble with spray adhesive. I'm using 120 grit paper as my first abrasive for the sole of this smoother. Notice that the iron is in the plane—although raised, of course—during the lapping process. This is so that lapping will remove any twist or arcing of the plane's body imposed by the stress of wedging the iron.

3

At this point, the sole of the smoother was nearly flat. A few more strokes brought the rest of the sole down to the level of the low patches on the toe and the heel.

4

The most important step in the patching process is determining the location of the back edge of the patch ahead of the cutting edge. Too close to the iron and the plane won't take a shaving without further mouth adjustment. Too far away and the plane won't perform as well as it should.

5

After I penciled in the limits of the patch, I cut the lines with a marking knife. This knife kerf gave me a place in which I could accurately register the tip of my paring chisel.

I used a router to remove wood from the patch mortise, taking about 1/16" of depth at a time.

When the mortise was cleaned out, I was ready to glue the patch in place. After I'd applied the glue and positioned the patch, I laid a piece of waxed paper over the patch, placed a small flat scrap of wood on top of the paper, and clamped the whole sandwich together overnight.

The patch mortise should be about 1/16" shallower than the thickness of the patch so there is patch thickness to plane down to the surface of the sole.

A stable cutting edge depends in part on the fit between the legs of the wedge and the wedge slot. With a toothpick, I'm pointing to the intersection of these surfaces. You can see how well they mate on this particular plane.

There probably isn't any good reason to do it—at least any good reason relating to the performance of the plane—but I always sand away the rust on both the iron and the cap iron.

Bench Planes: Restoring a Metal Plane to Use

This virtually unused but rusted #7 is a perfect choice for restoration to user status. It's a plane without any collectible value, so there's no incentive to retain original surfaces, and it's a first-rate example of Stanley's tool making during a period—the 1940s—when they were still making good planes. Nearly all the japanning is intact, and the exposed metal showed only a light rime of surface rust. In addition, both the lateral-adjustment lever, and the depth-of-cut adjustment worked freely. Plus, it had the frog adjustment screw that Stanley later removed from their offerings, a non-essential but desirable feature. All in all, except for correctable cosmetic issues and the need for a heavier iron and cap iron, this #7 is the equal of many good-quality modern jointers.

Rust removal is accomplished through one of three methods: the use of a rust-removal chemical, the use of electrolysis, and the use of sandpaper. Because I nearly killed myself as a result of 40 years of exposure to finishing products (Stage IV non-Hodgkins lymphoma in 2003), I'm wary of introducing new chemicals into my shop routine. For that reason, I won't use any of the rust removal compounds now available. I avoid electrolysis for a completely different reason, although it too involves the use of some chemical reactions that worry me. The fact is that I don't like the arid, denuded surfaces electrolysis leaves behind. Tools cleaned in this way have a barren, cratered, moonlike look, an appearance that lacks the inviting warmth of a tool you might take into your hands for the sheer pleasure of holding it. So I remove rust by wearing it away with sandpaper, then following that up with a non-toxic preservative like camellia oil or wax. This particular method doesn't expose me to any potentially dangerous chemicals, and it leaves behind very natural looking metal surfaces.

Of course, sanding should be avoided in the case of any tool having historical importance. (Please see the chapter on tool restoration.) Fortunately, I don't own any important tools.

The next step is to endow that plane with all the characteristics attributed on pages 17-18 to a "good plane," specifically a flat sole, a securely bedded iron, a tight mouth, and a certain degree of comfort in the hands.

While it's important to check the flatness of the soles on metal planes before purchase, there's not much point to checking those soles again before restoration. Any defect in flatness—twist or bow or a combination of the two—will be removed in the same way: by patient lapping. Plus, progress toward flatness doesn't require a straight edge; it can be checked simply by looking at the sole from time to time during lapping.

I flatten soles on a marble windowsill which is siliconed to a 2 x 6. I fix sandpaper to the marble with a spray adhesive which holds the paper in place during use but relinquishes its hold easily when it needs to be changed. If the sole is badly out of whack, I start

Before taking the plane apart, with the iron raised above the sole and clamped in place under the pressure of the lever cap, I work the sole back and forth on my long marble lapping surface. I begin with a good-quality 120 grit paper that is fixed on the lapping plate with a coat of spray adhesive. It's hard to do this wrong when you're lapping such a large plane, but a much smaller plane might rock very slightly as it's worked back and forth on the lapping surface.

with a fairly coarse abrasive—in one instance 60 grit paper. More often, though, the first grit will be 120 or 150, followed by 220 and then possibly 320. If you don't have a dedicated flat surface like mine, you can use spray adhesive to fasten sandpaper to the ground surface of your tablesaw or your power jointer. Some craftsmen prefer sheets of heavy glass as substrates for their adhesive.

As you can see here, the high spots are revealed after only a few passes.

Lapping should be done with the iron fixed in place—with the cutting edge raised, of course—clamped under the lever cap just as it would be during use. This is because the force of the lever cap cam clamping down might cause a slight distortion of the sole that needs to be removed during flattening.

While it's important to continue working a sole that has significant errors of flatness, perfection isn't required. If, after a half hour of lapping, the sole has a spot a couple of thousandths low (you can check this with a set of feeler gauges for spark plugs), don't put in another hour of lapping to work the rest of the sole to that depth. The plane will work just fine with that one low spot.

When the sole is sufficiently flat, I disassemble the plane and clean up the individual parts. Mostly, this means removing rust, which I do with sandpaper, finishing usually with 220 grit. The threads in tapped holes and on screws can't be sanded so I lubricate them liberally with a light machine oil. I then turn the screws in and out of their tapped holes enough times to loosen the action. I clean japanning with a dilute solution of Murphy oil soap on a damp rag, scrubbing into tight spots with an old toothbrush.

I also check all the mating surfaces of the plane: the top and bottom of the frog, as well as the ground surfaces on the body of the plane with which the frog mates. Any dirt or metal burrs on these surfaces will impair the plane's performance, so I remove them by scraping or filing.

For years, I refinished the japanning with a Rustoleum product that lays down a thick black surface, similar to the asphalt product Stanley used. More recently, however, I've restrained my urge to repaint. Today, if I'm restoring a plane with a few areas of missing black, I just accept them.

I then reassemble the plane and put it to work.

After working the plane back and forth for a half hour through a couple of abrasive changes, the sole of the jointer is noticeably flatter, flat enough in fact for use, although I took a few more passes before I quit lapping. Once I'm satisfied with the flatness of the sole, I switch to 150 and then finish up with 220 grit lapping abrasives. Many people think that a plane—particularly a jointer used to flatten—must be perfectly flat to perform. Not so. While it is possible for a plane to be so badly out of whack that it can't be made to work, any plane with a reasonably flat sole will perform. In fact, the sole of this jointer was probably flat enough to function before I lapped the sole.

After the sole is flattened, I break the plane down to its constituent parts. A little tray—like the oval box lid you see here—is ideal for keeping small parts from being lost.

I then clean the rust off of individual parts, typically beginning with 120 when the rust is fairly heavy, then finishing with 220 or 320 if I'm feeling ambitious.

6

I clean up the japanning using soap and water applied with a toothbrush to get into tight corners.

7

This #7—made during the 1940s—can match the performance of any of the jointers made during Stanley's golden age.

8

Although it lacks the perfect beauty of a new Lie-Nielsen jointer or new Veritas jointer, restored tools, like this 70-year-old Stanley, have a beauty of their own, one less dependent on physical perfection, more dependent on their decades of history.

9

This frog is not from the #7 shown in earlier pictures. It's from a #606 restored by another craftsman who wasn't sufficiently careful with the paint he used to touch up the japanning. Some had gotten onto the machined surfaces on the top and bottom of the frog. I scraped away most of the paint and filed away the remainder. This surface, which mates with a ground surface on the body of the plane must be kept clean of crud or, in this case, paint.

10

This top surface of the frog is just as important as the bottom surface because this is where the iron mates with the frog. The previous owner had left paint here, too.

39

Bench Planes: Restoring an Infill Bench Plane

A couple of years ago, I asked Tony Murland, the English tool dealer, if he had a project plane, one I might be able to pick up cheap and restore to usefulness. Maybe a week later, after he'd finished a buying trip somewhere in the British Isles, he e-mailed to say he had a little Spiers smoother that would be just perfect. He sent me a half dozen photos, and I bought the plane. At my request, he also included two blocks of rosewood to help me with the repairs.

The plane's shell was sound with only superficial pitting on the sole and sides. The dovetailing was clean and the mouth tight. "Spiers Ayr" was lightly stamped on the tarnished brass of the lever cap. The iron was a good heavy replacement, stamped MAWHWOOD, with about an inch of metal left below the slot. The wood, however, was in bad shape.

The horn had been broken off the tote and lost, and there was a second tote break, nearly clear through, just above the base. Also the bun (the squarish block of rosewood on the front of the plane) was missing two fairly large chunks of wood.

But the most troublesome aspect of the plane's condition was the large number of screws and nails someone had pounded or driven into the tote and bun to hold the plane together. There was a nail and a heavy brass screw in the bun and two screws and two nails in the tote.

I began the repair by removing the embedded metal. While this was fairly straightforward at the rear of the plane, the head of the heavy brass screw in the bun had been twisted off, so I had to use a screw removal kit to work it to the surface.

If the break in the tote had been recent and unrepaired, I would have been able to put it back together with nothing more than a bit of glue. Unfortunately, when I brought the two broken surfaces back together, I could see that some material was missing. Plus, the material that was present had been fouled with adhesive during an earlier, unsuccessful attempt at repair.

This sad puppy was the project plane Tony Murland found for me. Notice the broken-off brass screw imbedded in the bun. *Courtesy of* Woodwork *magazine.*

I decided the tote needed to be broken in half with the top and bottom surfaces of the break planed flat. I could then graft in a piece of new rosewood, using flat clean surfaces as glue joints, taking care to align the grain direction of the replacement stock to match the grain direction of the original tote. I then added a second piece at the top of the tote for the new horn. Here, too, I had to begin by planing the top of the stub flat in order to get a good glue surface.

In a perfect world, I would have restored the tote to its original magnificence, but unfortunately, I didn't have quite enough good rosewood, so I settled on a modified horn that would restore the tool to usefulness if not its original appearance.

I cut out the 1/4" thick replacement stock for the base of the tote and the replacement horn, clamping in turn each of the tote's three loose sections in place with my hands until the glue grabbed. When the glue had cured, I worked the replacement stock with a rasp and sandpaper to fair together the new elements and the original stock. I finished the repair by driving a 3-1/2" woodscrew up through the tote from the bottom. This is a feature some original makers of infill planes included in their work. *Courtesy of* Woodwork *magazine.*

The bun required similar repairs. After deciding to graft on two pieces of replacement rosewood, I planed and pared flat surfaces for good glue joints and then glued the replacements in place, clamping each piece with my hand until the glue grabbed. These, too, I faired with rasps and sandpaper. *Courtesy of* Woodwork *magazine.*

This little Spiers will never be mistaken for an all-original plane. It will, however, provide me and future owners with years of good use. And that was my only goal in making these repairs. If the plane had been unique or one of only a small population, I would have placed it on a shelf to admire, but since it is one of a fairly large number of existing Spiers parallel-sided smoothers, I felt it was appropriate to make the repairs I made. *Courtesy of* Woodwork *magazine.*

Bench Planes:
Sharpening the Iron

In the world of hand planes, the cutting edge is the point where the rubber meets the road. It is the point where a plane's singular purpose is realized, and a plane's ability to realize that purpose is totally dependent on the sharpness of that cutting edge.

Part 1: Flattening the back

The sharpening process begins by flattening and polishing the back of the iron. This often overlooked procedure is critical because the cutting edge doesn't consist only of the ground primary bevel and the honed secondary bevel. It consists, instead, of the intersection of two planes: the honed bevel and the back. If the back is rough and uneven, the cutting edge will be rough and uneven, no matter how much attention is lavished on the bevels.

Unfortunately, even some new irons must have their backs flattened and polished before they're used, and every antique/used plane I've ever purchased had an iron the back of which was badly in need of attention. If the back problems are relatively minor—for instance on a new iron—it can be polished on lapping plates. I use diamond plates in three grits: 250, 600, and 1200. But often, used irons need a more aggressive treatment. Sometimes, if the surface irregularities are too much for my diamond plates, I'll lap the back first on sandpaper, beginning typically with 120 grit before switching to 150 and 220, then moving to the diamond plates. This sandpaper work must be done a truly flat surface, so I'll lay the strips of sandpaper on one of my diamond plates or on the ground outfeed table of my power jointer.

If the back of the iron shows signs of significant rust degradation, I'll first attempt to flatten it with sandpaper on a flat surface, like the 120 grit paper I'm using here. Where the rust is lighter, my first abrasive is a 250 grit diamond plate.

Flattening the Backs of Badly Rusted Irons

Sometimes I'm wrong even when I'm absolutely convinced I'm right. Take the business of flattening the backs of badly rusted irons.

For years I flattened them on the sides of grinding wheels. I did this because the rust had eaten too deeply into the steel to be removed with hand lapping, even with a very coarse abrasive. I did this reluctantly because I knew this use of a grinding wheel wasn't recommended, but—I reasoned—since there were grinding wheels out there specifically designed for side grinding, it was probably a safe enough practice with grinding wheels in general.

Plus, I didn't know of any other way to work down through a century and a half of rust pits. True: other craftsmen recommended flattening these encrusted irons on a belt sander, but I knew that wouldn't work because I'd tried it. When I looked back into my memory, I saw myself in various past shops at various ages, working steel on a belt sander fixed upside down in a vise, and in my memory, the abrasive always wore out too quickly and the heat began to build up—also too quickly. In the confident clarity of my memory, I saw the repeated failure of my best efforts to flatten pitted steel on a belt sander.

I clung doggedly to this packet of beliefs until—as I was working on this book—a friend suggested that I might be wrong about the existence of grinding wheels that were certified safe for side grinding, that I might be wrong also about the use of belt sanders to quickly and efficiently flatten the backs of badly pitted irons.

I didn't scoff. I had too much respect for the friend who suggested I might be wrong. Instead, I spent an hour searching on the internet in pursuit of grinding wheels certified for side grinding. Nothing. Absolutely nothing. Maybe they were out there for some obscure manufacturing process, but it was clear that grinding wheels certified for side grinding were not accessible to ordinary people like me. I was convinced. These wheels existed only in my imagination. My confidence shaken, I went out to the shop to see if I was also wrong about flattening the back of plane irons with a power sander.

After installing a new 80-grit belt, I clamped a sander upside down in a vise and went to work. Wow. The 80-grit belt ripped right through the rust on the first iron. In less than a minute, I had flat clean steel. I searched for a more deeply rusted iron. In less than a minute, that iron also was clean. I grabbed a handful of irons from a supply cabinet, and buzzed through them one after another, working my way past deep rust inclusions in less time than it takes to tell about it. After cleaning up the rust, I then worked the backs of the irons with a succession of sandpaper and diamond plate grits—120, 220, 250, 600—before polishing the backs on my 1200 grit diamond plate.

(I've experimented with taking this polishing process to more extreme levels, in one instance going so far as to polish the back of an iron with a hard black Arkansas stone, but the effort such a polishing requires is not adequately rewarded by a commensurate improvement in cutting performance.)

When the iron is too badly degraded for hand lapping, I suggest a belt-sander treatment. First, clamp the belt sander upside down in a bench vise, then lay the bottom of the iron's back side on the running 80-grit sanding belt, holding it in place with a couple of finger tips. (I tried for an hour to shoot this image live, but the vibration of the running sander ruined every shot.) Check the progress every 15 or 20 seconds. Within a minute or so, the back should be reduced below the level of the deepest rust.

On the morning I tested this method, I did almost a dozen irons. Every one was quickly surfaced deep enough for me to hand lap with a variety of abrasive grits. The iron shown here had the most stubborn rust inclusion. If you look at that section a half inch above the cutting edge, you can see I'm not all the way down at that point; however, the half inch of clean surface below that inclusion is more than enough to polish. I then lapped the back with 120-grit paper, 150-grit paper, then switched to my lapping stones, working the back first with a 250-grit stone, finishing up with 600 and 1200-grit stones.

With a square, I determined that the width of the cutting edge wasn't perpendicular to either side of the iron.

I then jointed the end of the iron. Because the error was fairly significant, I touched it up on my grinding wheel.

I then fine-tuned the squared end by dragging it lengthwise across sandpaper and lapping plates.

Part 2: Jointing the edge

When the back is adequately polished, it's time to joint the edge. Almost inevitably the cutting edge of an antique/used plane iron is not square across its width, and most planes are easier to set up if that edge is perpendicular to the sides of the iron. I say "most" because there are exceptions to this rule. Some older plane irons taper not only in thickness but also in width; if you grind the cutting edge so that it's perpendicular to one side of the iron, it won't be perpendicular to the other. This taper across the width isn't always the result of an iron made that way deliberately. It can be simply the inadvertent result of the hand methods once used to make plane irons. In such a case, I average out the difference, creating an end perpendicular to an imaginary line drawn down the middle of the iron's width. The other exception to the perpendicular rule is more interesting. Some planes were simply built out of square and require an iron ground to match. I have a Spiers panel plane that slouches a bit to one side. You can't see the slouch when you look at the plane, but if you install a square iron, the cutting edge can't be set so that an equal amount penetrates the sole on both sides. With a plane like this, the only solution is to grind the iron deliberately out of square.

While that cutting edge may not be perpendicular to both sides of the iron, it should be straight all the way across or cambered in a regularized fashion. Irons intended for edge-jointing and some smoothing applications should be jointed dead straight across, with the corners relieved very slightly. Irons intended for leveling work and some smoothing work perform best with a slight camber. (Camber is an arc across the width of the iron.) And the irons in roughing planes should be ground with significant cambers across their widths. Cambering allows a plane to take a shaving—sometimes quite thick—without the iron digging in at the corners and stalling the plane.

In the case of irons to be assigned straight edges, I check the edge with a square. If there is significant error, I'll address that on the edge of a grinding wheel, holding the iron not flat on the tool rest, but perpendicular to the wheel's edge. If, however, the iron is generally straight across, I joint that edge by running it—with the iron standing straight up—across several grits of sandpaper and diamond lapping plates, ending with a 600 grit.

After experimenting with a number of different ways of creating camber, I've settled on the use of a series of cardboard patterns laid on the polished back of irons painted with layout fluid. With a sharp stylus, I trace one of these curves onto an iron. I then move to the grinder and create that camber, moving the iron freehand against the wheel while the front surface is flat on my grinder's tool rest. It takes a bit of practice, but the effect is rewarded by improved plane performance.

43

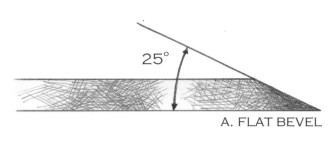

A. FLAT BEVEL

25°

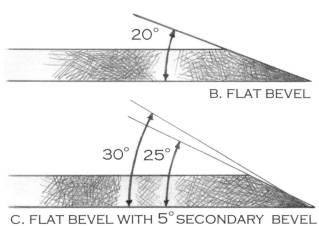

B. FLAT BEVEL

20°

C. FLAT BEVEL WITH 5° SECONDARY BEVEL

30° 25°

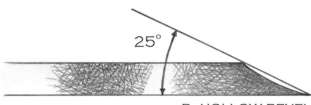

D. HOLLOW BEVEL

25°

The top three bevels are flat ground. The bottom bevel is hollow ground. The third bevel from the top illustrates how a secondary bevel can change the cutting angle, although this change comes into play only in the case of bevel-up tools.

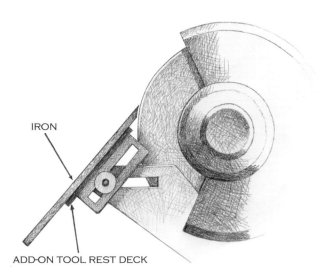

IRON

ADD-ON TOOL REST DECK

This drawing shows my grinding arrangement. The add-on tool rest gives me a larger bearing surface when I'm grinding plane irons. Notice also the way in which the roundness of the wheel is transferred to the end of the iron to produce a hollow-ground bevel.

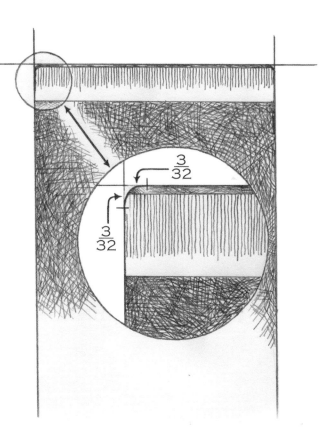

$\frac{3}{32}$

$\frac{3}{32}$

This is a desirable profile for irons used to joint or for final smoothing: dead straight across with the corners slightly relieved.

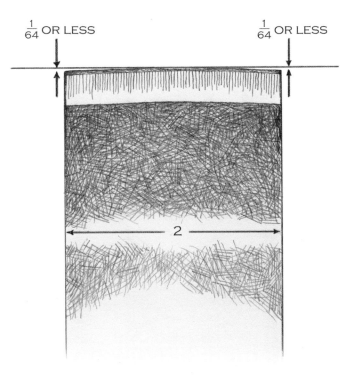

$\frac{1}{64}$ OR LESS

$\frac{1}{64}$ OR LESS

2

This is a profile for a smoothing plane iron which has been slightly cambered to produce a surface that will reveal to the hand that it has been worked with hand tools. (Please note that the amount of camber was exaggerated for clarity in the drawing.)

44

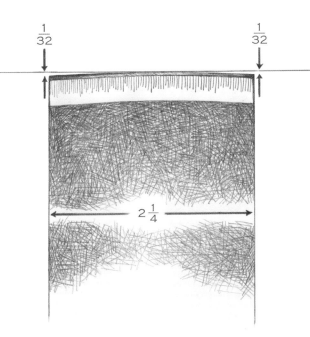

This is a profile for a leveling plane, a jack plane or longer used to level a panel prior to smoothing. (Please note that the amount of camber was exaggerated for clarity in the drawing.)

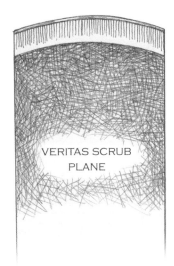

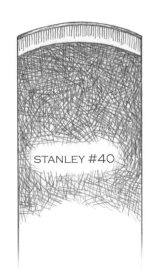

These are actual traced iron profiles for two popular roughing planes: a Veritas scrub plane on the left and a Stanley #40 on the right.

Part 3: Selecting a bevel

Grinding a bevel has only one purpose: to make it easier to hone the final bevel so that the cutting edge is as sharp as possible. At least in theory, a ground primary bevel isn't necessary. You can simply hone a final bevel that reaches all the way across the thickness of the iron, that is if you have the patience. The ground bevel is established simply to set up an approximation that will make it easier to hone that final bevel. The key word there is "approximation." It doesn't matter if that approximation is 20 degrees from the back of the iron or 22 degrees or 24 degrees. (There is one circumstance in which the angle does matter, and that is in regard to what is called the "clearance angle." A ground bevel must be ground with a shallow enough angle so that the heel of the bevel remains above the work surface when the cutting edge is engaged.) All you need is a bevel somewhere in the right neighborhood in order to give you a useful starting point when you begin to hone, a starting point that will allow you to produce a final bevel that is only, perhaps, 1/32" of the iron's thickness, rather than its full thickness. The truth is that the ground bevel is not involved in the cutting process at all. That process takes place only at that point where the honed bevel and the polished back intersect.

I have to admit that—prior to my work on this book—I had never made an organized attempt to measure the bevels I ground on my plane irons. In fact, it had been years since I'd measured any at all. My practice is to set the tool rest in what looks like the right position and begin work. When I'm regrinding an iron on which I've already shaped a bevel, I match the original angle. When I'm grinding the first bevel on the iron of a new acquisition, I use the angle on which the tool rest was left by my grinding of a previous bevel.

To judge the consistency of my work, I make periodic checks of the width of the cutting edge by examining the white line at the tip of the edge. If the white line is wider on one side than the other, the wider side needs additional work. This line is the same from side to side.

Because the tool rests that came with my grinder were too small, I epoxied (and later welded) larger sheet steel plates onto those rests. These give me surfaces on which I can securely stabilize a plane iron while passing it back and forth across the edge of the grinding wheel. The rest is set so that when an iron is laid flat on the rest, the grinding wheel will create a bevel in the 20 to 25 degree range. At the start, when the cutting edge is still thick, it's possible to take a fairly aggressive cut, but later, when the cutting edge has grown thin, passes must be lighter and move more quickly back and forth across width of the grinding wheel.

45

When I started measuring these angles for this book, I found that I have a preference for relatively shallow angles, in the 20-25 degree neighborhood. This is, I suppose, because I find it easier to quickly produce a really sharp edge on an iron ground to a shallow bevel. It would be possible to put a really sharp edge on an iron ground on a steeper bevel, even a 90 degree bevel, but such an angle wouldn't work in a bevel-down plane. The heel of the bevel would keep the cutting edge from contacting the work.

Traditionally, bevels in the 20-25 degree range are favored for the irons in bevel-up planes, while bevels in the 25-30 degree range are favored for bevel-down planes. I prefer the shallower (20-25 degree) bevels for all my planes.

Some craftsmen favor flat bevels; others favor hollow-ground bevels. Flat-bevellers usually cite the relative strength of flat bevels in order to defend their position. Hollow-ground bevellers usually cite the relative ease with which hollow-ground bevels can be honed in order to defend their position. Both arguments are powerful, but there are other elements involved in the bevel-style discussion, elements that, at least in my mind, tip the scales in the direction of the hollow-bevellers. First, if anybody is using a plane in a way that makes it likely that a portion of a hollow-ground edge might break off—well, they need to re-examine their technique because there isn't any right way to operate a hand plane that could result in breaking off bits of tool steel. But the second element is, I think, more persuasive, and that's the element of grinding machine cost. I don't have deep pockets, and when I spend money on tools, I would rather buy a good plane than a good grinder. In practice, this has meant that I have always done my bevel grinding on cheap machines, never costing more than $40, and these machines can't be set up to grind flat bevels in any safe way. Grinding a flat bevel requires a machine designed for that application, one that has a wheel mounted horizontally, and those machines are expensive.

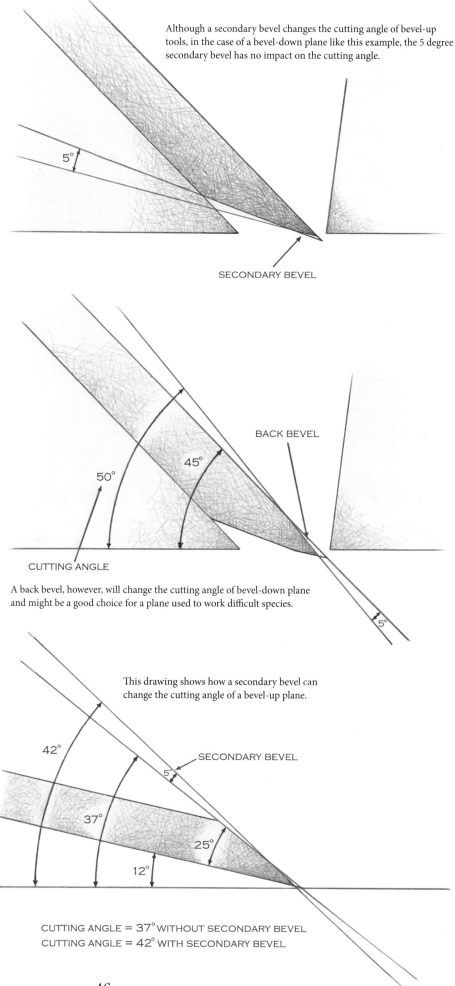

Although a secondary bevel changes the cutting angle of bevel-up tools, in the case of a bevel-down plane like this example, the 5 degree secondary bevel has no impact on the cutting angle.

SECONDARY BEVEL

BACK BEVEL

CUTTING ANGLE

A back bevel, however, will change the cutting angle of bevel-down plane and might be a good choice for a plane used to work difficult species.

This drawing shows how a secondary bevel can change the cutting angle of a bevel-up plane.

SECONDARY BEVEL

CUTTING ANGLE = 37° WITHOUT SECONDARY BEVEL
CUTTING ANGLE = 42° WITH SECONDARY BEVEL

46

Part 4: Bevel-grinding zen

Think about the way you learned to shoot a jump shot. If your coach had told you that your first jump shot *had* to go through the rim, would you have demonstrated the relaxed form essential to consistently good marksmanship? Probably not. And basketball coaches understand this. They know that in order to develop shooting form, you must begin by disregarding the end product. In fact, you could probably learn the fundamentals of the jump shot without access to a backboard and a rim.

We understand this about sports, but we don't always understand this about craftsmanship, which is—I suspect—closely related to athleticism.

Think about the first time you ground a new bevel on a plane iron. If your experience was like mine, you probably told yourself your first effort had to produce a usable bevel (after all, you were grinding that bevel because whatever it was you were doing required a new edge), and while your first effort might, in fact, have produced a usable bevel, it almost certainly didn't teach you how to efficiently produce a second one. The result is that you may have gone years producing usable—if labored—ground bevels without actually developing the rhythm, form, and touch necessary to grind consistently good bevels. At least, that's what I did.

Then, many years after I had become a professional furniture maker—even after I'd begun writing about woodworking for magazines—I realized I had little confidence in my ability to efficiently grind a consistently good bevel, this despite the fact that I'd been doing it for 25 years. I knew I could get there. My edges were certainly usable, but I knew I was spending way too much time on the process. Most telling was my comfort level at the grinder, or—I should say—my discomfort level. I re-ground bevels only when I absolutely had to, and it was work I never liked because I knew I didn't do it well.

Then, one day at a flea market, as I stood at a folding card table studying a vendor's oily mound of tools, I had an idea. I picked out several of that vendor's most battered planes—less than $10 each—took them home, pulled the irons, and threw the bodies away.

Then with the first of those irons, I went to work on my grinder. I squared up the cutting edge and began to grind. When I had formed a pretty good bevel, I studied it, ground it off, and started over. Then, when I finished the second bevel, I studied it and ground it off. Then I ground and ground off a third and a fourth. In fact, when I was done I had an iron the size—if not the sharpness—of a razor blade.

The process of forming a bevel I was never going to use was liberating. I felt no need to be perfect. I was free to fail, and that freedom to fail—by itself—allowed me to work more efficiently. That first bevel, which I had formed in less than ten minutes, was probably better than any of my previous efforts at the wheel.

As I ground away at the first iron, I paused from time to time to think about how I might improve my technique. I considered new hand positions, different speeds to pass the iron across the face of the wheel, different amounts of pressure I might apply, different angles for the tool rest.

As I finished each bevel, I checked it with a square and sighted it to assess my progress. It wasn't long before I could see that each was a good, clean hollow-grind, nicely perpendicular to the sides of the iron, and better yet, each one was a little better than the one before.

When I had consumed the first iron, I picked up another and went to work on it, grinding it away, one edge at a time. When an edge flared and scorched, I paused and thought about what I'd done wrong. Then I deliberately did it again. And I repeated this over and over until I learned to anticipate when the burning would occur. I then began to test techniques that would allow me to grind quickly without scorching. I surfaced the wheel with a dresser, wearing away the impacted bits of metal that might cause heating. I kept the iron moving continuously from side to side as it engaged the wheel. I experimented with a lighter touch as the bevel neared the tip of the iron. I lubricated the tool rest with water so I could move the iron across the rest while applying only the slightest pressure. I tried quenching the warming iron in water. I kept practicing, until I could work right up to the edge of disaster without burning the iron.

I don't think you can learn the necessary rhythm, pace, and touch that bevel grinding requires by reading a magazine article or by watching a video or even by watching an expert at work. I believe the only way to find that rhythm, pace, and touch is to experiment, to hold an iron in your hands, to pass it back and forth across the face of the wheel, while keeping your hands and eyes fully engaged in the process. And of course to really learn, you must do this repeatedly. Once or twice is not enough.

Bevel grinding—like so many other higher-level woodshop processes—isn't something that can be meaningfully expressed in an itemized list (first do this, then this, then this) because bevel grinding doesn't lend itself to being intellectualized in this way. That's because, I think, the knowledge doesn't accumulate in the brain; it accumulates in the hands and in the eyes.

I don't mean the sharpening process can't be studied empirically to good effect. The advances in sharpening technology we now enjoy reflect the usefulness of the scientific method. I mean instead that the actual practice of freehand bevel grinding is probably more art and athleticism than science.

You can't learn to shoot a jump shot by reading a book or by listening to a tape or even by watching a great shooter practicing his craft. You have to take the ball in your hands and take shot after shot after shot. If you do this often enough, gradually your body will do what it does so much better than your brain: It will learn.

Part 5: Creating a secondary bevel

When you're creating a secondary bevel for the iron in a bevel-down tool, that secondary bevel doesn't alter the cutting angle of the plane. The cutting angle of such a plane is the same as the plane's bedding angle, regardless what the secondary bevel might measure (see drawings on page 46). But the secondary bevel of a bevel-up tool can change the cutting angle. In such a plane, a secondary bevel of—for example—5 degrees will add 5 degrees to the cutting angle of that plane. What this means is that, in the case of bevel-down planes, you're only concerned with attaining a sharp edge, while in the case of bevel-up planes, you're concerned about not only sharpness but how that secondary bevel might change the plane's cutting angle.

This secondary bevel can be formed with the iron held in a honing jig, or you can hone the bevel freehand. Several years ago when I was working on a story about smoothing planes for *Woodwork* magazine (now sadly gone), I asked Lee Valley Tools for one of their honing jigs to test drive for that story. Although it looked a little intimidating, the MK II they sent me made achieving consistent secondary bevels ridiculously easy. I think that anybody new to the sharpening process should consider a jig like the MK II; however, in the years since I finished that *Woodwork* story, I've reverted to my old ways: I'm back to honing freehand, simply because it's the method I'm used to and because—at least for me—it's quicker and easier.

There are two different ways to form secondary bevels on hollow-ground irons. The easiest way is to form a secondary bevel with an angle identical to the angle of the primary bevel. To do this freehand, place the ground bevel on your stone (I use a 1200 grit diamond lapping plate) so that both the top and bottom edges of that bevel are resting securely. Then, holding the iron firmly in that same attitude using both hands, work the cutting edge up and down the length of your stone moving it in a roughly circular fashion. After a few of these circular strokes, check your progress by lifting the iron and examining the progress of your secondary bevel. If you see more wear on one side of the bevel than the other, adjust the pressure you're applying and take a few more strokes. Continue in this way until you can detect—all across the cutting edge—a burr when you slide your thumb up the back side of the iron. Then turn the iron over and lap the back side until the burr can't be felt from the back side. If the burr also can't be felt when you drag your thumb up the front side of the iron (across the bevel), you're done honing, although if the edge is unsatisfactory, you may want to raise a new burr. More likely, however, the burr will still be attached. In that case, lightly hone the bevel once again, and when the burr has been pushed to the back side of the iron, lap that back side. Repeat this process, if necessary, until the burr has fallen away.

The honing process is over when the burr falls away, but the sharpening process may not be. If you're not happy with your edge, raise another burr by honing the bevel and alternate between front and back side lapping-plate work until a new burr has formed and fallen away. Do this until the edge is sharp.

The other method for creating a secondary bevel is nearly the same as the one I just described. The only difference is the angle at which you hold the iron during honing.

After you've rested the bevel on the lapping plate, lift the end of the iron you're holding a few degrees so that the iron contacts the lapping plate only at the tip. Then hone the iron using the same circular strokes I described above. This produces a honed edge at a more acute angle than the one above, one that seems to last a little

This is the hand position I use when I establish secondary bevels. It allows me to balance out the pressure on both sides of the cutting edge, while holding the iron at a consistent angle.

To check for the presence of a burr, I push my thumb up the back of the iron past the cutting edge. (Never drag your thumb *along* a cutting edge.)

I then lap the back of the iron to begin the process of removing the burr.

longer than the cutting edge described above. Plus, this cutting edge seems to permit more honings between sessions at the grinding wheel. I qualify both these statements with the word "seems" because I've never tried to compare the two methods in any empirical manner, and I'm not sure that I could.

Part 6: Defining sharpness

How do you tell that an edge is sharp? Good question, and there are lots of different tests advocated by lots of different people. Here are a few:

1. Lay the polished back of the iron on your thumb nail. Gently push the iron forward about 1/8". If the cutting edge raises a thin shaving of thumbnail, it's sharp or so says this test.

2. Alternatively, hold the iron at a 90 degree angle to your thumbnail and lightly scrape the nail with the cutting edge. If the cutting edge raises a little roll of nail tissue, it's sharp or so says this test.

3. Hold a piece of paper up by one corner, grasping it between the thumb and forefinger. With your other hand move the plane iron down into the edge of the sheet of paper so that the iron's cutting edge is perpendicular to the edge of the paper. Push the cutting edge into the paper with a slight back-and-forth sawing action. If the cutting edge slices the paper, it's sharp or so says this test.

4. Lay the back of the iron on your forearm with the cutting edge 6"-8" from your elbow. Keeping the iron flat against your skin, push it gently toward your elbow. If it bulldozes a roll of arm hair ahead of the cutting edge, it's sharp or so says this test.

I think all of these tests can give you useful information about the sharpness of the cutting edge (I'm partial to the arm hair test), but the only test that matters is the test you make when you've installed the iron in a plane and you've used it to make a shaving. If the iron cuts cleanly, leaving behind a surface that gleams, it's truly sharp.

When I'm sharpening an iron for an audience at a woodworking school or a woodworking show, I sometimes employ one additional sharpening step. After I've ground the primary bevel, after I've honed the secondary bevel, I charge a fabric wheel on my grinder with an abrasive compound, and then buff the edge both front and back. I can then shave the hair on my arm, even if I did less than perfect work on my secondary bevel. This always works, but I suspect it's more parlor trick than technique because my impression is that the edge I form in this manner at the wheel is fragile, if very sharp. It's an edge that I suspect breaks down the first time I apply it to anything harder than arm hair. When I get a less than perfect edge in the comfortable confines of my shop, I simply rework the secondary bevel until the cutting edge comes out right.

Just to the right of the picture's center, you'll see a narrow white line angling up from the secondary bevel. This is a burr partially broken off by repeated honings on the cutting edge and the back of the iron. When the burr breaks off, it leaves a sharp cutting edge.

The back of a sharp iron will be polished enough to be reflective. The corrugations on the sole of this plane are reflected on the back of the iron.

Bench Plane: the Setup

I have a friend who collects English infill mitre planes, and I once sent him a link to one such plane that was being auctioned on eBay. The plane was stamped with the name of a maker I knew my friend collected, so I assumed he would immediately jump into the bidding.

But he didn't. "The mouth was too wide," he later explained.

I went back to the listing, which I had bookmarked. It included a number of sharply focused photos. I found the one showing the plane's sole, and I clicked on the image to enlarge it to life size. The mouth was the width of maybe half a sharpened pencil point. You could scoot a sheet of cheap copy paper through that mouth. Maybe.

For a jointer this would have been a tight mouth, but one of the defining characteristics of a good mitre plane is a tight—often extraordinarily tight—mouth, and a mitre plane with a mouth wide enough to pass a sheet of copy paper simply doesn't have the appeal of a mitre plane with a really tight mouth.

One of the keys to accomplishing good work with hand planes is recognizing that each plane must be set up to accomplish the specific task it has been assigned.

Part 1: The revolution

After a bench plane has been restored, after the iron has been sharpened, there are only two aspects of the plane's geometry that can be manipulated in order to affect the performance of the plane: the depth of cut and the width of the mouth. (I'm considering lateral adjustment as one aspect of depth of cut.) In fact, in the case of some planes, only the depth of cut can be manipulated. The English infill, for example, has a mouth that can't be adjusted. If a restorer should lap the sole of an infill in order to eliminate some rust pitting, the mouth will begin to widen and the performance of that plane will be forever compromised (well, "forever" unless the restorer has the ability to graft in new metal).

The mouths of classic wooden bench planes can be adjusted only by inlaying patches or by paring away at the throat. So it's simply not worthwhile to widen and tighten the mouth of such a plane in order to suit the same plane for different tasks. But most metal planes are different. Most metal planes have mouths that can be opened and closed simply by making a few quick adjustments with a screwdriver or an adjustment knob. The frog of a Bailey-style plane can be moved backwards and forwards after releasing a couple of screws, in effect changing the width of the mouth. Some block planes (and their larger cousins—bevel-up smoothers, jacks, and jointers—as well) have movable mouth plates that can change the width of the mouth.

This is a critical innovation in plane design, perhaps even more important than the depth-of-cut manipulations made so simple by the Bailey-style adjuster because depth of cut could already be adjusted to suit different applications, simply by tapping the iron into a new alignment. But a simple mechanism for changing the mouth to suit those different applications? That was revolutionary.

This Veritas # 5-1/4 is taking a heavy shaving through a gaping mouth. From this perspective, the shaving appears to be lifting cleanly. Notice the distance between the front edge of the shaving and the front edge of the mouth.

This image of the underside of that shaving reveals how much wood is breaking out and how rough the exposed surface has become as a result of the wide mouth and the excessive depth of cut.

By contrast, when the depth of cut and mouth have been reduced, the Veritas #5-1/4 leaves a beautiful surface.

Above:
This Lie-Nielsen #62 is being used to edge joint a short length of curly maple. Notice the distance between the front edge of the shaving and the front edge of the mouth. This is way too much mouth for finishing work on a curly species.

Above right:
This disturbed surface is the result of the wide mouth in the previous photo.

Right:
This photo shows how cleanly the LN #62 will cut curly maple if the mouth is closed up and the depth of cut fractionally reduced.

Part 2: Depth of cut

Anyone who has ever struggled to master hand plane use has experienced the disastrous consequences of working with too much iron exposed. Instead of gliding across the surface with shavings rising smoothly through the throat, the plane chokes on a too-thick shaving, grinding to a halt, and even if the mouth is open wide enough to pass that thick shaving, the first time the plane passes over a grain reversal or a patch of swirling grain, the thick shaving and open mouth leave behind a disturbed surface.

Depth-of-cut management is the mechanism by which plane users balance efficient cutting with clean cutting. In order to accomplish work in an efficient way, it's important to take the thickest shavings appropriate for a specific task without, at the same time, taking shavings of such a thickness that they do significant damage to the surface being worked. If you're using a scrub plane to remove 3/8" of bow from both ends of a walnut plank, you don't want to remove the bow a couple of thousandths at a time. That might take hours. Instead, you want to remove it 1/16 "at a time, even if that shaving leaves behind a disturbed surface. Leveling planes, too, may take a moderately heavy shaving. If you're working a large glued-up panel that has significant surface discontinuities where the individual boards come together, you don't want to take them down one gossamer shaving at a time. You want to take shavings heavy enough so that you can level the panel in a reasonable amount of time. In this situation also, you might decide that a combination of plane tracks and modest tearout is a satisfactory tradeoff for the speedy leveling of the surface.

And of course, finishing work has a different purpose, one requiring a much more minute depth of cut. When the object is not to level but to refine an already leveled surface, no amount of surface disturbance is acceptable. Your plane should be set so that it will take only those shavings that will leave behind a perfectly clean surface. However, there is considerable variation in the possible thickness of acceptable smoother shavings. If you're smoothing a straight-grained panel of white pine, you can do so with a relatively significant depth of cut, not as much as you used with your leveling plane, but much more than you would use for smoothing a panel of figured material. Even within these parameters, there is room for further refinement. If you're smoothing a panel of reasonably straight-grained walnut, you might start with a smoother set to take a shaving as thick as that taken when smoothing the pine panel described above. However, you may notice areas in which the walnut is not as cleanly cut as you'd like. You might then switch to a plane set to take a finer shaving. You might eventually end up with yet a third smoother set up to take shavings so thin they disintegrate as they rise in the throat, if that's what's required to create the clean and gleaming surface you want to achieve. Unfortunately, there's no way to spell out the exact shaving thicknesses a plane should be set up to produce in a specific context because wood is so variable. Two panels of the same species might appear to the eye to be nearly identical, even though they might manifest very different qualities under a cutting edge. This is why it's imperative for plane users—particularly inexperienced plane users—to proceed cautiously, to begin with conservative depth-of-cut settings, moving on to heavier shavings only if the material permits it.

Part 3: Matching mouth size to task

Depth of cut and width of mouth go hand in hand. You can't increase the depth of cut without also increasing the width of mouth because there's no way to take a shaving too thick to rise through the throat of the plane. That thick shaving will simply choke in the throat, stalling the plane. In practice, this means that the mouths of planes destined for rough work should be wide enough to accept the thick shavings those planes will be taking, and the mouths of planes intended for finishing work should be open only enough to take the much thinner shavings they are set up to take.

This is because mouths do more than simply pass shavings. They also retain the surface integrity of the material being worked. That side of the mouth ahead of the cutting edge presses down on the surface holding it in place while the cutting edge lifts a shaving. Without that front edge of the mouth, the shaving might run out ahead of the cutting edge, breaking out chips. This is why—when you're doing fine work—you want a mouth so tight that your gossamer shaving brushes both the cutting edge and the front edge of the mouth as it passes through.

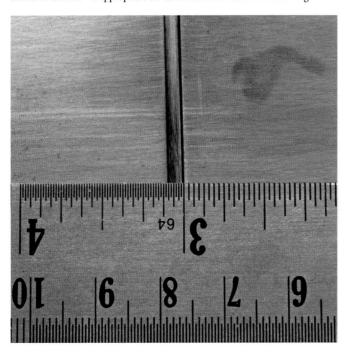

One of my favorite planes is a Spiers-style panel plane Chris Schwartz made from a Shepherd kit. The width of the mouth on that plane—less than a hundredth of an inch—is appropriate for all but the most extreme smoothing work.

By comparison the mouth on my Stanley #6—which I use for raising panels of drawer bottoms—is almost 3/32" wide.

I keep the mouth on my Lie-Nielsen #9, a miter plane, similarly tight.

The mouth of this Veritas scrub plane is over 1/8" wide, an appropriate width for a plane used for such rough work.

Part 4: Setting the cap iron

The primary function of the cap iron found on most bench planes is to stabilize the cutting edge, but the cap iron has a secondary function, as well. It directs shavings (chips) up into the throat of the plane. It's for this reason that the cap iron is sometimes referred to as the "chipbreaker."

In order for the cap iron to perform its two tasks, the leading edge of the cap iron must fit tightly against the polished back of the iron. Good quality new planes almost always manifest this tight fit, but many antique planes don't (and neither do many cheaply made new planes), and this has an adverse effect on the performance of these planes. A poor fit denies the cutting edge needed support, which can result in chatter. A poor fit can also allow shavings to become impacted in the gap between iron and cap iron, which brings your work to a halt.

A poor fit can be a result of rust degrading the lip of the cap iron or— particularly in the case of thin Stanley-type cap irons—it can be a result of bent metal.

To check the iron/ cap iron fit of a Stanley-type plane, position the cap iron against the back of the iron with the cap screw in place. Turn the cap screw just barely snug with your fingertips.

Then hold the iron/cap iron assembly up to a light, turning it until you can see the line of contact from the inside. Sometimes it's necessary to sight this contact in sections, one half from one side and the other half from the other side.

In the case of cap irons that fit tightly along their full lengths under the pressure of the cap screw—like the cap irons on antique infills or those on Lie-Nielsen planes—simply loosen the cap screw, and lay the tip of the cap iron on the polished back of the iron. If you see good contact on one side but not on the other, you know you need to remove material from the underside of the cap iron lip on the side that made good contact.

Remove the material cautiously with a file or lapping plate, making frequent checks of your progress by returning the cap iron to its position on the back of the iron.

Also the point of contact should be at the extreme tip of the cap iron lip. If you see that the contact actually takes place above that extreme tip, rework the angle on the cap iron lip until you get the fit you want.

Once you've achieved a proper fit, set the cap iron so that its lip is fractionally above the cutting edge of the iron—say 1/16"—and turn the cap screw tight. You're ready then to load this assembly into your plane.

The tip of the cap iron that presses against the iron to stabilize the cutting edge sometimes fails to make good contact all across the width of the cap iron, which reduces its effectiveness. This can be corrected with a little work on a honing stone.

Bench Planes: Putting Them to Use

In the 1950s—when the understanding of hand-held surfacing planes was in a state of free fall—craftsmen lacking the money for large surfacing machinery became adept at using affordable hand-held belt sanders to level and smooth, but the process of surfacing even a single large panel in this way can be exhausting, both because of the time it takes and because of the conditions under which the operator of such a tool must labor. These belt sanders are heavy, and the dust and noise they eject into the atmosphere of the shop wear on the stamina of the operator, and, while a dust mask and hearing protection will mitigate these conditions, the simple fact of having these devices clamped to the head causes additional fatigue.

Some power-tool enthusiasts explain their preference for power-tool surfacing by pointing to the skill that hand-plane use requires, but it could be argued that leveling and smoothing panels with a hand-held belt sander requires even more skill than the use of hand planes. Anyone who has attempted to surface a large panel in this way knows how easily a moment's inattention to the posture of the wrists can result in an edge of the sanding belt digging a furrow into the surface being worked. A bench plane, by contrast, has sole all around the mouth, so there is no possibility of the cutting edge digging in. It is a benign tool, less likely to penalize a moment of inattention.

Part 1: Establishing a hand planing workspace

No good hand plane work can be done without a decent bench. Fortunately, "decent" in the case of benches doesn't necessarily mean expensive, although it's easy to drop a grand or two on a bench. The example you see in Photos 1 and 2 is quite inexpensive, homemade, built with framing lumber, and equipped with several vises: two inexpensive side vises (each intended to be used with a catch block), and one good but home-made end vise which is paired with two long rows of dog holes along the length of the bench.

Although small parts or small subassemblies can be held in the side vises, their most important purpose is to clamp onto one end of a long board, the other end of which is supported by a catch block screwed to the side of the bench at the same height as the bottom of the side vise. This arrangement makes it possible to joint an edge of almost any length.

The end vise—when paired with two rows of dog holes—is the most important holding tool in the shop. It can function like a side vise to hold small parts or subassemblies. In connection with a set of

The side vise you see here is an antique that moves on a 4" wide bar of ribbed steel, not on slender metal rods, like most modern vises. This gives the vise great strength, enough to support a heavy load even when the vise is opened to its maximum capacity of 10" (wood jaw to bench). This capacity is about twice that of the new and inexpensive vise installed on the back side of the bench (for use when the bench is in other shop locations).

This end vise is home-made, assembled around a 17-1/2 " long vise screw, a pair of 24" black-iron pipes and a hardwood jaw. Although its capabilities might surprise users who have purchased vises costing hundreds of dollars, this example added less than $60 to the cost of the bench.

dogs, it can also hold boards or panels tight against the surface of the bench so they can be worked with planes. In addition, edge-jointing stock can be held between dogs, although that's a little more awkward than working an edge when it's held with a side vise and catch block. Plus, the dog holes can be used with holdfasts to secure odd-shaped stock so that it can be worked with hand planes or other tools.

Ideally, a bench is constructed of hardwood, with hard maple being the most popular choice for manufactured benches, but when I designed the bench you see in Photos 1 and 2, I wanted something that could be built for under $200, vises and all, so I substituted fir framing stock for hardwood.

After using this bench (and others like it) for several years, I'm convinced that softwood benches offer a level of service that might surprise many furniture makers accustomed to vastly more expensive hardwood benches. While it is relatively easy to dent and scratch this softwood top, I've always regarded a bench top as a surface on which work could be accomplished rather than a surface I should work to protect. And if the top gets too banged up, I just joint it and work it with some smoothing planes. The only other complaint I have about these softwood benches is that—after several years of heavy use—the dog holes do shift a bit. Those that I stress most often have taken on a pronounced lean, tilting away from the end vise; however so far, they all still hold my dogs as securely as they did when the top was new, and if they ever get so badly out of alignment that they can't be used, I'll simply remove the boards in which the dog holes are drilled and replace the boards and the holes.

A good planing bench must do more than simply hold material being worked; it must also be able to resist the considerable force generated during hand planing. It's surprisingly easy to get even a heavy bench in motion when you're surfacing or molding on it, and, unrestrained, a light bench like mine would run all over the shop when I'm working hardwood with a wide molding plane. To eliminate this, I've screwed steel L-brackets to the feet of my bench, and those brackets are screwed to the floor every time I reposition the bench.

Good hand plane work also requires good lighting. This means strong lighting directly above the bench as well as a source of side light. In my shop, I have a pair of 40 watt fluorescent bulbs directly above my bench, as well as other pairs of 40 watt bulbs scattered across my shop ceiling. This light washes over my bench, revealing the details of a surface or an edge I'm working with planes. The perfect sidelight is natural light streaming in through a window directly above and beside the bench. Unfortunately, the bench on which I choose to work most often is in the middle of my shop, well away from the windows. So I've learned to create a side light by turning off my ceiling fluorescents and laying a short unmounted fluorescent tube on the bench top beside the work. This light immediately reveals even the most insignificant areas of tearout, as well as any plane tracks that need to be removed with further work. I don't actually work in the light cast by this tube. I use it only to make periodic checks on my progress.

The use of a side light—like this unmounted fluorescent tube—can bring the smallest areas of tearout into sharp focus.

Part 2: Matching planes to task

Bench planes are most often used to perform one of two very common shop tasks. First they are used to prep individual boards, specifically to level, square, smooth, thickness, and edge joint them. Second, they are used to prep glued-up panels, specifically to level, smooth, and sometimes thickness those panels. In general, you begin this work by matching the size of the plane to the size of the task.

Edge-jointing short stock—less than say 20"—is best performed with a medium-sized plane. A Stanley #6 or even a #5 would do this work quite nicely. Longer edge-jointing requires a longer plane, for example a Stanley #7 or #8. And, of course, extremely short edge-jointing is best performed with even smaller planes. All planes used for edge-jointing should have irons ground dead flat across their width with, perhaps, the corners slightly rounded.

Surfacing individual boards or glued up panels typically involves the use of three different planes. The first is a roughing plane equipped with a wide mouth and heavily cambered iron for rapid stock removal. (The Stanley #40 and #40-1/2, as well as the Lie-Nielsen #40-1/2 and Veritas scrub plane are all designed for this singular purpose.

If the surface is relatively flat or if you're trying to reduce the size of your plane flock, you can begin with the second plane in this three-plane sequence. Traditionally, the second plane would have been a wooden plane of moderate length called a fore or try plane, but these terms are not widely used today. In the 21st century, you're more likely to hear plane enthusiasts talk about performing this rough work with a Stanley/Bailey style #5 or #6 (the #6 is about the same size as a wooden fore plane). This plane should be equipped with a moderately cambered iron and a moderately wide mouth. This is the leveling plane I've spoken about earlier in this book. It rides over the uneven surfaces left behind by the scrub plane scalping the high spots, in that manner reducing them to the level of the low spots. Smaller surfaces should be leveled with the smaller planes from this category—say the Stanley #5—and larger surfaces should be leveled with larger planes—say the Stanley #6 or, in the case of really large panels, perhaps a Stanley #7.

Once the leveling is done, you switch to smoothers, again matching plane size to task. If you're planing a really large surface—like a dining table—an English panel plane might be the best choice. But most craftsmen prefer a smaller plane for most smoothing work, one the size of a Stanley #3 or #4 because these planes can work into relatively small areas.

When you're matching planes to tasks, plane quality is also a consideration. While a Stanley #4 with its original iron is adequate for smoothing a pine panel, if you're working hardwood, you might want a better plane, a #4-1/2 for example, with a heavier aftermarket iron and cap iron. A Lie-Nielsen or Veritas smoother of either the conventional type or the bevel-up, low-angle variety would be even better choices. So, too, would an infill smoother.

And if you're working a really thorny wood, you might get the very best results with bevel-up, low angle smoothers. I know that high-angle planes, like the LN #4-1/2 with a high-angle frog, are designed for this work, but my subjective opinion is that the bevel-up planes really excel at this task.

Part 3: Assessing the work

Before you apply your bench planes to the work, take a few moments to evaluate the material. This process begins with your eyes and your hands, but it's also essential to check the work with a straight-edge and a pair of winding sticks.

First try to determine the direction of rising grain. You can sometimes do this by reading the grain lines on the edge of the board. You can also run your hand lengthwise along the work, with your skin just barely touching the surface. The wood will usually feel silky when your hand moves in the direction of rising grain and bristly when it moves against the rising grain. But sometimes your eyes and your hands will fail to conclusively identify the right direction. In such a case, you can take some shavings with a block plane or a smoother at several different locations and check the results with a side light for evidence of tearout.

Your visual and tactile inspection should also search out any defects in the material that will complicate planing, like knots or the kind of swirling grain often found in lumber sawn from tree crotches. This visual check will also help you identify how you can best cut needed parts from a board or panel. Sometimes, in fact, it's possible to lay out parts in a way that bypasses those areas that will cause the most significant surfacing problems.

Use the straight-edge to identify cupping across the grain, as well as bow, which is a lengthwise arcing of the top surface. Winding sticks are short lengths of material—carefully straightened—that can be laid across a board or panel at different locations along the length of the work. Sighting their top edges—comparing one to the other—will reveal twist in the board or panel.

Whenever possible, bench planes should be used in the direction of rising grain. One of the simplest ways to determine that direction is to look at the grain lines on an adjacent face.

You can also determine the direction of rising grain by sliding the palm of your hand very lightly over the surface of the board. In the direction of rising grain, the wood fibers will feel silky to your skin; against the direction of rising grain, they will feel bristly.

After forty years of working wood, I have yet to encounter my first piece of defect-free stock. Clear material is not that unusual, but the fact that boards are sawn out of a log which has a pronounced columnar structure means that boards will try to reassert that structure once they've been sawn flat. This is why plain sawn boards inevitably cup. Plus, trees are living things that respond to specific conditions in their specific environments—like wind, direction of sunlight, the angle at which the trunk rose from the earth. All of these things impact the tree's growth causing the tree to lean toward the sun, for example, and every saw log manifests these conditions in ways that may not be apparent when the log is in the round.

56

"Cup" and "cupping" refer an arcing of the board across its width.

"Bow" refers to a lengthwise arcing of the board's wide surface.

"Crook" refers to a lengthwise arcing of the edge of the board. Most boards—particularly those in the rough—will simultaneously manifest some, perhaps slight, degree of "cupping," "bow," and "crook."

Part 4: Edge jointing

Edge jointing begins with a proper stance. Because a tight joint is achieved as a result of an edge that is both straight and perpendicular (to the board's face) along its full length, it's imperative that you begin by establishing a good foundation to minimize the likelihood that an unstable lower body will affect the posture of your hands on the plane.

If I'm jointing a short edge, one that doesn't require me to take steps as I plane, I position my feet about 18" apart, the left one maybe 12" behind the end of the edge with which I'll begin, my right foot forward and 10"-15" away from the side of the board. (I should probably mention that I'm left-handed. Righties, as always, do things backwards.) As I begin my stroke, my weight is back on my left foot. Then as I move the plane forward, I transfer weight to my right foot, and when I finish the stroke, I'm leaning slightly forward.

If it's a board long enough to require steps, I first map them out with the plane held above the edge I'm going to joint. I start with my feet in the same position I use for jointing a short edge. Then I move forward dividing the distance up into an appropriate number of shuffling steps, enough so that I don't have to lean uncomfortably forward but not so many that they become choppy. I'll practice the movement a couple of times. Then I put the plane to the wood.

Hand position is important. Unlike surface planing when you often let the weight of the plane determine its posture, in the case of edge jointing you want to achieve consistent perpendicularity, and you simply can't do that if your hands are all over the place.

My method is to grasp the tote in my left hand. I place my right hand so that the web between the thumb and forefinger of that hand controls the knob, and I allow the tips of the other fingers of that hand to lightly trail under the plane along the face of the board I'm jointing.

I don't know that these are the best hand positions for edge jointing. I've seen other craftsmen position their hands in other ways. But I do think every craftsman should establish a routine and stick to it. Routine allows muscle memory to take over, and any time you can remove the brain from the business of craftsmanship, it becomes easier to do work the way it should be done.

Next slide a square along the edge you're going to plane. If it's perpendicular to the face of the board (it should be if it was sawn on a tablesaw), rest the plane at a slightly skewed angle on the edge you're about to plane. Then put your hands on the plane. That's what perpendicular feels like.

Then begin to plane the edge, maintaining perpendicularity and a slightly skewed passage forward throughout the entire stroke, keeping the plane in motion from end to end. Pay particular attention to the beginning and end of the stroke because at those points, only a portion of the plane's sole will be resting on the edge. At the start of each stroke, when only the first few inches of the plane's sole are resting on the edge, all of your downward pressure should be exerted through the knob. Similarly, at the end of the stroke, when the front end of the plane is riding the air, all of your downward pressure should be exerted through the tote.

Ideally, the edge you're working is fresh from your tablesaw because it's so much easier for your tablesaw to establish straight and square, but if it's not, if the edge you've selected to work is leftover from the sawmill, it probably has a crook. (A crook is an arc along the edge of the board.) This is almost always seen on sawmill edges cut when the board was still green. A crook requires a slightly different edge-jointing procedure. Begin by knocking off the high spots of that crook with a shorter plane with a wide mouth. Then as the crook has disappeared, switch to your jointer.

When you're working an edge, it's important to move your plane in the direction of the rising grain in order to avoid the tearout that can occur when you work against that grain.

Good edge-jointing technique is built on a foundation of practice and repetition. Establish a planing body posture and a method of grasping the plane that gives you control throughout the jointing stroke. Then repeat the stroke over and over, periodically checking your work with a square.

Unfortunately, it's rare for a long board to have grain rising in the same direction all along its length. More often, the grain will rise in one direction on one end, then switch at some point, and then perhaps switch back. Sometimes, if the angle of the rising grain is relatively shallow, it's possible to ignore grain that's rising against your plane's direction of travel, but sometimes, you have to stop and change your approach.

You might first try reducing your depth of cut. Often this will allow you to plane against rising grain, but sometimes— on a really difficult board—even that won't work. You might then switch to a different plane. A low-angle, bevel-up jointer is the very best option for such a board, but if you don't have one or you're working an edge that even that plane can't tame, simply disregard the tearout in that section of the edge—that is if you're constructing a glue joint— because a short section of tearout there won't pose any danger to the panel's structural integrity, and of course, it will never be seen.

If, however, the problem edge is one that will be visible in the finished piece—like the edge of a table top—the solution is even easier: simply switch directions with your plane as you proceed along the edge.

When I first began to plane edges by hand, I used the method I just described to prove to myself that I could get usable glue joints in this very traditional way, but now I use a different approach, one that incorporates the best of power jointing and the best of hand jointing. First, I run the edge over my power jointer. This quickly and effortlessly straightens the edge while simultaneously making it perpendicular. Then I take one single pass with a jointing plane to remove the ripples the machine jointer left behind. This two-step method gives me the ease and speed of a power jointer and the cleanliness of a hand-jointed edge.

And there is one other method you might consider: That is the use of a jointing plane equipped with a fence. A fence is simply a piece of flat stock projecting below the sole of that plane, mounted at a 90 degree angle to the sole. This isn't a new idea. Stanley used to sell a metal fence, the #386, to mount on their planes. And Lee Valley offers fences today that can be attached to their planes. But you can also make a fence yourself, and if you choose to try this, it might be easiest to work with a wooden plane or a transitional plane because something with a wood body makes the attachment process easier.

And a fence really does work, transforming this fairly tricky hand-planing task into something anyone can do with a minimum of practice.

Your progress can also be checked by examining the shaving your jointer is taking to see that it is continuous from end to end and from side to side.

The final check of any jointed edge is made when you stack jointed boards on their edges. If the stack aligns vertically and if there are no light leaks between the boards, the joints are good. In this photo, I'm using a straight edge to check the flatness of a stack of four jointed boards.

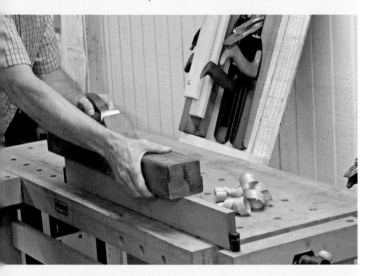

A wooden jointer weighs less than a metal jointer and might be a good choice for craftsmen who have trouble stabilizing a heavy metal plane on a narrow edge. Notice that here, the material is being held between two dogs on the surface of the bench.

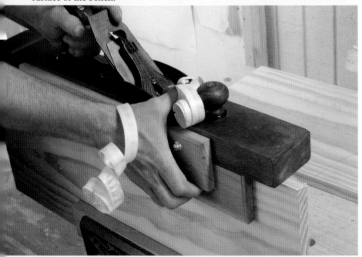

I added a wood fence to this Sargent jointer to make it easier to joint perfectly perpendicular edges.

Part 5: Surfacing a board

If you're preparing boards narrow enough to be flattened by your power jointer (mine cuts a six-inch track), you may want to flatten one face on that machine, then flatten the other in your thickness planer—if you have one, saving your planes for the panel these boards will become. But if you're flattening boards too wide for your power jointer, you can use hand planes for this preliminary work.

Most boards are narrow enough to be fixed between a single pair of dogs, one in the bench top and the other in the jaw of the end vise. The dogs should be placed so that their top surfaces are below the surface you will ultimately create with your planes. Otherwise you may nick the dogs with your irons, damaging the cutting edges. If the board has a pronounced twist, you may want to shim it in a couple of places so that it won't rock as you work it. If the board has a pronounced bow, you have to decide whether it will be easier to work it with the two high-ends down on your bench or the high-middle down on your bench. Usually, I find that the board is more stable if the two high ends are down.

As in the edge-jointing process, the grain in the material being worked sometimes complicates the surfacing process, so it's important to begin with a visual inspection of the work. Ideally, the grain in a board or panel will run the same direction across the full width and along the full length of the surface being worked. Unfortunately, you may never encounter this ideal. In the real world, grain rises and dives and swirls in response to the many forces which were at work on the living tree. Sometimes you can recognize these complications with your eye, but at other times subtle changes in grain direction only reveal themselves as the surface is being worked with a plane. For this reason, it's important that the leveling planes (and, later, the smoothing planes) begin their work tentatively, taking only thin shavings. Then, if you see no tearout, you can increase the depth of cut.

With a straight edge and winding sticks, carefully check the surface. Note the high areas you're going to reduce with your roughing plane. I sometimes mark these with scribbled pencil lines, particularly if they are oddly shaped.

Stance isn't much of an issue when you're surfacing because you're not as concerned with a perfectly planar result. This surface only needs to be generally flat, generally in the same plane, a surface flat enough to convince the eye and a caressing hand, not a surface that needs to mate perfectly with another surface during a glue-up.

Begin by attacking the high spots with your roughing plane, taking fairly thick shavings. Don't labor for perfection with this first plane. All you want to do is to knock the peaks down.

Then switch to your leveling plane. Your first few shavings with this tool should be thin until you've determined that there are no areas tearing out under the cutting edge. If the surface remains clean, you can then increase the depth of cut and widen the mouth. However, if you see areas where the grain is reversing, areas in which the iron is tearing out bits of the surface, you may want to keep the depth of cut relatively shallow, and you may want to try reversing the direction you're planing. These decisions are based on the depth of the tearout. Minor tearout can be cleaned up through careful work with a good smoothing plane. Significant tearout, however, is a whole other matter. In such a case, a relatively thick shaving taken with your leveling plane may do more harm than good.

If the board is narrow—say a couple of plane-widths wide—work it end-to-end with a leveling plane pushed at a skewed angle. The angle does two things. First an iron cuts more easily when skewed. Second, at a skewed angle, your leveling plane isn't creating a narrow trough on the surface; its nose and heel are riding on stock to the left and right of the track the iron is cutting, so you are—in effect—leveling a wider track. If the board is wide, use the 45 degree leveling procedure described in *Part 5: Surfacing a panel.*

When your straight edge, eye, and winding sticks all tell you that the surface is level, it's time to switch to your smoothing planes. For me, this is when the fun begins because there are few workshop experiences that can compare with the pleasure you get from using a well tuned smoother to lift tissue-paper-thin shavings, leaving behind a surface so cleanly cut that it reflects light, a surface glowing with a brilliance you simply can't achieve with abrasives.

Smoothing work should be done—generally—in the direction of rising grain, working the boards from one end to the other, with the plane pushed at a slightly skewed angle. But when the grain changes direction enough to cause tearout, you should change the direction in which you're pushing your smoother, reversing it when the rising grain reverses. In fact, in the case of some areas of swirling grain, the best results may be achieved by working the plane in short semi-circular passes around the center of that swirling grain.

This means that in difficult areas in which you're working to remove tearout left behind by your leveling plane, you may be working down, reducing the height of the surface in that small area. If you have to go deep enough to be noticeable, you may need to feather that area out to conceal the depression. This is why smoothers are so much shorter than other bench planes: Their small stature allows them to work small areas that couldn't be accessed with a longer plane.

If the board you're smoothing will later be glued-up into a panel, it isn't necessary to work the surface to perfection with your smoothing planes. Once it's reasonably smooth, set it aside and go onto the next board.

A scrub plane, like this Veritas, has a heavily cambered iron and a wide mouth enabling it to quickly remove material from the high spots on a board or panel. Notice that the shavings it takes are thick in the middle and taper to nothing on each side. Notice also the winding sticks in the background which were used to assess the amount of twist in the board.

After the scrub plane has knocked down the highest areas, a longer leveling plane like this Stanley #606 with a cambered iron, can bring the entire surface down to the same level. This plane should be used diagonally along the full length of the board or panel, then diagonally again in the other direction, producing a pattern of overlapping X's across the surface.

The final surfacing is done with a smoother, like this antique Spiers. This plane—like most of my smoothers also has a cambered iron, although the arc is much less pronounced than the arc on my Veritas scrub plane or my #606. Smoothers should be used in the direction of rising grain.

I began work on this board with the scrub plane on the extreme right. I then switched to the #606 in the middle right. Instead of one smoother, I used two (as I often do). The first smoother-- in the middle left—takes a thin shaving. The second smoother on the extreme right—takes an even thinner shaving. The surface these planes produce is ready for finish, although the cambered irons on my last smoother left the surface very slightly undulating.

As this close-up reveals, a good set of hand planes can produce a remarkably smooth and level surface.

Once one face of a board is surfaced, it can be used as a reference for creating other faces.

Part 6: Surfacing a panel

First, fix the panel on your bench between dogs. Two pairs of dogs will keep the panel from racking as you work. Then inspect the panel, looking for areas that could tearout under your plane. Panels will have all of the problems of boards—knots, swirling grain, diving grain, etc.—but they will also have one additional complexity: board-wide reversals in the direction of rising grain. In a perfect world, you would align all the boards in a panel so that the grain is rising in the same direction in every board, but in the imperfect world in which most of us work, board alignment never seems to happen that way. This is because when we're laying out a panel, our goal isn't to make planing easy; it's to create panels in which the color and figure of the overall panel makes some kind of visual sense. This means that two adjacent boards are just as likely to have their grain rising in two different directions as in the same direction. When you extend those odds out to the four or five boards that make up some panels—well, you realize you're almost inevitably going to face some board-wide reversals in rising grain in most of the panels you surface.

Next, check the panel with a straight edge and winding sticks. If you were successful at straightening and leveling each of the individual boards from which the panel is made up, you would think that the panel would already be flat all across its surface, but that never seems to happen. Always, there are slight surface discontinuities where two boards come together. Sometimes these are the result of insufficient work flattening the individual boards but at other times, it's just the luck of the draw. If, for example, a board with an almost imperceptible dip is glued up next to a board with an almost imperceptible hump—well the difference suddenly becomes perceptible.

If the panel has any high spots, use a roughing plane to knock those down, but surface irregularities at this stage are usually minor, so you may be able to move directly to your leveling plane: a jack-sized tool for small panels, a larger tool for large panels.

Begin by planing the entire panel using a stroke pattern laid out at a 45 degree angle to the lengthwise direction of the boards in the panel, taking extra shavings from any high spots you marked. Then plane the entire panel again, this time using a stroke pattern laid out in a direction perpendicular to the strokes in your first planing pattern. What you'll see emerging then is an X-ing of plane strokes all across the panel. When you're done with the second planing pattern, the panel should be reasonably flat, a circumstance you can verify with your straight edge and winding

When a panel is short—like this cherry example—the leveling can be done with a jack plane working diagonally. The surface then can be worked with the two smoothers in the foreground, each set to take a different shaving.

sticks. You should also check your plane tracks with a side light to see if any areas are tearing out. Wood is usually pretty forgiving when you're working it at a 45 degree angle, but you may be able to identify some of the areas that will cause problems when you're smoothing. If there are any still-high areas, give them some extra attention with your leveling plane.

You're ready then to use your smoothing planes. Smoothing a panel is exactly like smoothing an individual board—with one important exception: the board-width changes in the direction of rising grain. By this point in the surfacing process, you can usually tell which way the grain goes in each of the panel's boards. If not, take a few moments to determine rising-grain direction using the palm of your hand or a few careful shavings with a block plane. When you've established the panel's

A panel planed to smoothness has a visual depth that abraded panels can't approach because the planed surface is made up of wood fibers cut cleanly, not wood fibers made ragged by repeating grinding with abrasive particles.

62

dominant direction of rising grain, work the panel in that direction, setting your smoother to take very thin shavings. Make frequent checks of your work under a side light. If you see some tearout (it should be very shallow since you're using a very shallow depth of cut), try working that area by skewing your plane. Sometimes, in fact, it's best to work small problem areas on the "north" side of a knot by planing in the opposite direction, but this will leave a slightly disturbed area where the two directions of your smoother's travel meet.

Patience is the key. When I began to make a serious effort to incorporate bench planes into my shop routines, I wasn't always patient enough. If—after a half dozen strokes of the plane—I couldn't see progress, I would increase the depth of cut. While that would create progress, it also sometimes created significant tearout problems. And these were often more trouble to remove than the tracks of the leveling plane I originally set out to eliminate.

Remember: As long as the plane is lifting shavings, it's doing its job, even if you can't identify any naked-eye progress on the work.

Part 7: Thicknessing

I don't often thickness with hand planes—at least not in a rigorously controlled fashion. I usually flatten narrow individual boards on my 6" power jointer, then run them through my power planer to bring them to something close to the desired final thickness. When those boards will be used in a panel, I leave an extra 1/32"—the amount of material I estimate I'll remove during hand plane leveling and smoothing one side of the panel. When I'm working with boards wider than the capacity of my 6" power jointer, I flatten one side with hand planes, before feeding them through my 12" power planer, which then establishes the correct approximate thickness.

Sometimes, however, I will use hand planes to thickness even individual boards to accurately represent 18th or 19th century shop practices, so that an examination of the interior surfaces of a piece built of such material reveals the passage of hand planes.

The first step in thicknessing with hand planes is to establish one flat surface using the methods described above. Then—with a tri-square and a pencil—create lines on all four edges of the

Using the leveling and smoothing techniques discussed in this chapter, reduce the surface of the work all the way to the line.

With a pencil point running along the end of the square's blade, slide the square along the full length of the work's edge, keeping the square's fence tight against the surface.

work indicating the depth of the work's other flat surface. You then simply bring that surface down to the line using the same techniques you used for the reference surface. Well, it's not really that simple. For a panel on which both sides will show, the goal is to bring the board's thickness down to the line at the very same moment you have created a perfectly smooth and tearout-free surface, and that may take some effort.

Part 8: Finishing the job

When the hand plane work is done, you have to decide what additional surfacing attention—if any—should be given to a panel or a board. If the hand planes left behind no areas of tearout that need the attention of card scrapers and sandpaper, you can move directly to the first coat of finish, and there are good reasons to consider this approach. Wood that's been cleanly cut with a well-set-up hand plane has a glow and reflectivity you can't achieve with scrapers and abrasives. But on most glued up panels, there will be some areas where the surface is troubled, maybe around a knot, maybe where two boards with different directions of rising grain came together. These will require a bit of scraping, followed by some hand sanding.

Plus, no matter how careful you are with your smoothing planes, they leave behind a faint record of their travels. Sometimes this can't be seen with the unaided eye, but it can be felt under the hand. If a hand-planed surface is inappropriate for a particular application, a bit of work with fine sandpaper wrapped around a sanding block will take out those faint tracks.

Bench Planes: Type Studies

Stanley plane enthusiasts have organized the long and convoluted manufacturing history of many of the planes made by this company into type studies which make it possible to date individual tools. For example, the tool scholar Roger Smith (with a later assist from Patrick Leach) divided Bailey-style bench planes (numbers 1-8) into 20 different types, with Type 1 representing those planes manufactured between 1867 and 1869 to Type 20 representing those planes manufactured between 1962-1967 with Types 2-19 falling chronologically in between. Each of these 20 types manifests the basic features of the type preceding it in the type progression, in addition to several characteristics which mark it as identifiably different than those earlier planes. While some of these identifying characteristics are pretty esoteric, others are part of the *lingua franca* of even casual Stanley enthusiasts.

For example, in my collection of Stanley users, I have a #4-1/2 with a hard rubber depth-of-cut adjustment wheel. That detail, together with the unusually thick casting identifies the tool as a WWII-era plane.

The presence of a lateral adjustment lever—which first occurred in 1885—is one of the most important Stanley bench plane dating characteristics. The presence of that lever identifies a tool as a post-1885, Type 5 or later plane. Another key marker is the kidney-shaped hole in the lever cap, which was based on a July 18, 1933 patent. That shape replaced the upside down keyhole that formerly appeared on Stanley lever caps. The variety of wood used for knobs and totes is another critical marker. Rosewood was the material of choice for planes manufactured prior to WWII. At that point—with the exception of a brief post-war return to rosewood—Stanley shifted to a non-descript hardwood finished with either red stain or black paint and then later with a lighter stain.

But with a little effort, even the subtler aspects of plane construction can be used to put a relatively firm date on a plane. For example, my favorite Stanley bench plane (for reasons I would find it hard to explain) is a #6 that has U.S. Pat. APR 19-10 as the only info cast onto the body behind the frog. This identifies the plane as one made after 1925. Another identifying mark of this particular #6 is the lack of a raised cast support ring around the knob, a feature that came into existence in 1929. These two details together date the plane's probable manufacture between the years 1925 and 1929.

I say "probable" because the Stanley company also produced hybrids, planes possessing characteristics of two different types as a result of the company's disinclination to throw out good parts that belonged to earlier editions of the plane. My #6—while likely produced between 1925 and 1929—could have been produced in 1930 or even later if Stanley found itself in possession of not-yet-used castings lacking the knob support ring after the official year of the ring's introduction in 1929.

Additionally, Stanley collectors and users have created their own hybrids, adding, for example, tall knobs to planes that originally came equipped with low knobs or perhaps putting a Sweetheart iron in a plane manufactured before the creation of the Sweetheart planes in 1919. I know that few of the planes in my collection of users have remained in their original configurations because I have—over the years—mixed and matched parts in order to put together a group of well-appointed users.

This hard rubber depth-of-cut-adjustment wheel on this #4–1/2 is one of the characteristics of Stanley planes manufactured during WWII.

The plane on the left is the #4–1/2 shown in the previous photograph. The plane on the right is a #4 of more recent vintage. The difference in casting thickness is easily seen. Thick castings are another identifying characteristic of WWII-era Stanley planes.

The WWII-era #4–1/2 is, I believe, the cheapest premium-quality smoother available to contemporary craftsmen. Used examples in good condition can be had for $75 or less. (I picked up this one at an antique show in Washington, Pennsylvania, for $45.) Their quality is, first of all, a result of the quality of all Stanley bench planes of that period. In addition, the heavier castings of WWII-era planes adds to their weighty presence in use. Plus, the #4–1/2 has two inherent advantages over other Stanley smoothers—for example the #4—even those made during the War. The #4–1/2's greater width (2-3/16" compared to a #4 at just 2-7/16") adds even more to its weight. In addition, that extra width makes the plane more stable on uneven surfaces. I include in this group of desirable smoothers those #4-1/2s that lack a throat adjustment screw (at the base of the frog) because the absence of that screw in no way diminishes the quality of these planes. The frog on planes lacking the screw can be moved simply by loosening the frog attachment screws and repositioning the frog.

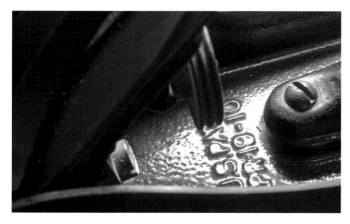

The presence of this single line of patent information on my #6 means that this plane was probably manufactured after 1925.

The plane in the rear has a cast support ring around the knob. My #6 in the foreground lacks this cast support ring. This means the #6 was probably manufactured before 1929.

The finish on this rosewood tote—so thick it has crazed—suggests that the plane bearing this tote is likely a Type 19, the type on which this excessively thick finish on rosewood is typically found. That detail—together with other details—suggest a manufacturing date in the late 1940s.

Right:
Post-war planes—like this #7—were made at a time when Stanley was still producing planes of exceptional quality, and when you can find one—like this example—that has seen little or no use—you should snap it up. Once restored, it's the equal—except of course in the realm of aesthetics—of many modern-day jointers. (This is the plane I refurbished on pages 37-39)

In addition, type studies of some of the other notable Stanley lines have appeared. The web is home to type studies of the ubiquitous #45, the Miller's patent line, the Bedrock line, the routers and so on, and John Walter's book "Antique and Collectible Stanley Tools" includes even more Stanley type studies. I have also seen a web-based type study for Miller's Falls planes. In addition, David Lynch has an exquisite website which presents what is, in effect, a type study for Record planes, although the material isn't arranged in quite the way the Jay Sutherland Stanley bench plane type study is organized. These all provide collectors with information about the tools they own or hope someday to own, information that can enhance the pleasure they find in collecting. In addition, a knowledge of type studies can be important for tool buyers who wish to purchase wisely because, for example, the price difference between a Type 1 Stanley #4 and a Type 5 Stanley #4 can be significant. This is particularly true for buyers pursuing planes with across-the-board high-dollar-value like those in the Miller's patent line in which the price of a single plane in good condition can run into hundreds or—in the case of pristine examples—even thousands of dollars.

These studies have been criticized, sometimes by knowledgeable collectors and dealers. Type studies are not infallible. New information is constantly coming to light as the field of plane scholarship moves forward, and sometimes that new information contradicts earlier information. This, isn't surprising because, in the absence of detailed shop floor records identifying exactly what Stanley was manufacturing during each week of the company's 150-year history, the information in the Type studies must be assembled from secondary sources—for example patent dates and descriptions in the company's many catalogs. Plus—as I noted above—Stanley did routinely produce hybrids during the manufacturing process. Nevertheless, I suspect that most collectors would agree that type studies have enhanced the pleasure they find in the tools they own.

* Type studies of the Bailey-style bench planes are available on several different websites. The one to which I refer is maintained by Joshua Clark at www.hyperkitten.com/tools/stanley_bench_plane/type_study.php. This study is one originally presented on the web by Jay Sutherland, a study based on the work of Roger Smith, later updated by Patrick Leach whose own website (www.supertool.com/StanleyBG/stanO.htm) is an important resource for anyone with an interest in Stanley planes.

Bench Planes:
Bench Plane Values

This is a golden age for those of us who take pleasure in owning and using high-quality bench planes. We are blessed by the presence of a community of toolmakers who have committed themselves to quality in much the same way as Stewart Spiers and Thomas Norris during an earlier golden age. In addition, these current makers have access to materials (A2 and O1 steel, for example) that were not available during any earlier golden age. Plus, via the internet, we have access to the offerings of toolmakers all across the planet. In addition, through web-based tool sellers and web-based auction sites, we also have access to some of the best period planes ever made.

If you choose to buy new metal bench planes, you can't go wrong with the offerings of Lie-Nielsen Toolworks or Lee Valley Tools. Both manufacturers offer first-rate quality at reasonable prices. A Lie-Nielsen #3 is priced at $265 with a #8 priced at $475 with the intermediate sizes falling in between. Veritas doesn't offer an entire line of the classic bevel-down bench planes, but they do offer a #4-1/2 smoother for $225, a #5-1/4 jack at $225, as well as a #6 foreplane at $259.

Lie-Nielsen Toolworks also makes a bevel-up line with the smoother priced at $265, the jack at $245, and the jointer at $350. Lee Valley Tools offers a similar line of bevel-up planes with their smoother offered at $189, their jack at $215, their jointer at $269.

The planes in the Lie-Nielsen line of bevel-down bench planes are all based on the Stanley Bedrock series, but that doesn't mean that the Lie-Nielsen planes are simply reproductions of those originals. Tom Lie-Nielsen has reimagined those classic planes, making his better in every important way. The castings of Lie-Nielsen planes are heavier than the Bedrocks, giving the planes a greater mass. The irons and cap irons of the Lie-Nielsens are much thicker than those on any of the Stanley planes, increasing the stability of the cutting edge, and, of course, he took advantage of modern metallurgy to build his tools from materials which, in some cases, weren't available during the Stanley golden age. In addition, the Lie-Nielsen shop lavishes a level of care on every aspect of the tools' finish not seen in the Bedrock originals. The cherry knobs and totes of the Lie-Nielsen planes are silky under the hand. All edges of the irons and cap irons are smoothed and buffed with the corners slightly relieved. What you get when you purchase a Lie-Nielsen bench plane is classic styling in a meticulously executed modern package.

The designers at Lee Valley Tools took another route to plane superiority. Instead of basing theirs on period originals, they decided to build new tools from the ground up, borrowing details from the past but packaging those details in designs that don't evoke any particular period original. When you look at a Veritas bench plane, you're not looking at anything you've seen before, but—like the Lie-Nielsen bench planes—the Veritas line offers a level of performance not found in period planes. The irons are heavier than period planes, and the machining is done to more exacting standards. The shape of the lever cap (it doesn't actually involve a lever), the shape and species (bubinga) of the wood knob

While the celebrated Bedrock series does have features not found on the Bailey-style series, there is little apparent difference in performance, probably not enough to justify the difference in cost. The #6 shown here (background) and the #606 (foreground) are essentially the same plane.

and tote are not quite like anything in any earlier hand plane. Perhaps the most appealing detail on the Veritas bevel-down bench planes (and their bevel-up line as well), is the use of an adjuster that combines depth of cut and lateral adjustment in the same knob. It's reminiscent of the Norris adjuster, but built to a simpler and more robust design.

If you prefer the look and feel of wooden planes, you can buy them new from Clark and Williams at prices ranging from $315 for a small smoother to $520 for a jointer. While I haven't had a chance to use the company's full range of bench planes, the smoother I have used was everything you could want in a wooden plane: clean crisp execution and solid performance.

If you just inherited a bundle from your favorite aunt, there are still other choices you might consider in the realm of new tools. Tools for Working Wood offers the Ray Iles version of the Norris A5. Several years ago, one of the Iles's A5s spent a couple of weeks in my shop, and I fell in love. The plane's clean and neat execution, coupled with its performance (better than my Norris A5), make it a good value at $995. Plus, there are quite a few modern planemakers producing one-off bench planes of incredible beauty at still higher prices.

If, however, your aunt died penniless and you've just been laid off, there are other still good choices available to you, namely period planes in restorable condition, and while these period planes don't hold up in comparison to the best modern planes, they can certainly be made to do beautiful work.

During the months I worked on this book, I tracked the selling prices of over 100 planes on the online auction site eBay, so that I could make some useful statement about the real value of these tools. To make the comparisons as meaningful as possible, I confined myself to those planes accompanied by a thorough enough photo record to make it possible to assign some kind of condition to each plane based on the condition standards enumerated by "The Fine Tool Journal."

If you're looking to purchase planes from Stanley's premier line, the Bedrocks, be prepared to spend $100 or more. I did spot one #605 in what I estimated to be good+ condition that went for

$89, but the overwhelming majority of usable Bedrocks sold for higher prices. Planes in Stanley's Bailey-style #1-#8 line, however, were much more reasonably priced. For example, a #5C (the "C" identifies a plane with lengthwise corrugations on the sole) from the 1920s sold for $50 and a WWII-era 4-1/2 sold for $41. And sometimes these planes went for incomprehensibly low prices. In one instance, a #6 in good condition sold for just $1. If you spend enough time on the site, you'll be struck by other vagaries of on-line selling. I watched two nearly identical post-WWII-era #5s in Good+ condition sell back to back for two different prices: $15 and $25. Either would have made a good user in someone's shop.

During the period when I was monitoring eBay sales, some transitional bench planes did sell. Stanley transitional smoothers sold for $10-$25, but more went unsold with typical starting bids of $10-$20. Stanley transitional jacks experienced similar fates. If the starting bids were low and the planes were in usable condition, they usually went for $10 or $15. Usable transitional jointers— much rarer—did sell, sometimes for as much as $50. Transitionals made by other companies tended to do even worse. I tracked several usable Fulton jacks, for example, that didn't sell at all, even with starting bids as low as $10. However, a Winchester #3040, a transitional smoother, did sell for $51.

In 2007 as part of my research for a story in *Woodwork* magazine on infill planes, I tracked the eBay selling prices of 24 of these tools. Six were made by T. Norris and Son, eight by Stewart Spiers, two by Edward Preston, and one by the New York maker J. Poppin. The rest were unmarked, probably craftsman made. The most expensive infill sold during that period was a pre-War Norris #1 panel plane in rosewood in what I estimated to be Good+ or Fine condition. This plane sold for $822. The least expensive was a crude wedged smoother that sold for $64.50. Several magnificent infills went unsold, including a 20-1/2" dovetailed Spiers jointer in what the seller estimated to be Good++ condition. Based on what I saw in the photos, I couldn't disagree with his condition estimate, and I wasn't surprised when the bidding topped out at $1,047 with the Reserve unmet.

Based on those selling prices, I was able to generalize that to buy a good, name-brand, user-quality infill smoother, you should expect to pay $300 or more. For a panel plane, you should add a couple hundred to that amount. Jointers—well, they were way out there on the outer limits of price.

In my 2009 price checks, however, things were a little different. A Norris A5 with beech infill went unsold at $280, and a handsome little toted Spiers coffin smoother did sell but only achieved a price of $180. But most surprising was a 14" Spiers panel plane in what I estimated was good+ condition that brought only $415.

The best eBay bargains were in the area of wooden bench planes. It's impossible to accurately evaluate the

conditions of these planes because you can't sight down the soles for twist and bow, so I sidestepped that condition issue by assuming that all soles would require flattening and mouth patches. I then eliminated any tools with missing parts or blown cheeks. I also eliminated any with broken totes, deep body checks, or those which had been generally brutalized by a hammer during iron setting. In other words, I confined myself to planes in pretty good shape.

The truth is that many of these wooden planes didn't sell (because, I think, the opening bids were too high), but those listed with low opening bids—$1 for example—seemed to find buyers at $10-$15. In fact, in one instance, I followed the sale of a group of four wooden bench planes in sound shape that sold for $51. That group—two jacks, a smoother, and a second smoother with a radiused sole—would have equipped a craftsman with enough tools to level and smooth medium-sized panels.

But there is one caveat: An inexperienced plane user buying these wooden planes would have to restore them before they could be used, and then they would have to learn to set wooden plane irons on their own. It can be done. That's they way I learned, but in the 19th and early 20th century shops in which the original owners of these planes worked, that how-to information was communicated by an older more experienced craftsman who likely stood by, offering advice, while the novice struggled to master these tools.

For that reason, a novice might be better served by purchasing period Stanleys which—while still in need of restoration—come equipped with an easy-to-master depth-of-cut adjustment, a simple lever to establish lateral adjustment, and a mouth that can be opened or closed by simply loosening a couple of screws.

Of course, the easiest option would be to buy something from Lie-Nielsen Toolworks or Lee Valley Tools because those planes are ready to go right out of the box.

Today, there is a growing number of individual makers of bench planes producing one-off work of investment quality. This little smoother is the work of Jim Leamy, a Pennsylvania planemaker best known for his reproductions of period plow planes.

Chapter 3

Joinery Planes

Joinery planes, like this Melvin Copeland dado plane, dating to the mid-19th century, can produce crisply executed joinery without the noise and dust generated by the machines typically now used for the same purposes.

Assembling a Collection of Users

Joinery planes make it easier to accomplish precise work. A miter plane and a shooting board allow you to take feathery parings from the end grain of a miter cut, reducing the part's length fractionally until you achieve a perfect fit. Shoulder planes make it possible to incrementally reduce the height of a tenon shoulder in a highly controlled fashion. They can also be used to take thickness from a tenon cheek, one shaving at a time, as you work your way toward an optimal fit. In addition, joinery planes make the shop a more pleasant place in which to work. You can replace the screaming whine of a router or the rumble of a tablesaw by switching to dado planes, plow planes, and moving filletsters when you cut rabbets and grooves. These planes don't fill the air

with dust because the wood they remove stays intact, bound up in shavings you can sweep up and throw away.

Nevertheless, these are the hand planes you are least likely to find if you visit the shop of a contemporary woodworker. Everybody, it seems, has a block plane and a couple of bench planes, usually a smoother and a jack. And many have a molding plane or two, although they might be more decorative than useful. But few craftsmen whose shops I have visited have shoulder planes or dado planes or moving filletsters, despite that the fact that in a one-man, one-off shop, these planes may be more time-efficient and less expensive than the machines a craftsman might buy to cut grooves, rabbets, or to dress miters. This is rooted, I believe, in the notion that hand planes in general, and joinery planes, in particular—with their unfamiliar fences and stops—require an esoteric set of skills some modern craftsmen find forbidding.

Part 1: Joinery plane types

The joinery plane group is larger than you might think, and it includes at least one plane that is typically viewed as a bench plane: the jointer. Although this plane is, in fact, a bench plane because it can be used to level large panels and clean up edges, the jointer could also be placed in the joinery class because its most important function is the creation of glue joints used to join individual boards into wide panels. (Jointing planes are covered in this book in the bench plane chapter.) The joinery plane group also includes shoulder planes which—as the name suggests—are designed to trim tenon shoulders, although you may find them handy in lots of other, non-shoulder applications. For example, when I'm fairing the surfaces of two pieces of mitered molding with imperfectly matched heights, I'll use a shoulder plane to remove material from fillets and convex shapes because of its ability to work the full width of its sole. The joinery group includes all those ingenious planes designed to cut grooves and rabbets, both in the direction of the grain and perpendicular to the grain: dado planes, plow planes, moving filletsters, and rabbet planes. It is also home to those planes used to fractionally adjust these grooves, the side rabbets. Although grooving and rabbeting planes are underappreciated in most modern shops, it is a group of planes on which tool designers have invested perhaps more ingenuity and passion than on any other group of planes. Finally, the joinery plane class includes the miter plane, which 200 years ago was viewed more as a bench plane for stock preparation, but today serves a more specialized function: the fine tuning of end-grain cuts.

Part 2: Choosing wisely

Shoulder planes and rabbet planes look very much alike. Both planes have narrow bodies. Both planes have irons that reach all the way from one side of the body to the other. In fact, the terms are sometimes used interchangeably. But the term "shoulder plane" is probably best reserved for those planes with the irons bedded bevel up with support underneath the irons all the way to the cutting edges in order to support those edges when working end-grain shoulders. Traditionally, shoulder plane sizes are given in each plane's width of cut, although the Stanley Company varies from this tradition, identifying their rabbet (shoulder) planes as part of the same numbering sequence used for all of their other planes. Smaller shoulder planes—say 1/2"—are easier to handle on narrow

The 1-1/2" shoulder plane in the rear is ideal for removing thickness from a tenon cheek. The next two planes—the Lie-Nielsen #042 (3/4" wide) and the Veritas medium shoulder plane (11/16" wide)—are good sizes for cleaning up tenon shoulders. The three bullnose planes in the foreground make it possible to work in tight quarters.

A good miter plane, like the Lie-Nielsen #9 shown here, and a shooting board make it possible to reduce the length of a mitered part in a highly controlled manner in order to achieve a perfect fit. The plane also removes any roughness left on the cut by the miter saw.

shoulders, but wider planes make it much easier to take accurate shavings from a tenon cheek, so ideally, a craftsman should have a pair of shoulder planes: one maybe 1/2" with the other maybe an 1-1/4" or more. Shoulder planes are not often found on the antique tool market, and when they are, they typically command good prices. During my price-tracking of eBay sales, a 1-1/2" Spiers sold for $705, and unmarked shoulder planes in Fair to Good condition sold for $160 and more.

Fortunately, two modern manufacturers are offering new, good-quality shoulder planes at better prices than those often realized for antique shoulder planes. Lie-Nielsen Toolworks sells a small (5/8") shoulder plane, an improved version of a classic Record plane, for $165. There are two larger sizes in this series, also improvements on Record originals, with the largest (1-1/4") selling for $250. Veritas also offers three sizes, ranging from 11/16" to 1-1/4". The small carries a $175 price and the larger is priced at $209. The medium-sized Veritas and the large Veritas both feature rotating lever-cap knobs that can be positioned to best fit your grip.

Antique wooden dado planes are relatively inexpensive. The three I tracked on eBay while I worked on this chapter all sold at the same price of $30, despite the fact that these three examples represented a range of widths. The Stanley dado planes, the #39s, are more expensive planes. I did track one heavily rusted #39 that sold for $45, but the others went unsold for $86 because the seller's reserve prices hadn't been met. While most #39 widths fetch good prices, there is one—the 13/16" that would take a great big chunk out of your wallet because of the rarity of that particular size. One knowledgeable collector told me that a 13/16" in Fine condition could bring $1000 or more.

While it is possible to use a bench plane with a shooting board to clean up end-grain cuts (I used a Stanley #3 for years), a dedicated miter plane like the Lie-Nielsen #9 has a more stable presence in this application, a presence which I think results in more accurate cuts. I have also used traditional wooden miters on my shooting board, but their lack of mass seems to make them less effective than heavier metal planes which can more easily maintain the momentum necessary to cut cleanly through tough end grain. Plus, the thick iron of the Lie-Nielsen #9 is very resistant to chatter, so despite the $375 price, this is a tool any serious craftsman should consider, and if the price is too high, use a good bench plane while you save up for the #9.

Most modern craftsmen use the tablesaw to cut rabbets, but prior to the 20th century, this work was accomplished with rabbeting planes or moving filletsters. A simple rabbet plane is nothing more than a block of squared up beech into which a throat has been cut and an iron wedged, an iron that reaches across the full width of the plane's body. Although I know some very knowledgeable craftsman continue to use these planes in their day-to day work, I've used mine only rarely. That's because these planes lack features to control the depth or width of cut. To use a simple rabbet plane, you must first establish a fence—either by attaching a batten to the work or by starting a rabbet with a fenced plane—and then work down to a line. For this reason, I prefer a moving filletster of either wood or metal construction.

A wooden moving filletster resembles a fat molding plane in its overall shape, but unlike a molding plane, the moving filletster has a moveable fence attached to the sole with a pair of woodscrews. In addition, it comes equipped with an adjustable brass depth stop instead of fillet cut into the sole. Sometimes these are found without a fence and/or a depth stop in which case they would be of no more use than a

wooden rabbet so shop carefully. User-grade antique wooden filletster planes made of beech can be purchased for as little as $50. Rosewood examples or examples built with a screw-arm fence are much more expensive.

But for craftsmen who prefer metal planes to wooden planes, there are lots of excellent metal moving filletsters available as antiques. Stanley, for example, offered a wide range of rabbeting tools, some with fences and depth stops and some without. The easiest to find is the #78. In fact, I'm not sure I've ever searched for planes in an antique mall without encountering at least a couple of #78s, although most were lacking a fence and depth stop. These planes come equipped with a slitter having three sharpened teeth so the plane can cut across the grain as well as in the direction of the grain. The plane also has a second bed near the toe so it can be used for bullnose work.

When they appear in the booths of antique dealers lacking tool knowledge, #78s can be priced ridiculously high—even when they're missing parts. I recently saw one such example—with a rust-frozen adjuster and without a fence or depth stop—priced at $60, but when I tracked the selling prices of complete user-grade #78s on eBay, I saw each one sell for $10-$16. I also tracked a badly battered, rust-encrusted Sargent moving filletster, and I was surprised to see that this plane sold for $20. Wooden examples are a bit more expensive, and here too dealer knowledge plays a role. Because they're often mistakenly identified as molding planes, sometimes dealers will offer them for $20-$30. But if you buy one from a tool dealer or on eBay, you're likely to pay a bit more. The most expensive example I own I purchased for $50 on eBay.

Modern toolmakers are today offering new moving filletsters. E.C. Emmerich sells a wedged wooden example for $185. Stanley is still selling the #78 for $64, although it's designated with a new number #12-978. But the Veritas skew rabbet at $249 may be the best bargain, despite the price. Like other Veritas tools, this isn't simply a copy of an antique; it's a 21st century design, new-built from the ground up.

The most beautiful planes in the joinery class—and perhaps the most beautiful planes of all—are the plows. Like the moving filletsters, these are found constructed of both wood and metal. In general, the wooden plows predate the metal versions, although some makers still offered wooden examples after the metal plows had saturated the market.

Because of its rarity and beauty, I would be reluctant to use this rosewood moving filletster. *Collection of Max Stebelton.*

Antique wooden English plows are typically of the wedge-arm variety with the arms and attached fence held in place by a pair of long wedges fit into tapering slots in the body beside each arm. "Yankee plows" are among the first American plows. The fences on these planes are attached to arms that slide through mortises cut in the body of the plows, arms which are secured with boxwood thumbscrews. Later in the 19th century most American planemakers dropped slide-arm plows in favor of screw-arm planes with the arms locked in place through the use of a pair of threaded washers and a pair of threaded nuts. In addition to thousands of user-grade plows, some planemakers also sold smaller numbers of presentation plows made of rosewood or ebony decorated with ivory, brass, and even silver. These are tools best left to collectors because of their high dollar value. A case in point: in 2004 a Sandusky Tool Company presentation plow made of ebony and ivory brought the highest auction price ever realized for an American tool: $114,000.

User-grade plows are surprisingly reasonable. I've purchased usable wedge-arm plows for $40 on eBay. Usable screw-arms tend to be a bit more expensive, but several years ago I bought my best plow—an Ohio Tool Company screw-arm made entirely of boxwood with perfect screw arm threads—for just $50 on eBay. That purchase was a fluke, however. It was offered by someone who didn't know plows, so it was listed simply as a wood plane. Plus, the plow was coated with 100 years of thick grime, so it made a poor first impression. However, after spending some time studying the photos, I came to suspect—because of the plane's color—that it had a boxwood body (more desirable than beech), and the threads all looked to be intact, at least those not concealed by the body of the plane.

At the rear is an English wedge-arm plow. The plow with the orange cast is a boxwood untoted screw-arm plow. To the right of that example is a Yankee plow with boxwood thumbscrews. In the left foreground is a toted screw-arm plow.

Unfortunately, you'd need some luck to get a usable screw-arm plow for less than $80, so shop carefully. In particular, check for thread damage. A few localized broken threads don't make a plane unusable, but if there's a patch in which all the threads are gone, that plane won't perform in your shop.

I have used wedge-arm plows and Yankee plows, but I find the screw-arm style to be the easiest type to adjust, and they are certainly the most common of the wooden plows available on the antique tool market.

This ivory-tipped rosewood plow made by the Ohio Tool Company is an example of the premium-grade plows made by some 19th century manufacturers. *Collection of Max Stebelton.*

In the field of metal plows, Stanley of course led the way, and most of the antique metal plows available today are Stanleys. The most beautiful of the Stanley plows are the Miller's patents which were first offered in 1871. These plows are ornamented with elaborate floral designs cast onto the body, the fence, and the top of the filletster bottom. Today, these planes have considerable value and should not be used to cut grooves.

Some of Stanley's other offerings are less costly and, in fact, make good users, like the #46 which is designed to cut on the skew. Unfortunately a full set of cutters for this—or any other antique Stanley plow—can be hard to acquire.

Also, there are some companies offering new plow planes. E.C. Emmerich offers a wooden plow with six irons (ranging from 1/8" to 9/16") for $380. Veritas sells a small metal plow plane, similar in size to Record #044. It comes with five irons: 1/8", 3/16", 1/4", 5/16", 3/8". This is a slick little plow, easy to set up and easy to use.

The Stanley #41 is one of the most beautiful plows ever made. *Collection of Max Stebelton.*

With a set of five irons, the price is $269. They also make the tool in a left-handed configuration for those of us who do everything backwards, but it's not something I'd consider for myself because all of my other joinery and molding planes are right-handed which has required me to learn how to work backwards, and I'm afraid the wiring in my head might begin to arc and smoke if I tried to work a plow plane left-handed. Finally, Clark and Williams offers a wooden wedge-arm plow with a full set of eight irons for $1295. It's a beautiful tool, worth—I suspect—every dollar, but if I had ever paid that much for a plow plane, I could never make myself use it.

Part 3: The elephant in the room

The 1926 Stanley Tools catalog identifies the #55 as "A Planing Mill Within Itself." The text goes on to say that: "This tool, in addition to being a beading and center beading plane, a plow, dado, rabbet, filletster, and match plane, a sash plane, and a slitting plane, is also a superior moulding plane."

That might be overstatement. The plane is a remarkably versatile engineering accomplishment, a single tool that can operate a total of 98 different cutters, but the complexity that makes that versatility possible can also make shifting from one function to another immensely frustrating. By contrast, if I want to switch from using my wooden moving filletster to using a wooden side bead, all I have to do is pluck the side bead from my plane cabinet and begin working. That side bead—like every other molder in my collection—is already set up, with the depth stop and the fence built right into the sole.

Plus, there is the problem of the #55's solelessness. Molding planes all have soles into which are cut reasonably tight mouths.

This means that these individual molding planes can successfully work material that is less than perfect without leaving behind significant tearout. To use the #55 as a molder—successfully—you need material that is essentially flawless and straight-grained because there is no mouth to control tearout.

I think the #55 makes a reasonably good plow plane, if you subtract the frustration of setting it up to perform this work after using it to perform some other task. Unfortunately, all but a handful of the cutters sold for this plane are designed to cut moldings, and if you look at the most famous Stanley #55 advertising image, you'll see a plane poised in space, surrounded by moldings (not stock in which grooves have been plowed) disappearing behind the plane in bold one-point perspective.

All but a few of those moldings require multiple cutters, and that's where the use of the #55 goes way off the frustration charts. To create a molding containing several shapes, not only do you need to install sequentially several different cutters in the #55, you also need to align each one so it meets the work of the previous cutters where it should, and this can be immensely frustrating work, particularly when you realize that the same group of shapes could be cut with a single complex molding plane on which the fence and depth stop are always correctly set.

I think the #55 (and it's older brother, the #45) could be mastered, but it would take an enormous amount of study and practice, and even then, you'd be working with a plane that has no sole and one that requires set-up time to shift from one function to another.

This isn't a plane I would recommend to anyone but a collector.

Joinery Planes: Miter Planes and Shooting Boards

Few shop-made devices will do more for the quality of your work than a shooting board (or perhaps several shooting boards, each designed to meet a different need). With a shooting board and a plane of even average quality, you can pare tissue-paper thin shavings from the end grain of stock crosscut to any angle, and in this manner remove sawmarks and reduce the part's length one shaving at a time in order to achieve a perfect fit. Plus, the shooting board/miter plane combination will allow you to rectify any errors in angle that might be present in the sawn miter.

For many years, my miter plane was an ordinary bench plane, a Stanley #3, which I'd taken the time to tune carefully, with the iron sharp and the plane set up with a tight mouth. This inexpensive antique performed ably for many years in this role, but eventually when I began to get more serious about finding ways in which the use of dedicated hand planes could enhance not only the quality of my work but also the pleasure I find in doing that work, I decided it was time invest in a miter plane.

My first purchase was an American-style wood miter plane I picked up on eBay for $10. It was listed on the auction site as a smoother because it does look like a smoother. Both planes have their irons bedded bevel down. The only difference is the angle at which the iron is bedded. A smoother typically has its iron bedded at a 45 degree angle. An American wood miter plane, on the other hand, has its iron bedded at a much shallower angle, usually between 30 and 40 degrees. The English also made wooden mitre planes, but the irons in these English planes were bedded bevel up, usually at an even shallower angle than their American counterparts. These planes also often included a boxwood block fit on end into a through mortise just ahead of the iron. This block could be tapped down to rebuild the sole if the area in front of the mouth began to wear.

Eventually, I also purchased a Lie-Nielsen #9. This updated version of the classic Stanley #9 is a true low angle with its bevel-up iron bedded at an angle of 20 degrees. It has an adjustable mouth and features a sole and sides machined so that they are precisely 90 degrees apart, which is critical when you're using the plane to shoot miters.

In the realm of antique tools, you might find several other types of miter planes as well. Some of these were intended to be used only with a shooting board. For example, a tool collector in my hometown has an enormous antique cast iron shooting-board plane with two skewed mouths, one on either end. I've never put this behemoth on a scale, but I'd be surprised if it weighed less than 15 pounds. Also, some shooting board planes were made of wood with a skewed iron and a handle for driving the plane, a handle which rises from the side that would be uppermost when the plane is in position on a shooting board. And of course, some of the most beautiful planes ever made were the English infill mitre planes of the 19th century. These usually dovetailed boxes of steel were stuffed with exotic hardwoods, then topped with a shallowly bedded iron held in

Traditionally, American miter planes were made of wood, like the two examples in the rear. Then, in the 19th century, when metal planes began to compete with wooden planes, miter planes made of metal made their appearance. The Stanley #9, on which the Lie-Nielsen #9 shown here in the foreground was based, made its first appearance in 1870. *Courtesy of* Woodwork *magazine.*

Miter planes make it easy to produce clean, accurate miters. *Courtesy of* Woodwork *magazine.*

place with a wedge fitted against a metal bar joined on either end to the sides of the box.

A miter plane without a shooting board is just a bench plane with an unusual bedding angle. It's when it's used in conjunction with a shooting board that a miter plane is best able to do the work it's designed to do. I have a variety of shooting boards in my shop, each one designed for a particular job. Some are used for shooting frame miters, the kind of miters you cut for picture frames. Others are used for shooting case miters, the kind of miters you might use on the sides of a box. And there are other kinds of shooting boards you might consider, some set up to pare cuts at non-right angles, as well as adjustable commercially manufactured shooting boards, like the Stanley #52.

Part 1: Preparing a miter plane

Since a miter plane is used most often to pare tough end grain wood, it's important that the iron be as sharp as possible. The business end of the iron should also be ground straight across its width, without the slight camber or rounded corners you might want on an iron intended for a smoothing plane.

If you're preparing the iron for an American wood miter plane, you must grind the bevel to an unusually shallow angle (a bit less than the plane's bedding angle) in order for the heel of the bevel to clear the work. If the angle isn't sufficiently shallow, the heel will rub on the work preventing the cutting edge from engaging, and no matter how hard you press on the plane or how sharp its cutting edge, the plane won't take a shaving. This problem doesn't occur with the irons on bevel-up miter planes. These can be ground to any angle you like, with something in the area of 20-25 degrees being the norm.

The mouth for a miter plane is typically set very tight, often just a few thousandths wide. The mouths on the finest English mitre planes—the gold-standard for this genre of tool—are so tight that only the slightest glimmer of light will penetrate.

You should also check to see that the sole and the sides of the miter plane are exactly 90 degrees apart. Error is relatively easy to correct in a wood miter plane, more difficult in a metal miter plane like the Stanley #9 which would require some fussy work on a lapping plate.

Part 2: Using a miter plane

When you're cutting a part to length that you will later treat with a miter plane and shooting board, remember to leave extra length on the part. The amount of extra length is best determined by experimenting on a bit of scrap using your miter plane/shooting board combination.

My shop-made shooting boards have no hold-down devices, so with my right hand. I simply press the work against the shooting-board fence, positioning it so that just a sliver of the work's end hangs out beyond the fence. I then grip the plane with my left hand and

The miter plane iron in the foreground has a much shallower ground bevel than the smoother iron in the background. This shallower bevel is necessary if the heel of the bevel is to clear the work. *Courtesy of* Woodwork *magazine.*

move it past the work. I'm left-handed so this is my normal way of working, but if you're right-handed, you'll prefer a mirror image set up. Also while it's possible to turn some moldings upside down in order to plane the miter on the right hand end of the work on the left side of the shooting board, the back side of some moldings will splinter if planed this way. In such a case, I use the #9 right-handed on the right side of a shooting board.

I ordered a "hot dog" attachment for my Lie-Nielsen #9. This is a short tube of metal that is attached to the frame of the miter plane through the use of a set screw. It can be positioned anywhere along the frame that feels comfortable. When I'm using this miter plane, I grip the "hot dog" and use it to push the plane into and past the work. When I'm using a wood miter plane, I simply grip the plane in a comfortable position, with a couple of fingers tucked into the plane's excavation.

Because the work of a miter plane is most often performed on tough end-grain material, it takes a bit of power to drive it through a cut, particularly if you're truing a wide miter on a hard wood. While you must maintain control of the plane, you also need to move it past the work with some authority if you want to avoid hesitation marks, which will require additional passes to clean up. You might practice on a bit of scrap before you attempt to true a cut on a part intended for a project.

Sometimes you don't want a dead-on-perfect 45 degree miter because perhaps the case to which you're attaching your mitered stock might be a bit out of square or because the mitered element to which the current part will be joined might have an imperfect miter. In such a case, you may want the new miter to be a bit less than or a bit more than 45 degrees. Fortunately, when you're using a shooting board, it's easy to cheat.

You cheat with a bit of folded paper pressed between the part and the shooting board fence. If you want an angle greater than 45 degrees, you slip the folded paper into position between the fence and the part near the miter cut, then use your fingers to pin the work to the fence near the right-hand side of the shooting board. If you want an angle a little less than 45 degrees, you slip the folded paper into position away from the miter cut and pin the work to the fence near the cut you're planing.

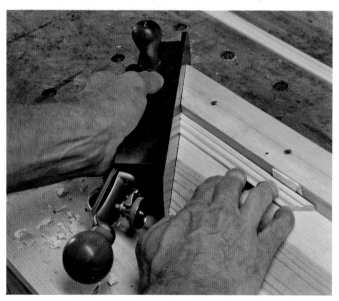

You can make minute adjustments of mitered angles with bits of folded paper as is shown here. *Courtesy of* Woodwork *magazine.*

The Stanley #51 is a different animal, one requiring a different approach. This combination miter plane and chute board was offered by the Stanley Rule and Level Company up until World War II for the use of—in the words of their 1909 catalog—"Pattern Makers, Cabinet Makers, Printers and Electrotypers." The chute board itself is adjustable for many different angles, and the plane is designed to ride in a track on the chute board. In addition, the plane's iron is mounted at a skewed angle to make "a smooth, keen cut" and the tote is also mounted at an angle, one which tilts the tote up from the chute board so the user won't bark his knuckles on the chute board or the bench on which it's mounted. It is, in short, a very well designed tool, which unfortunately comes with a price commensurate with its quality. Although I've been searching the antique tool markets for several years, I have not been able to find a #51+#52 in good condition, with all essential parts, for less than $1200.

In order to keep the plane running smoothly, you should keep the channel clear of dust and chips. Plus, a bit of lubrication facilitates the easy movement of metal on metal, but you should avoid using oil for this purpose. Oil attracts and retains dirt, and—in the long run—will create more problems than it solves. Charles Murray, the craftsman shown demonstrating his Stanley #51 in this chapter, recommends rubbing the contact areas with the lead from a #2 pencil, using graphite as a non-dust-attracting lubricant.

Like the wood miter plane and the #9, the #51 works best when the operator generates a bit of power. Before he pushes the work into the iron, Murray slides the plane back and forth in the track several times to establish pace and momentum. He then feeds the work into the iron incrementally by scooting it along the fence with his left hand.

The trick with any miter plane is taking thin passes and maintaining momentum throughout the stroke. If you do this and your tool is set up well and the iron sharp, you will be rewarded with cleanly pared cross cuts and a pile of intact end-grain parings.

Charles Murray, a cabinetmaker from Canal-Winchester, Ohio, is demonstrating his Stanley #51 and Stanley chute board, the #52. *Courtesy of* Woodwork *magazine.*

The #51+#52 has a hold-down to secure the work. Notice the intact end-grain parings. *Courtesy of* Woodwork *magazine.*

Part 3: Bevel up or down

Traditionally, block planes were said to be superior to smoothing planes for end-grain work because block planes offer a lower angle of attack, and it's pretty easy to demonstrate—at least anecdotally—the effectiveness of a shallow attack angle on end-grain work by applying a hand-held paring chisel to a bit of end grain. When the chisel is held at a low angle—one with the back of the chisel nearly parallel with the end-grain surface being worked—the chisel pares effectively with its approximately 25-30 degree cutting angle, but when that same paring chisel is held in a more upright posture, increasing the cutting angle to—say—40 or 50 degrees, the chisel performs much less well. In fact, it might not perform at all.

The superiority of a low cutting-angle bevel-up plane for end-grain work, in my mind, seems pretty clear, but the reason why is less clear. A block plane is typically bedded at—say—20 degrees, which might at first seem to be just about twice as good as the smoother's 45 degree angle. Unfortunately, the cutting angle of a block plane consists not only of the bedding angle; it also includes the bevel angle because block planes have their irons bedded bevel up. This means that the cutting angle of a block plane with its iron bedded at 20 degrees and having a bevel angle of 25 degrees is exactly the same as the cutting angles of most smoothers.

So is there an advantage to using a block plane for end-grain work? Tom Lie-Nielsen cites the issue of cutting-edge support. The sole of a block plane, like the Lie-Nielsen #9, offers support almost directly under the cutting edge, whereas the sole of a plane with an iron bedded bevel-down offers its closest support a short distance from the cutting edge. The bottom 1/4" of the iron on my #3—the part that most needs support—is simply hanging out there in space when the plane is in use. In the case of wooden miter planes, even more of the iron behind the cutting edge is unsupported, nearly 1/2" on my two wooden miter planes.

As a result, I believe, of this lack of support immediately under the cutting edge, sometimes when I'm using one of my wooden miter planes to clean up a cross cut in really hard wood, the iron will chatter as that unsupported cutting edge stutters on the hard end grain. This is not, however, something I've seen when I'm using my #3 to clean up miters. Like my #9, the #3 seems pretty resistant to chatter, which could be due to the fact that support is closer to the cutting edge on the #3 than it is to the cutting edge of my wood miter planes. Also, metal miter planes carry more weight, enabling them to maintain momentum as they engage and then power their way through tough end-grain material. This might also reduce the likelihood of chatter.

If you can afford it, a carefully restored Stanley #51 +#52 chute board is probably the best option for truing up sawn cross cuts. If not, the #9—either the Stanley original or the Lie-Nielsen version—is a first-rate alternative.

Shooting boards can be used on no-standard miters like this half-mitered part for the plate rack shown on page 106. *Courtesy* Popular Woodworking *magazine.*

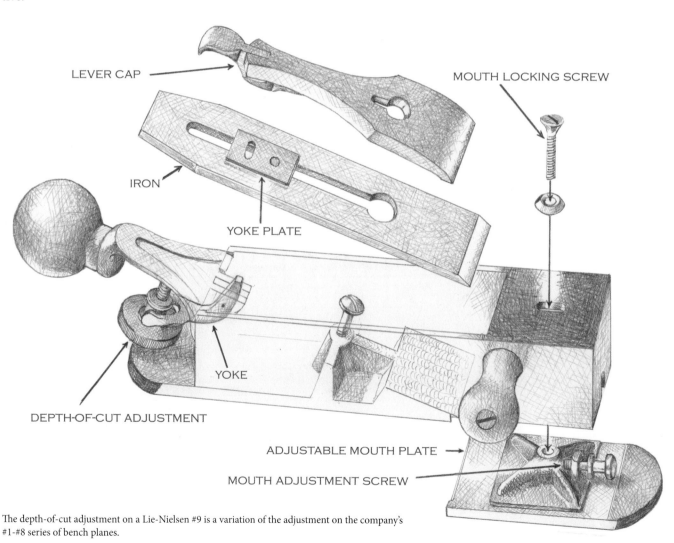

LEVER CAP

MOUTH LOCKING SCREW

IRON

YOKE PLATE

DEPTH-OF-CUT ADJUSTMENT

YOKE

ADJUSTABLE MOUTH PLATE

MOUTH ADJUSTMENT SCREW

The depth-of-cut adjustment on a Lie-Nielsen #9 is a variation of the adjustment on the company's #1-#8 series of bench planes.

Joinery Planes: Grooving and Rabetting Planes

If you're going to cut rabbets on a hundred parts, it makes sense to remove the ripping blade from your tablesaw and replace it with a stack of dado cutters because the brutal efficiency of the tablesaw can quickly render rabbets on these 100 parts, but in my shop, because I tend to build things one at a time, I rarely find myself facing such a large number of rabbets. More typically, I find myself cutting them on two parts or maybe four.

In such a case, I take a moving filletster of either the wooden or metal variety, set the fence and go to work. The set up time? Maybe 30 seconds. Set up time for removing the tablesaw's ripping blade, installing a stack of dado cutters, attaching a wood fence to the tablesaw's metal fence (to protect the blade), and then setting that fence? Well, all that takes a good bit longer.

And hand planes are equally efficient when you're cutting just a few dadoes or a just a few grooves.

While this work *can* be done on the tablesaw, these machines are noisy and dusty and not much fun to use. Grooving planes, on the other hand, are clean and quiet and profoundly pleasurable to use because let's face it: A tablesaw doesn't require any skill to operate. A grooving plane, however, gives us an opportunity to demonstrate—if only to ourselves—that we really are craftsmen.

Part 1: Plow planes

There are three different kinds of channels typically used in the assembly of casework: (1.) the groove, which is plowed some distance from the edge of a board in the direction of the running grain; (2) the rabbet which is cut along the edge either in the direction of the running grain or across the grain, and (3) the dado, a channel cut across the grain.

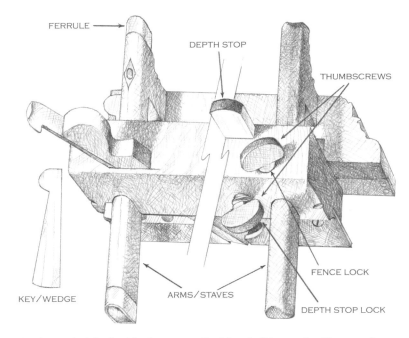

The plow on the left side of the drawing is an English-style slide-arm plow. The arms of this type are locked in place with tapered wedges. The plow on the right is a Yankee-style slide arm. The arms on Yankee plows were locked in place with thumb screws, usually formed of boxwood.

The plow plane is the hand tool of choice for cutting grooves in the direction of the running grain. Drawer bottoms, for example, are installed in grooves cut on the inside faces of drawer sides. The plow plane—either the classic wooden-bodied type or the metal-bodied type made famous by Stanley—was designed to cut such grooves.

Wooden plow planes typically were purchased with a set of eight interchangeable irons graduated in 1/16" width increments from 1/8" to 5/8" (skipping the 9/16" stop in the progression). Unfortunately, plows are almost never found with full sets of irons. I own about a dozen plows, and each one came to me with only a single iron. However, it is possible to buy loose irons from tool dealers, and in that manner assemble a set. But not all irons will fit all plows, so when you buy, make sure that the irons are stamped with the name of the maker of the plow in which you hope to use them. With an unmarked iron, the only thing you can do is try it in your plane. Despite several years of searching I still don't own a complete set for any individual plow. The closest I come is a grouping of five different Ohio Tool irons.

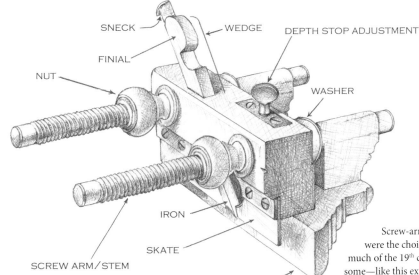

Screw-arm plows, like the one shown here, were the choice of American craftsmen during much of the 19th century. Some were toted, and some—like this example—were not.

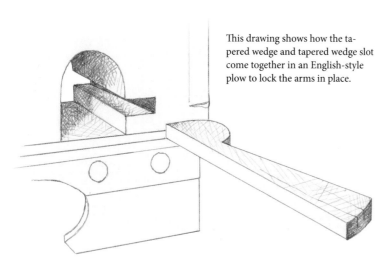

This drawing shows how the tapered wedge and tapered wedge slot come together in an English-style plow to lock the arms in place.

There are several different ways of locking the fences on the plows available on the antique tool market. The arms and the attached fences of most English plows are held in position by tapping wedges into tapered mortises cut in the sides of the arm mortises. The arms and fences of early American plows are often held in position with thumbscrews—usually made of dense, durable boxwood—passing down through the plane's body to make contact with the fence arms. Later American plows are equipped with threaded screw arms, also made of boxwood which pass through unthreaded mortises in the plow bodies. The fences of these plows are held in position by trapping the plane bodies between threaded boxwood washers on the left side (as you're using the plow) and larger threaded boxwood nuts on the right side.

The irons are quite heavy on the business end, 1/4" or more, tapering in thickness to less than 1/16" at the top of the tang which protrudes above the wedge of the plane. Sometimes these tangs are snecked

The plow in the rear is an English-style slide arm. The plow on the right is a Yankee plow. The two plows on the left are screw arms, one toted (front left), the other not. *Courtesy of* Woodwork *magazine.*

This boxwood screw arm plow does a beautiful job. So far, I have only five of the eight irons that would have come with this tool. *Courtesy of* Woodwork *magazine.*

The broken down untoted screw arm in the front illustrates the way the pieces come together. The toted screw arm in the rear breaks down in exactly the same way. *Courtesy of* Woodwork *magazine.*

Every iron has a groove milled on the lower back. This groove mates with the leading edge of the back skate section. *Courtesy of Woodwork magazine.*

to make it easier to set an iron. A sneck is a tab of metal sticking out of one side of the tang to make it possible to raise the iron by tapping upward on that sneck. The iron is held in place with a tapered wedge tapped into a tapered mortise which passes vertically through the plane at a 45-50 degree angle. The bottom end of the iron bisects a metal skate screwed to the plane's body. The iron is stabilized through the use of a groove milled into its back side which fits over the leading edge of the back half of the skate.

The plane is fitted with a moveable depth stop which can be set to create grooves up to about 1" in depth. Most plows have a depth stop fixed in a vertical through-mortise. On the top side of the plane, a brass thumbscrew emerges from a brass plate. On the bottom side of the plow, there is an iron or brass shoe which is raised or lowered by turning the top-side thumbscrew. On most plows, it's then locked in place with a second thumbscrew on the left side of the plane body.

The depth stops on some early plows are simply narrow blocks of boxwood friction-fit into mortises cut vertically in the planes' bodies.

To prepare a plow for use, set the sharpened iron so that cutting edge just barely peeks above the bottom edge of the skate when you're sighting the bottom of the plane's skate from the front. Make sure the groove on the back side of the iron is engaged with the leading edge of the back half of the skate. Then tap the wedge firmly in place with a mallet. Some craftsmen use metal mallets for this purpose, but I've seen too many mushroomed tangs and broken down wedge finials resulting from blows from metal mallets, so I use mallets with wood heads. Specifically, I use a large-headed wood mallet for removing stuck wedges, and smaller wood mallet for tapping the iron into position and for tapping a wedge into its tapered mortise.

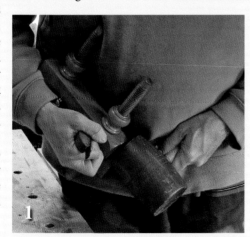

If the iron is stuck, hold the plow as shown against your body with your thumb and forefinger wrapped around the finial. Then rap the heel of your plow with a mallet. (Please: No metal hammers.) *Courtesy of* Woodwork *magazine.*

After the iron is set to the correct depth, rap the top of the finial with a wood mallet to lock the iron in that position. *Courtesy of* Woodwork *magazine.*

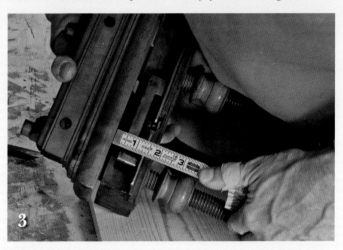

The distance from the groove's outside edge and the edge of the board is established by measuring from the outside edge of the iron and the inside edge of the fence. Then measure between the inside edge of the fence and the outside edge of the skate at both the toe and the heel in order to make sure the fence is parallel to the skate. Finally trap the plane's body in that position by turning the nuts and washers snug against the body. (This will seem to be very tricky at first, but if you're patient with the process, you'll learn how to correctly position these parts when setting up a cut.) *Courtesy of* Woodwork *magazine.*

To operate the plow, press the fence against the outside edge of the board with your left hand, and—while pressing downward—push the plane forward with your right hand.

After you've determined the necessary distance between the edge of the board and the outside edge of the groove, set the fence and snug up the washers on the left-hand side of the plow's body, checking the distance at both the front and back. Remember that the inside edge of the groove is measured from the iron, not the skate. You measure from the fence to the inside edge of the skate only to ensure that the fence and skate are parallel by checking that measurement at two places along the length of the skate. Once you've properly positioned the fence, draw up the nuts to trap the body in that position.

Set the depth of cut by measuring from the bottom of the depth stop to the bottom of the iron's cutting edge, adjusting the depth stop as necessary.

You're now ready to apply the plow to the wood.

Metal plow planes, like this Stanley #46, operate in much the same way as the wooden counterparts. Because this Stanley #46 uses skewed irons, the shavings come out in twists, like those made by a spill plane.

With your left hand, press the fence against the edge of the board while your right hand presses the skate (and the cutting edge) down onto the top surface of the board while simultaneously pushing the plow forward.

If this is your first time using a plow, your depth of cut might need to be reset after your first attempt to take a shaving. You might have too little cutting edge exposed, making it impossible to take a shaving or so much exposed that you're taking a shaving thick enough to rip away material from both sides of the intended groove. A proper shaving will be thin enough to curl but not quite so thin as those produced by a smoothing plane.

Metal plows, like the Stanley #46, are set up and used in much the same way although the fences and depth stops are configured in different ways.

Part 2: Rabbet/moving filletster planes

Rabbets are grooves along the edges of boards, open on one side, running either in the direction of the grain or across the direction of the grain. They can be formed with simple rabbet planes (rebate if you're English), and judging by the numbers of simple rabbet planes still found at antique malls, these must have been widely used in the 19th century. These planes aren't among my favorites, however, because they lack the fence and depth stop present on moving filletsters.

Both the #78 (and its moving filletster equivalents made by other manufacturers) and the wooden moving filletsters function in about the same way, although the planes look very different. In each case the iron—bedded bevel-side down—just barely peeks out from the right side of the plane. This allows the plane to work right up to the shoulder of the evolving rabbet.

Both the metal and the wooden planes have depth stops: probably a brass shoe in the case of the wooden plane and an iron shoe in the case of the #78. Both planes have a fence

The Stanley #78 is the most common moving filletster on the antique tool market. Unfortunately, most are unusable because they're found without the fence, the fence arm, and the depth stop. Stanley is still making a #78 look-alike, and although I asked to be given one to test for this book, Stanley chose not send me one.

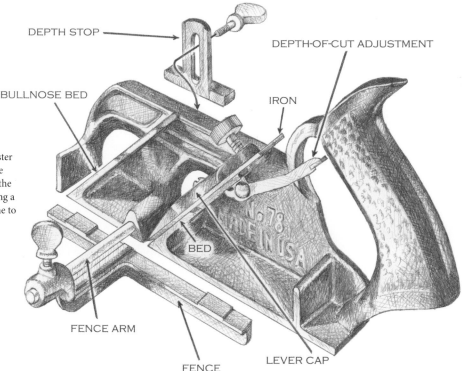

DEPTH STOP

DEPTH-OF-CUT ADJUSTMENT

BULLNOSE BED

IRON

BED

FENCE ARM

LEVER CAP

FENCE

80

which controls the width of the exposed cutting edge on the plane's sole and the consequent width of the rabbet being cut. In the case of the wooden plane, the fence is a 2" wide, 9-1/2" long board attached to the sole via a pair of heavy woodscrews passing through brass channels mortised into the fence. In the case of the #78, the fence is a narrow steel bar mounted just below the sole on a rod that protrudes from the left side of the plane. Both planes also have slitters/nickers just ahead of the iron in order to score the wood so that the plane can take clean cross-grain shavings. The slitter on the wooden moving filletster is usually a small iron set sideways and wedged in place on the right side of the plane body ahead of the primary iron. The slitter on the #78 is a little different. It is instead a three-pointed star housed in a shallow mortise just ahead of the iron. Each of those legs can be set to hang below the sole of the #78 scoring the wood ahead of the iron.

Typically slitters need to be sharpened before they're used. The slitter on a wooden plane should be filed or stoned so that the bevel on its front-facing cutting edge is formed on the inside only (the side adjacent to the plane). It should then be set so that its sharpened point extends below the plane's sole between 1/32" and 1/16". Any more than that, and the slitter becomes a drag on the plane's forward movement; any less and you may not achieve clean cross-grain severing of wood fibers ahead of the primary iron.

Because most wooden moving filletsters have skewed irons (actually every one I've ever seen), you may feel that the wooden planes take a shaving with less effort than the #78. I know I have that feeling, but it's hard to devise a shop test to determine if this perception is authentic or simply part of my general preference for wooden moving filletsters. My general preference is probably rooted in the fact that metal moving filletsters are nowhere near as comfortable to hold in use as their wooden-bodied counterparts, but they are much easier to find, and the truth is they perform rabbeting work in an efficient manner.

The #78 features a three-armed star slitter just ahead of the iron. These should be sharpened if the plane is to be used for cross-grain work. If you're working in the direction of the grain, position the star so that none of the legs are protruding from the plane.

The teeth on the adjustment lever of the #78 engage these grooves milled into the back of the iron.

Crowd the fence of the #78 against the edge of the board you're working. Then begin taking passes until the depth stop rubs the top of the board.

The iron in a wooden-bodied filletster is sharpened and installed just like the iron in any other wooden plane having a skewed iron—with one exception. You must be very careful to get it positioned with the right outside corner of the iron aligned so that just a whisker protrudes from the right-hand side of the plane.

Setting the depth of cut on a wooden moving filletster is essentially the same thing as setting the depth of cut on a wooden bench plane: Tap the iron into position and once it's there, tap the wedge to lock the iron. You'll want a more exposure of the cutting edge through the sole than you would with—for example—a smoothing plane.

The fence on a wooden filletster is set by backing off the woodscrews that attach the fence and then tightening them once again when the fence has been moved where you want it. To move the fence on the #78 loosen the fence thumbscrew, then tighten the thumbscrew when the fence has been slid to the correct position.

To cut a rabbet with a wooden plane, crowd the fence against the edge of the stock being rabbetted with your left hand. Then, with your right hand applying downward pressure, push the plane into the cut.

Cross grain rabbets require a bit of extra preparation. In order to prevent the plane from tearing out long fibers at the end of each stroke, you need to clamp a backer strip onto the far edge of the stock being worked. Also, even with a slitter, sometimes when you're working in a relatively brittle species, you might want to first score across the grain with a sharp knife.

The #78 has one feature not found on the wooden planes. It's equipped with two beds: a conventionally placed bed near the midpoint along the plane's length and a second bed near the front for bullnose work.

Like the iron in a wooden moving filletster, the iron in a #78 is bedded bevel side down. Depth of cut is set by moving the adjustment lever on the back side of the plane's central bed up or down. This causes gear teeth on the lever to engage a series of horizontal grooves milled into the back side of the iron, which scoots the iron up and down along the bed.

To use a #78, you simply crowd the fence against the edge of the work with your left hand while simultaneously pressing down and forward with your right hand in much the same way you propel the wooden moving filletster through a cut.

To set the fence on the bottom of a wooden moving filletster, loosen the screws, move the fence into position, then tighten the screws.

The slitter on a wooden moving filletster is a small second iron just ahead of the primary iron.

You operate the wooden moving filletster just like its metal cousin.

Crowd the fence against the edge of the board with your left hand. Then push the plane forward and down with your right hand.

To do clean cross-grain work, use a backing strip.

You can even use a moving filletster on plywood.

Anybody who's ever used a bench plane knows that planes cut more efficiently when they're pushed at a skewed angle. Since it's not possible to hold a #78 (or any other non-skewed rabbet plane) at a skewed angle and do any meaningful rabbet work, Veritas introduced a skew rabbet, with the skew built right into the bed of this plane, and I believe it does make a difference. In addition, the generally superior design and manufacturing present throughout the Veritas line makes an even greater difference.

The Veritas skew rabbet has a comfortable wooden tote at the heel and a comfortable wooden knob at the toe. Depth of cut is controlled with a brass knob set up in a manner much like the depth-of-cut control on antique Record shoulder planes. The fence is locked in place through the use of a pair of brass nuts that draw down on the metal collets by which the fence is attached to the rods. There is also a depth stop similar to the one on the #78. It is, in general, a rock-solid rabbeting plane.

For years, I've used either a wooden side rabbet or a chisel when I needed to make slight increases in the width of a dado or a rabbet. Neither tool does this work particularly well. The chisel has no control surfaces. It's just a wedge of sharp iron only partially controlled by my own unfortunately human hands. And the wooden side rabbet is more a good idea than a good tool. It's too light, too flimsy to do effective work on end grain, although it handles long grain reasonably well when I'm widening a plowed groove.

Stanley of course made side rabbets. So, too, does Lie-Nielsen, but I've never had an opportunity to use either. I have used the Veritas side rabbet, and it's every bit as effective as the skew rabbet I described in the preceding paragraph. The side rabbet is a fistful of carefully machined iron with a flat ground sole, a mouth and a pair of irons, one for working in one direction and the second for working in the other direction. It also has a comfortable handle that can be shifted from one side to the other in order to match up with either iron.

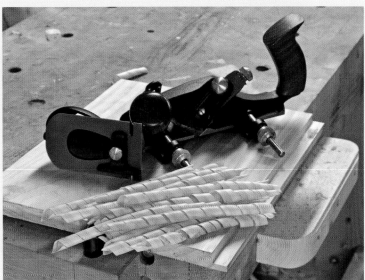

Shown here are the Veritas skew rabbet (rear) and the Veritas side rabbet (left front). Because the iron in the skewed rabbet is—well— skewed, shavings come out as twists, like those made by antique spill planes. This skewed rabbet/moving filletster is the finest filletster plane I have ever used. If you can afford it, you won't regret the decision to purchase this magnificent rabbeting tool. The side rabbet makes it possible to fractionally widen a rabbet, dado, or groove in an accurate and controlled manner.

Part 3: Dado planes

I don't own any Stanley dado planes (the #39 series) because they're quite expensive, much more so than equivalent wooden dado planes. (I borrowed the #39s you see in this chapter from Lancaster, Ohio, tool collector Max Stebelton.) Plus, like the #78, the planes in the #39 series are less comfortable to use than their wooden counterparts because, instead of pressing fingertips against smooth, rounded wooden surfaces, users of Stanley dado planes have to press their fingertips against hard metal surfaces (strangely) lacking the carefully designed contact points found on some other Stanley classics. However, the Stanley series does offer one advantage over the wooden equivalents. The soles on the antique Stanleys typically have remained straight, while the soles on many wooden-bodied dado planes have developed significant twists, as a result, I suspect, of the fact that the soles of these planes are bisected at two points along their lengths.

A wooden dado plane has two irons. The primary iron is positioned about halfway along the length of the plane, set skewed across its width (to cut more efficiently). The secondary iron—close to the toe of the plane—terminates on its bottom end in a pair of slitters that score the cross-grain wood fibers ahead of the primary iron. Viewed from the front, this slitter iron looks like a squat upside down "U" with its short legs sharpened on their inside leading edges. The depth stop typically resembles the depth stop of a plow plane with a thumbscrew on the top that raises and lowers a metal shoe on the bottom of the plane, but sometimes, wooden dado planes have depth stops mounted on the right side of the plane like the

Dado planes cut a trench the width of the sole, not the plane body. Even though the body widths of several of these planes are the same, each cuts a trench of a different width.

depth stops on the wooden moving filletsters discussed earlier in this article.

While I love using these wooden dado planes, they do require some advance planning. These planes have no fences. They're aligned instead against a batten, so in addition to fixing the stock being dadoed between bench dogs, you must also either clamp or tack a batten beside the dado you wish to cut. Plus, because they're designed to cut across the grain, you need a backer strip clamped to your stock on the finishing edge in order to avoid ripping out long splinters when you complete your cut.

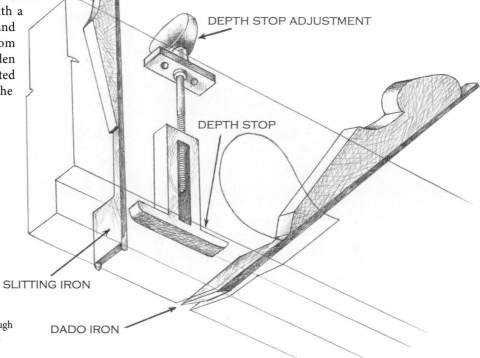

In addition to the plane body, every dado plane has three key components: the depth stop, the slitting iron, and the primary iron. The irons in all wooden dado planes will look very much like the ones in this drawing, although there are several different styles of depth stops.

DEPTH STOP ADJUSTMENT

DEPTH STOP

SLITTING IRON

DADO IRON

84

Detail.

To cut a dado, clamp a batten across the board, a batten aligned with the right side of the intended dado. Clamp a backing strip along the opposite edge of the board to prevent wood fibers from tearing loose at the end of each plane stroke. Then push the plane across the board while keeping the right side of the plane snuggly against the batten.

The Stanley #39 series consists of eight planes ranging from a narrowest of 1/4" to a widest of 1", graduated in 1/8" increments. The exception to this is the 13/16" plane which the Stanley Company made by grinding thickness from a 7/8" plane.

The set up for using a #39 is the same as the set up for using a wooden dado plane, employing a batten as guide and a backer strip in order to prevent breaking out wood fibers at the end of a stroke.

Instead of a single slitting iron with two prongs like the wooden dado plane, the #39 uses a pair of slitters, one mounted on either side of the plane, each one fixed in place in a machined groove by a pair of screws. These slitters should be sharpened before use.

The Stanley Company also made a couple of adjustable dado planes—the #46 and the #47. Although I've never used the #47, I have used the #46, and it makes an excellent plow plane, the best, I think, in the Stanley line. They both, however, share the same—in my eyes—conceptual problem: too many options are packed into a single tool. This makes set up a bit of a headache. To switch, for example, from a 3/8" dado to a 1/2" dado, you have to change out the iron (blade/cutter). You then have to adjust the correct cutting edge exposure. Then you have to move the slitters to this new width. By contrast, a dedicated 1/2" dado plane of either the wood or the Stanley variety is always ready to go. Just blow off the dust and start planing.

The set up for using a #39 is exactly the same as it is for cutting dados with a wooden plane.

Stanley 39s cut dados in a variety of widths from 1/4" to 1". Nevertheless, the planes were all built in the same configuration. The slitters are located just ahead of the iron, partially concealed on the left side of the plane by the depth stop. The iron is held in place via a lever cap pivoting on a central point.

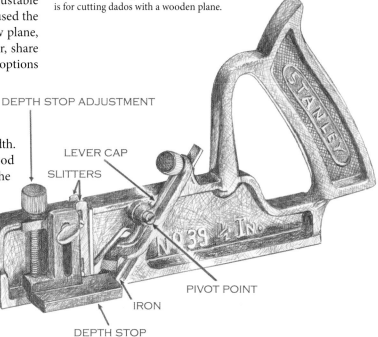

DEPTH STOP ADJUSTMENT

LEVER CAP

SLITTERS

PIVOT POINT

IRON

DEPTH STOP

The Veritas Small Plow Plane

Joinery Planes: Shoulder Planes

In 2007, Veritas began selling a small, eminently usable metal plow, more usable, in fact, than any of the Stanley plows or combination planes. Based on the Record #044, the new Veritas plow is executed in the familiar Veritas manner—black steel body, bubinga tote, brass knobs—all nicely finished. The plow has a brass depth-of-cut adjustment nut with a collar that engages a notch machined into the side of each iron/cutter, making precise adjustments possible by simply rotating the brass knob. The two brass nuts that lock the fence down each close over collets that not only lock tight, but—because of their length—also serve to keep the fence parallel to the skate, making it unnecessary to check fence/skate distance at more than one location, a real advantage over the plane's wooden-bodied equivalents. The depth stop is a machined shoe—relieved on the bottom side at the front and back to keep it from getting stuck when entering a cut—which is locked at the desired height through the use of a fat brass knob on the right side of the plane.

The plane comes with a single iron/blade—a 1/4"—but there are four more available as extras, ranging from 1/8" to 3/8" in 1/16" increments, and the irons/blades arrive virtually ready to use. All I did was polish the backs a bit before loading them into the plane.

The Veritas plow performed exactly as expected, quickly cutting one clean-bottomed groove after another. Because it is a small, light tool, it does require a bit of concentration to keep it properly oriented on its vertical and horizontal axes, but the fence is drilled so that a larger wood fence can be attached, and such a fence will, I suspect, make the tool easier to stabilize.

Because there are no slitters ahead of the iron/blade, this plow—like the wooden-bodied plows appearing elsewhere in this chapter—is intended only for work on the direction of the grain, but thanks to a pocket machined into the inside face of the fence that allows the fence to envelope one side of the iron/cutter, the plow can also be used as a rabbet plane.

This small Veritas plow could be used to cut grooves on the inside of drawer components to receive the drawer bottom.

At first glance, a wooden rabbet plane might be mistaken for a shoulder plane. The body of each is made up of a block of nicely squared up material. The iron in each penetrates the plane at an angle sloping toward the toe, ending with a cutting edge that reaches across the full width of the body. But that's where the resemblance ends. Tenon shoulders present a craftsman with tough end-grain material, and the cutting edge of a rabbet plane is unsupported, hanging out there in space, a full quarter inch from the stabilizing influence of the bed. Any attempt to work a hardwood shoulder with such a plane will likely result in chatter as the cutting edge stutters along the end-grain. However, the iron in a shoulder plane—a plane designed to work stubborn end-grain surfaces—does have support almost to the point where the cutting edge feathers away to nothing because a plane of this type has its iron bedded bevel up. Plus, a shoulder plane is either entirely made of metal or is built around a metal shell, and metal can provide substantial support even when it's milled thin in cross section as it is at the back of the mouth.

A bevel-up, full-width iron and a bed that reaches almost to the cutting edge are the primary identifying characteristics of a shoulder plane. Another is the bedding angle. The irons in shoulder planes are typically bedded at approximately 20 degrees. However, while the 20 degree pitch is 30 degrees less than the 50 degree bedding angle of the garden-variety rabbet plane, that detail isn't the difference-maker it might at first appear to be. The fact that the iron of a shoulder plane is bedded bevel up means that—if the iron is bedded at 20 degrees and if the bevel is ground at a standard 25 degrees—the actual cutting angle is not much different than the cutting angle of a common rabbet plane.

Another identifying characteristic is the presence of beauty in the design and execution of most shoulder planes and the relative absence of beauty in common rabbet planes. Wooden rabbet planes are just blocks of wood into which an iron is fit. Shoulder planes, however, are tools on which plane designers have lavished attention. Classical shoulder planes have sleek wedges cut from ebony and rosewood, fit into narrow but elegant cigarette-case bodies. Modern shoulder planes are designed with a contemporary sensibility, delineating shapes with sweeping curves, combining brass and polished steel and then contrasting both against pebbly black japanning.

Part 1: Shoulder plane tune up

The iron of an antique shoulder plane will probably need some attention before the plane is put to use. Check the cutting edge with a square to see if it is straight across and perpendicular to the sides of the iron. If you need to regrind, the processes of grinding the primary bevel and honing the secondary bevel are much the same as those for bench plane irons. (See page 49) New shoulder planes from Lie-Nielsen and Veritas are shipped in essentially ready-to-use condition.

Also check to see that the sole and sides of the antique shoulder plane are perpendicular to each other. Sometimes the shells of older, dovetailed shoulder planes are not as square as you'd like them to be. I've seen this in planes I own, and I'm not sure if the error was built into the planes or is something that occurred over time with use and abuse. If you find significant errors in perpendicularity, you may want to set the plane aside. Otherwise you may be creating shoulders angling in such a way that gaps will occur where the shoulder meets an adjacent component.

I'm not sure that a tight mouth does much for end-grain work, but because I use my shoulder planes in so many side-grain situations, I usually have the mouth set quite tight.

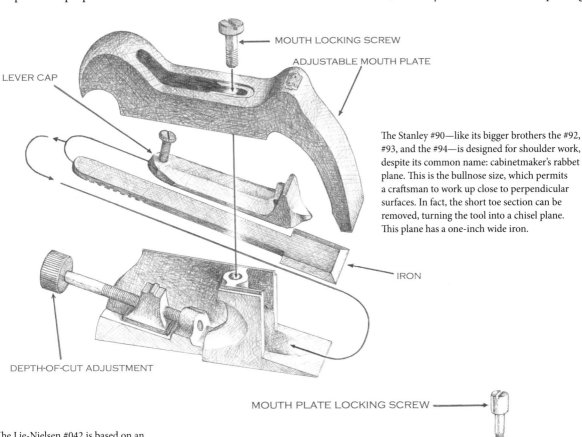

MOUTH LOCKING SCREW

ADJUSTABLE MOUTH PLATE

LEVER CAP

IRON

DEPTH-OF-CUT ADJUSTMENT

The Stanley #90—like its bigger brothers the #92, #93, and the #94—is designed for shoulder work, despite its common name: cabinetmaker's rabbet plane. This is the bullnose size, which permits a craftsman to work up close to perpendicular surfaces. In fact, the short toe section can be removed, turning the tool into a chisel plane. This plane has a one-inch wide iron.

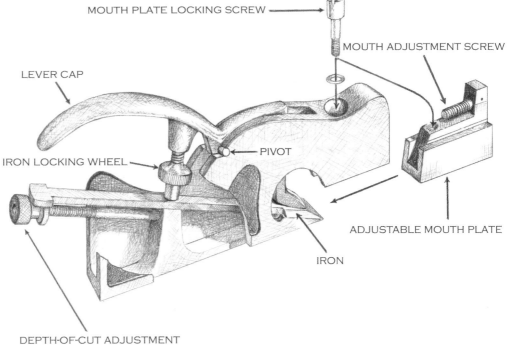

The Lie-Nielsen #042 is based on an earlier Preston shoulder plane. Depth of cut is controlled by a knurled knob at the heel of the plane. There is also an adjustable mouth plate to permit easy expansion or contraction of the plane's mouth. This plane has a 3/4" iron.

MOUTH PLATE LOCKING SCREW

MOUTH ADJUSTMENT SCREW

LEVER CAP

IRON LOCKING WHEEL

PIVOT

ADJUSTABLE MOUTH PLATE

IRON

DEPTH-OF-CUT ADJUSTMENT

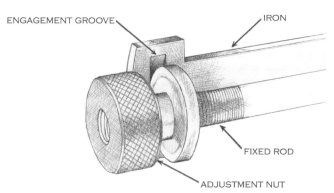

ENGAGEMENT GROOVE — IRON

FIXED ROD

ADJUSTMENT NUT

The metal disk at the base of the knurled knob engages a groove cut into the under side of the tang of the #042's iron. When the knob is turned, the knob moves up and down on the fixed threaded rod, taking the iron along with it.

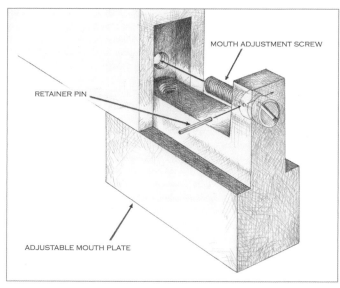

MOUTH ADJUSTMENT SCREW

RETAINER PIN

ADJUSTABLE MOUTH PLATE

The mouth plate is locked with a screw that vertically penetrates the body of the plane and turns into a hole in the top of the mouth plate. When that screw is loosened, a second screw—located on the toe—can be turned right or left to advance or retreat the mouth plate.

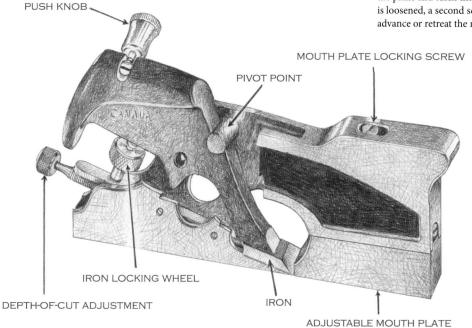

PUSH KNOB

MOUTH PLATE LOCKING SCREW

PIVOT POINT

IRON LOCKING WHEEL

DEPTH-OF-CUT ADJUSTMENT

IRON

ADJUSTABLE MOUTH PLATE

Left:
Like the Lie-Nielsen #042, the Veritas medium shoulder plane applies stabilizing pressure on the top of the iron via a pivoting lever cap. This plane has an 11/16" wide iron.

Below:
The Veritas shoulder plane also has an adjustable mouth plate, but it operates in a slightly different way than the mouth plate on the Lie-Nielsen shoulder plane. A screw on the toe of the plane is turned into a threaded hole in the body of the plane. That screw has a collar that engages a fixed pin rising from the mouth plate. When the screw is turned, it moves either forward or backward, taking the pin and the mouth plate in which the pin is fixed along with it.

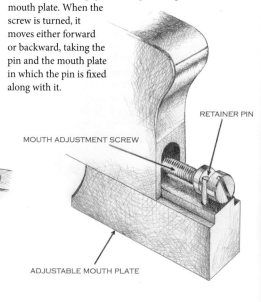

RETAINER PIN

MOUTH ADJUSTMENT SCREW

ADJUSTABLE MOUTH PLATE

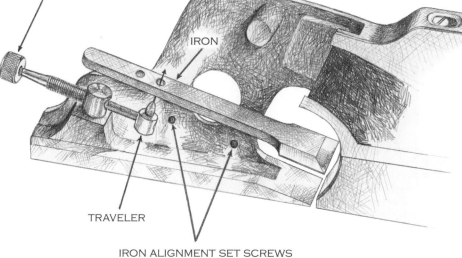

DEPTH-OF-CUT ADJUSTMENT

IRON

TRAVELER

IRON ALIGNMENT SET SCREWS

The Veritas shoulder plane uses an abbreviated form of the adjuster found on the company's bench planes. That adjuster combines lateral adjustment and depth-of-cut adjustment in the same knob. Turning the knob changes depth of cut. Racking the knob from side to side changes lateral adjustment.

Part 2: Small shoulder planes

My approach to the tenon-making process is a result of the fact that I have several good shoulder planes. These enable me to work my way to a precise fit one shaving at a time. If I have just a couple of tenons to form, I'll create them with a backsaw, but if I have a large number of tenons to form, I'll use a stack of dado cutters on my tablesaw. In either case, I leave a bit of extra material on the tenon shoulders and the tenon cheeks. This enables me to work my way gradually toward a perfect fit. I know it would be more efficient if I cut the tenons to their finished sizes right from the start, but I run less risk of creating undersized parts using my method. This is particularly true in my shop because I chop mortises by hand and each probably manifests the slight width variation typical of hand work.

Plus, in my shop, there's no urgent need to get stuff out the door in a timely fashion.

When I'm laying out tenons, I mark shoulder locations with a marking knife laid against a square. I once used this scoring as a registration point for the paring chisels with which I fine-tuned shoulders. This did work, but sometimes it left an imperfect shoulder line where two paring-chisel cuts abutted at slightly different angles. Now I use that scoring as a finish line for my shoulder plane. As a result, my shoulders now are more crisp than they used to be.

I find that smaller shoulder planes are better suited to actual shoulder work than their larger cousins. Anything up to 3/4" seems to work well in this context. That's a group that includes the Stanley #90, as well as they Lie-Nielsen #041 and #042, and the Veritas small and medium shoulder planes. It's more difficult for me to "feel" what the plane is doing when I'm maneuvering a large plane past a narrow shoulder, and "narrow" describes almost every shoulder I've ever trimmed.

You can't do good shoulder work when you're holding the part in one hand, the plane in the other—although I have certainly tried this. The best way to do good shoulder work is to fix the part securely between dogs on your bench top or to press it against the fence of a bench hook.

I find I use several different hand positions with my shoulder planes, each depending on the kind of work I'm performing. If I'm working a shoulder beside a short tenon, I loop the fingers of one hand underneath the plane to support it and keep it tight against the shoulder, with the fingers of the other hand being used to drive the plane forward and keep it flat on the cheek. If the tenon is long enough to interfere with fingers underneath the plane, I work the plane one-handed with the fingers of that hand doing double duty by keeping the sole pressed against the shoulder and keeping the side of the plane flat on the tenon. If I'm using the plane to clean up a rabbet, dado, or plowed groove, I use a two-handed grip similar to the grip I use on a bench plane.

Because shoulder work is done with the plane in an atypical operating position (either lying on its side and/or with one side of the plane pushed up tight against a finger-barking adjacent surface), it's easier to take inaccurate partial strokes than it would be if the plane were standing up straight with nothing crowding your hands on either side. Unless you're removing a high spot, an incomplete stroke can cause more problems than it solves by creating a sloping shoulder. For this reason, shoulder work requires

This large Mathieson shoulder plane is typical of many shoulder planes made by British makers, most notably Stewart Spiers and Thomas Norris. Lee Richmond photo

When you're working a shoulder, keep the plane flat against the tenon and take firm even strokes. To avoid breaking ot splinters at the end of the stroke, work from both sides toward the middle. Courtesy of *Woodwork* magazine

Larger shoulder planes, like this dovetailed infill example, are very effective at removing material from tenon cheeks in a highly controlled manner.

a greater degree of concentration than some other kinds of plane work. You must focus on keeping the plane square against the tenon cheek. You must focus on taking a shaving throughout the full length of the stroke.

A full stroke, however, doesn't necessarily mean the full length of the shoulder. If the material is prone to breaking out at the end of a stroke—say oak, ash, or hickory—you may want to start the shoulder work on one end of the shoulder either with the shoulder plane or a paring chisel. Then reverse the part and take full shoulder plane strokes toward and past the partial strokes you took on the other end. If the wood is dense, not prone to breaking out at the end of a stroke—say hard maple—you might take the shoulder down with full-length strokes. Or you could work the shoulder with the stock on a bench hook or shooting board.

The most difficult shoulders to plane are those on narrow stock. A wide shoulder on wide stock is easy to plane because there's a long bearing surface for the sole of the plane, but a shoulder that's only an inch wide is more problematic. It's just too easy to create an out-of-square shoulder on such a piece. If that shoulder is one of several (and this is just about always the case), I'll use a square to line up a group of parts to be shouldered and then work those shoulders together. This works nicely, as long as you have the work adequately clamped between bench dogs. If they begin to slip around during the shouldering work, you could have a mess.

Part 3: Large shoulder planes for cheek work

Although I don't think it would have occurred to me in the years before I began to use shoulder planes, the larger versions are actually better cheek planes than shoulder planes. It's difficult to do accurate cleanup on a 2" long tenon cheek if you're using a 5/8" wide shoulder plane, but if you use a 1-1/2" shoulder plane on that same cheek, there's enough bearing surface to keep the plane stabilized in an upright position throughout each stroke. It's less likely, then, to end up with a tenon that tapers toward one end or toward one side.

If the cheeks were formed with dado cutters, there are always some irregularities where blade tracks come together, and as long as you allowed some extra thickness for this purpose, it's easy to clean up those irregularities with a wide shoulder plane. And handsawn cheeks often need cleanup, too. Plus, my practice

of cutting each tenon a bit too wide allows me to baby my way toward the desired final thickness.

There is a risk to the business of fine-tuning cheeks with a wide shoulder plane. The plane is so good at performing this work that you have to be careful not to get lost in the planing experience and remove too much material.

Part 4: Miscellaneous work for shoulder planes

A magazine editor for whom I've done a good bit of work once asked me how I decided which molding planes to purchase. I told him I simply buy what I see and then find ways to need them. I think the same rule also applies to other kinds of planes. Before I owned a shoulder plane, I didn't think the plane would be useful for anything except trimming tenon shoulders.

But as it turns out, that's not true at all. Once you have a few shoulder planes in a rack near your bench, you find all kinds of situations in which these planes can more easily do work you once did with other tools. Sometimes I use a shoulder plane to deepen or widen a rabbet cut with a moving filletster because it's easier to simply grab a shoulder plane than it is to reset the moving filletster. If I've cut a bunch of dadoes or grooves or rabbets with my tablesaw, I'll use a shoulder plane to deepen or simply to clean-up these channels.

Perhaps the most unusual place in which I use shoulder planes is at miters of moldings created with hand planes. These moldings aren't quite as uniform as those cut by machines, so sometimes at the miter, one side will be slightly higher than the other. I could bring the high side down to the level of the low side with a paring chisel and sandpaper, but a shoulder plane is even better suited for this work. Because it allows me to work the full width of its sole, I can get into places I could never reach with a block plane, and because it is a plane, rather than an uncontrolled chisel, I can feather the correction out over a longer distance, making it more difficult for anyone to see the correction.

Shoulder planes can also be used to clean up or deepen dadoes, plowed grooves, or rabbets as shown here.

Joinery Planes: Restoring an Antique Plow Plane and Sharpening a Plow-Plane Iron

In 19th-century American woodshops, a cabinetmaker's plow plane was a tangible expression of his status. A great craftsman owned a great plow plane with an ebony or rosewood body and brass and ivory details. A craftsman who was merely good might have owned a boxwood plow plane with a few bits of brass hardware. A journeyman likely owned a simple plow plane made of beech.

Despite its significance as a status symbol, a plow plane is a _____ ask. A plow plane doesn't shape. It _____ ready for the application of fin- _____ It simply excavates flat-bottomed _____ grain.

_____ he is more than an historical cu- _____ ftsman plowing the grooves for a _____ ight want to do this work with a _____ if you're plowing grooves for just _____ ane makes good sense. Not only _____ to set up and use.

_____ w in a box of household goods _____ en table at a local antique mall. _____ e previous owner had sprayed it _____ s—with a coat of red paint that _____ side of a barn.

The most serious damage was a series of age cracks in the nuts.

Part 1: Disassembly, repair, cleaning, and re-assembly

I began my restoration by removing the wedge from its mortise. With my right forearm (I'm left-handed), I pressed the plane against my side, wrapping the thumb and forefinger of that hand around the top of the wedge and iron. Then, with my wooden plane mallet in my left hand, I rapped repeatedly on the heel of the plane, striking each blow with more authority than the one before. At just about the time I'd decided to clamp the wedge finial in a vise and drive the plane up off of it, the wedge came loose in my hand, loose probably for the first time in over a century.

I then removed the screw-arm nuts and pulled the arms through their mortises in the plane's body, separating the body from the fence. Both nuts were cracked. One fell apart in my hand as I removed it.

The brass thumbscrew that controlled depth of cut was attached to a brass plate fastened to the plane's body with two steel screws. These screws had their slots filled by red paint and a hundred years of rust and grime. I selected a sharp screwdriver of the correct size and pushed one corner of the screwdriver's tip through the slot, driving the muck ahead of it. I then removed the screws and turned the thumbscrew until it had disengaged from the shoe housed in a mortise on the bottom of the plane. I removed the depth stop and the thumbscrew from the plane's body.

_____ but when I saw it in an area antique _____ t, and nearly all of the screw arm

_____ e nuts, fence, and washers. Then I _____ pth-stop thumbscrew until the shoe _____ e loose.

The red paint—as well as the underlying original finish came off with several applications of paint stripper.

After applying the glue to the split sides of the nuts, I clamped the halves of the nut together with rubber bands.

The next step was removing the paint. One light coat of stripper was enough to clean the paint from the smooth surfaces of the plane's body, wedge, and fence, but it took several applications of stripper and some vigorous scrubbing with a toothbrush to clean the red from the plane's threaded parts. I then cleaned the parts with water using a wet rag to remove the traces of stripper.

I took a look at the wedge to determine why it had been so hard to remove. Sometimes a wedge will stick because a century of grime seals it in place in much the same way a window sash becomes permanently closed after being painted. But in this case, the problem was a plane body that had dried (and shrunk) more than the wedge it contained. This problem could be corrected in two ways. I could plane a shaving or two from the side of the wedge or I could pare down one side of the mortise. Because planing the wedge would remove the patina that remained after stripping, I decided to pare down one side of the mortise.

The two-part skate, as well as a steel wear strip on the fence, was badly rusted, pitted in fact. I decided to do what I could with sandpaper. This practice is frowned on by most collectors and tool conservators—with good reason. Sanding does remove a surface which could be of historical interest. After all, that layer

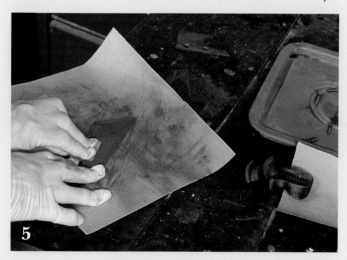

I sanded the rust from both halves of the skate

of rust and grime provides a record of the circumstances in which the plane had spent the last century. But this was not a tool of any historical importance. It's only future was as a user plow in my shop, and a rusty skate and wear strip could streak the surface of furniture components on which I might use the plane.

I first sanded the parts with 220 grit paper, keeping at the work until the abrasive stopped removing rust from the surface. Particles buried in rust pits I left behind. I then did a light sanding with 320 grit paper.

The most troublesome repair was the broken nut. Because the outside of the nut had shrunk more than the threaded interior surface, there would be visible cracks, even after it had been glued together. Being careful to keep glue from that threaded interior surface, I glued the broken surfaces of the nut, then clamped the two parts together with a rubber band until the glue cured.

Like the skate, the iron was crusted over with rust and a little paint. I sanded all four surfaces, then turned my attention to the bevel.

The iron had a convex bevel, instead of the concave, hollow-ground, bevel I prefer. I lightly touched the end of the iron to my wheel until it was perpendicular to both sides of the iron, and then I began changing that convex bevel to a concave bevel.

This required the removal of a fair amount of metal, but because I wasn't working at the tip where the heat would build up in a hurry, I was able to press the bevel firmly against a wheel in one continuous grinding session. I created the primary bevel by resting the back of the iron on my grinder's tool rest, which was pre-set to an angle that would produce the kind of hollow grind I prefer.

When I had ground the bevel to within 1/16" of the tip, I lifted the bottom of the iron, while keeping the end of it in contact with the wheel until I had created a convex bevel on the last 1/8" of the iron.

This unusual bevel—concave over most of its length, then convex in the 1/8" closest to the tip—has the advantages of both a hollow-ground bevel and a flat ground bevel. Like the traditional hollow-ground bevel, the radius cut along most of the bevel's length reduced the amount of material I would have to remove to hone new edges. But the convex bevel on the final section gave me a much stronger tip than I would have had if I had feathered that hollow grind all the way to the tip.

I then flattened the back of the iron on a sheet of 220 paper and finished it off with some lapping on my 600 grit diamond stone. Finally, I honed a microbevel on the front edge of the iron, working a burr back and forth on the stone until the burr fell away, leaving behind a sharp cutting edge.

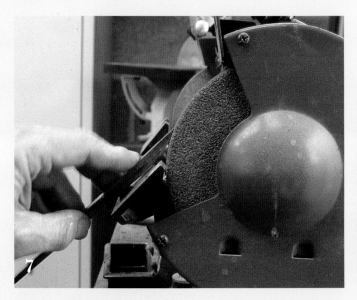

7

8

I hollow grind much of a plow-plane iron's bevel. Then I lift the tang while the iron remains in contact with the wheel. This leaves behind an ogee bevel, with some of the advantages of a hollow-ground bevel, without the fragility of a thin cutting edge. (Wheel is shut off for clarity.)

I then flatten the back of the iron on sandpaper and a diamond lapping plate. I finish sharpening by honing a secondary bevel, working the burr back and forth until it falls off, leaving behind a sharp cutting edge.

9

With a fresh coat of finish, the plow was ready for use.

Chapter 4
Molding Planes

Our generation (or possibly our children's generation) will probably be the last to enjoy the wealth of richly diverse (and still usable) antique molding planes now being pulled from attics, basements, barns, and garages all across the Eastern United States. Unfortunately, when this national treasure is gone, there is nothing on the horizon set to take its place.

Assembling a Collection of Molding Planes

Today, in the opening decade of the 21st century, architectural wood moldings are machine made, typically by enormous multi-head behemoths spitting out completed moldings as fast as they can be stacked by human hands. But in the 19th century, this work was accomplished in a very different manner. Once the necessary profiles had been determined, a 19th century builder had to locate the planes those profiles would require. Sometimes those planes were in the toolkits of his craftsmen. At other times, a job might require a profile not immediately available, so the builder or finish carpenter would order the planes from a catalog of standard profiles or from the shop of a planemaker able to create custom profiles. The finish carpenter then selected molding stock from the lumber delivered to the job site, choosing clear, straight-grained

stuff that wouldn't tearout under the molding plane irons. Then, if the profile was a simple one—a side bead, for example—he might have turned the task over to an apprentice who would have then spent hours working with a side bead plane in the shade of a tree on the building lot or perhaps in one of the rooms of the house under construction. If the profile involved deep cuts into the molding stock, those cuts might have been first roughed out with a filletster or rabbet plane, as well as hollows and rounds, before the molder was introduced. The molding plane then might have been pushed along the prepared stock by the master, himself. In the case of a truly enormous cornice molder, the efforts of the master would have been augmented by an apprentice or two pulling at a dowel or a rope attached to the cornice plane via a mortise drilled through the plane's body. In some situations, however, if only a short length of a complicated molding was needed, the master might have created that molding from scratch, without the use of a dedicated molder, employing, instead a variety of planes, including filletsters, rabbets, hollows, rounds, and snipe bills. Although this approach was more exacting than the use of a dedicated molder, in situations requiring only a short length of a complicated molding, this process could have saved the builder the cost of an expensive molding plane.

Molding planes used for architectural applications were intended for use in softwoods. These planes had their irons bedded at 45 degrees. Furniture makers, who typically worked with cherry, walnut, maple, or mahoganies as primary woods employed a different type of molder, one having the iron bedded at a steeper angle, often 55 or 60 degrees.

This doesn't mean that molding planes intended for softer architectural woods can't be used with hardwoods. I use them on hardwoods today, and I would be surprised if 19th century furniture makers didn't occasionally use an architectural molder on hardwoods if the profile they needed was readily available only on a plane with a 45 degree pitch.

Even 19th century Shakers—committed to lives of material simplicity—couldn't resist decorating their dwellings with shapes created with molding planes. This woodwork from the kitchen of the Centre Family Dwelling of the Pleasant Hill, Kentucky, community required the use of half a dozen molding planes.

If you were to remove the simple molding shapes in this fireplace surround from the kitchen of the Pleasant Hill Centre Family Dwelling, it would lose much of its visual appeal.

Part 1: Molding plane varieties

Molding planes are traditionally broken into three general categories: shaping, simple and complex. Shaping molders are those that create elements of more complicated shapes. The hollows, rounds, and snipe bills mentioned above are shaping planes. Simple molders are unfenced molding planes intended to create a single complete shape, like the ubiquitous side bead planes. Complex molders are dedicated planes that can—by themselves- be used to create complicated shapes having two or more elements. These planes are typically equipped with both depth stops and fences.

In the 19th century, anyone who made a living working wood probably had a few hollows and rounds in his kit. "Hollows" are planes that have concave "hollows" cut across their widths. "Rounds" are planes with convex rounds across their widths. In both cases, the arc described by the sole of an individual plane is 1/6 of a complete circle. The 1872 catalog of the Greenfield Tool Company of Greenfield, Massachusetts, lists 24 different sizes of hollows and rounds. The Sandusky Tool Company catalog of 1925 has reduced that number to 15, reflecting perhaps the impending demise of molding plane manufacture. Planes of the smallest size in the Sandusky catalog—the #1—cut arcs of a circle measuring only 1/2" in diameter, while the largest size—the #15—cuts arcs of a circle measuring 4" in diameter. Typically, these planes were sold in sets of matching pairs, consisting of one hollow and one round, the soles of which each represented 1/6 of a circle of the same diameter. A full set of American hollows and rounds typically included 24 matching pairs while a half set included the odd or even pair sizes, for example the #2, #4, #6, #8, #10, #12, #14, #16, #18, #20, #22, and #24 pairs. It's interesting to note that hollows

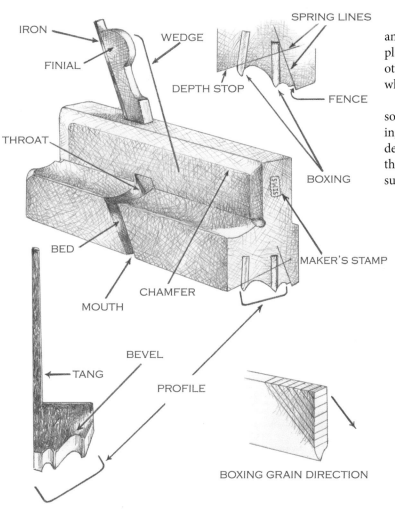

IRON
FINIAL
WEDGE
SPRING LINES
DEPTH STOP
FENCE
THROAT
BOXING
BED
MAKER'S STAMP
MOUTH
CHAMFER
BEVEL
TANG
PROFILE
BOXING GRAIN DIRECTION

and rounds are the only molders named for the shape of the plane soles, rather than the shape they create on the work. All other molders are named for the shape they create on the work, which is the mirror image of the shape of the plane's sole.

Snipe bills—rarely seen on the antique tool market—were sold in pairs. When the hollows and rounds creating the sweeping ogee shapes of complicated moldings were executed without dedicated planes, the snipe bills defined the quirks separating these elements. They were also used the clean up the convex surfaces of ogee shapes.

The detail in the upper right shows the control surfaces of a molding plane. The plane is ready to use when the fence is crowded against the left hand (from the user's perspective, not the left hand side of the drawing) edge of the work and the plane body is oriented so that the spring lines match true horizontal and true vertical. The profile is complete when the depth stop reaches the surface of the work. Notice the strips of end-grain boxwood inlaid into the wear points on the sole.

The sole of each hollow and each round is an arc comprising 1/6 of a circle.

Maker's marks can also be found stamped onto the tangs of some irons.

The nose of each molder is stamped with the mark of the planemaker. Many of these marks also include the city in which the maker lived.

That 19th century woodworker also probably had a few bead planes in his kit. The most common of these is the side bead. This plane is designed to cut a bead on the face of a board immediately adjacent to the edge. To define that bead, the plane cuts a quirk—a small groove—on the right hand side of the bead. (Directions are given from the plane user's perspective.) Less often, that kit would have included a center bead plane or two. These unfenced planes cut beads anywhere across the width of a board defining them with grooves cut on both sides.

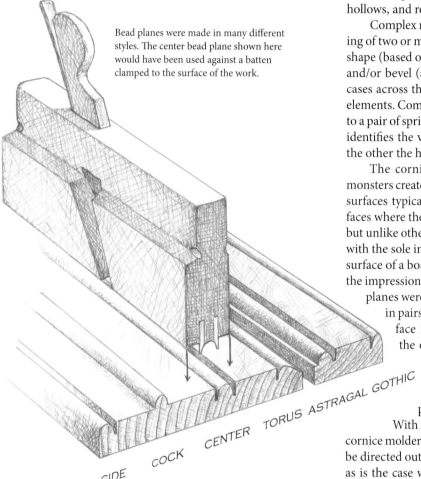

Bead planes were made in many different styles. The center bead plane shown here would have been used against a batten clamped to the surface of the work.

SIDE COCK CENTER TORUS ASTRAGAL GOTHIC

Unlike the shaping planes, simple molders usually have both fences and depth stops. In use, the fence is snugged up against the left vertical edge of the horizontal surface the plane is working. The craftsman then pushes the plane forward while crowding the fence against the edge. The depth stop is a fillet cut on the right side of the sole. When the depth stop bottoms out on the horizontal surface of the board being worked, the profile is complete. The simple planes cut ovolos, coves, ogees or thumbnail shapes, often in graduated sizes. These planes are still relatively common in the antique tool world, but they are found much less often than hollows, and rounds.

Complex molders are planes designed to cut profiles consisting of two or more simple elements. These might include an ogee shape (based on the cyma curve) along with a quirk and/or bead and/or bevel (a narrow flat titled at an angle), totaling in some cases across the sole of a single plane, a bewildering number of elements. Complex molders are designed to be aligned according to a pair of spring lines etched onto the nose of the plane. One line identifies the vertical alignment of the properly oriented plane, the other the horizontal alignment.

The cornice plane is the supreme molding plane. These monsters created the wide moldings installed on a home's exterior surfaces typically under roof overhangs and on its interior surfaces where the ceiling and walls meet. They were fenced planes, but unlike other complex molders they were intended to be used with the sole in a horizontal alignment working across the entire surface of a board, which was then installed at an angle, creating the impression of a heavily stacked molding. Sometimes, cornice planes were used as singletons; at other times they were used in pairs; one plane in the pair worked one half of a board's face in one direction, while the other plane worked the other half in the other direction, in this manner creating a very wide profile. This paired practice must have been fairly common because the 1872 Greenfield catalog lists only four sizes of cornice planes, all of them pairs.

With the exception of some very wide ogee planes and cornice molders, molding planes were built so that shavings would be directed out the side of the plane, rather than through the top as is the case with bench planes. The iron of a typical molding plane consists of a blade wide enough to encompass the profile on the business end. That blade is attached to a tang rising from its upper left side, and the tang then is the only part of the iron that reaches through the plane to protrude from the top. Most complex molders have a single iron, but some have two and—much more rarely—three.

The sole of each of these complex molders is composed of two or more shape elements.

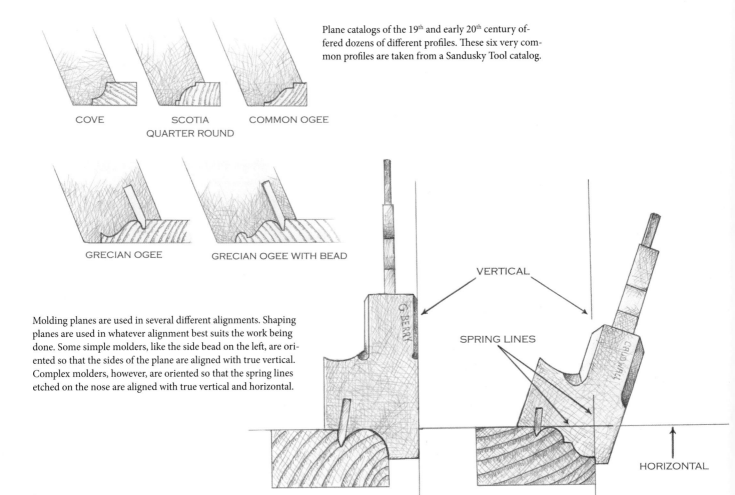

COVE

SCOTIA
QUARTER ROUND

COMMON OGEE

GRECIAN OGEE

GRECIAN OGEE WITH BEAD

Plane catalogs of the 19th and early 20th century offered dozens of different profiles. These six very common profiles are taken from a Sandusky Tool catalog.

VERTICAL

SPRING LINES

HORIZONTAL

Molding planes are used in several different alignments. Shaping planes are used in whatever alignment best suits the work being done. Some simple molders, like the side bead on the left, are oriented so that the sides of the plane are aligned with true vertical. Complex molders, however, are oriented so that the spring lines etched on the nose are aligned with true vertical and horizontal.

American molders made prior to 1800 had narrow flat chamfers on their upper surfaces with slender wedges surmounted with a round finial. Molding planes made in the early years of the 19th century have wider chamfers which become even wider and slightly crowned during the later decades of the 19th century. Wedges became wider as well, ending in larger, less rounded finials.

Some of the planes appearing today in the inventory of antique tool vendors look like molding planes, but were, in fact, built to perform other tasks. Sash planes were intended to create window sashes, and coping planes were used to create the joinery that brings together two elements of a sash. These are technically not molders although they were built with tanged irons in a side escapement form like molders. Table planes were built in the same fashion, and they may resemble rounds and hollows and quarter round planes but they were, in fact, sold in pairs to create the components that meet when the leaves of a table are raised. The rule joint is the most widely known joint of this type. In addition, there are other incidental planes which, in their general configuration, resemble molding planes, but which were designed for some other purpose.

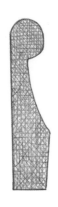

FRANCIS NICHOLSON
C. 1728

CESAR CHELOR
C. 1750

WILLIAM WILLIAMS
C. 1845

GREENFIELD TOOL CO.
C. 1870

Wedge finials were slender and elongated in the 18th century. They became shorter and stockier in the 19th century.

Part 2: Naming names

There is general agreement about the naming of many of the simpler molding plane profiles. Side beads, astragals, coves, and center beads are essentially the same from one reference to another. But that's not the case with more complicated profiles. In part, this may be a result of our chronological distance from the golden age of molding planes, but it is also a result of the fact that different 19th century planemaking shops used different methods to name the tools they produced. And there were many shops. "A Guide to American Wooden Planes and their Makers" by Emil and Martyl Pollack lists over 4,000 American planemakers, working in the 18th, 19th, and very early 20th centuries.

John Whelan, the author of "The Wooden Plane: Its History, Form, and Function" has systematized the naming of complex molding planes. His method begins by providing clear definitions for each of the 13 basic shape elements he uses to construct the names of complex molders. He then establishes the order in which a profile's elements will be listed in its official designation "…the name begins with the name of the element that the plane cuts at the greatest distance from the edge of the work." His method makes sense, but it is by no means universally accepted.

Part 3: Changing fashions

In the 18th and 19th centuries, as new furniture styles appeared in the United States, American planemakers introduced new molding planes designed to cut profiles suited to these new furniture styles. The new styles—like the old ones—were still based on classical architectural principles, and—at first glance—the differences between one style of molding plane and another may seem slight. For example, in Thomas Chippendale's "The Gentleman and Cabinetmaker's Director," most molding elements were constructed from arcs circular in cross section. Then early in the 19th century, as a result of shifting tastes, "Greek Revival" moldings—better known by the term "Grecian"—came to dominate the field. Instead of molding components consisting of arcs circular in cross section, these Grecian moldings featured elements which were constructed from arcs elliptical in cross section. This may not seem like much of a difference, but if you compare a group of Roman ogees with a group of Grecian ogees, you'll notice that the Roman shapes have a stately upright posture, while the Grecian elements have a more stylized stance, leaning to one side.

Like automobile manufacturers today, the cabinetmakers of the period realized that—in order to encourage their clients to purchase new pieces—they themselves had to produce newer, more fashionable designs which meant the purchase of molding planes with the new profiles these fashionable pieces required.

This evolution of molding shapes continued throughout the 18th and 19th centuries with new forms periodically supplanting the old. For furniture makers/molding plane collectors in the 21st century, this means that while each of the molding planes in our collections is representative of a particular era, together our planes typically represent many eras. Some might have been made in the late 18th century with circular (Roman) elements. Other planes from later years might include Grecian elements. What we have in our tool cabinets then is likely a mishmash of molding profiles plucked at random from a century and a half of American and British planemaking.

You could certainly argue that moldings for a particular piece of furniture should be fitted only with those moldings that can be traced to the era in which that piece originated. But that's something I've never done with any period piece I've built. Instead, when I'm planning the moldings for a period piece, I sort through the molding planes in my cabinets until I find planes that cut profiles that seem to fit the space and style in which I'll place them, sometimes combining molding plane profiles that span a century in a single piece of furniture.

Part 4: What to buy

The process of acquiring molding planes in the 21st century—when new planes are no longer being produced—turns the whole business of tool purchase on its ear. Here's the reason: If you were to decide the piece you're building should be ornamented with an ogee-with-scotia-and-bevel profile about 2" across, where would you find a plane to cut that profile? You can't open a catalog and order one from a planemaker*, and it might take years of searching the inventories of antique tool vendors to find that particular plane in that particular size. That's why molding plane purchases require a different shopping mentality: When you look for molding planes, you don't buy what you need; you buy what's available, and then you learn to need it. It's kind of like going to Sears because you need a tablesaw and walking out with a drill press because Sears only had drill presses in stock.

*Several small planemaking shops—among them Clark and Williams—will create molding planes to your specifications, but the prices are quite high.

When inspecting a molder prior to purchase, be sure to examine the straightness of the sole.

It may sound unlikely, but it's true. If I'm looking to assemble molding profiles for a specific piece of furniture, I don't draw up profiles and then search out planes that will cut them. Instead, I look at the 75 or so restored-to-use molders in my collection and think about ways to combine profiles cut by those tools on that piece, ways that will make some kind of visual sense.

So here's how molding plane purchase actually works: Yes, you'll need some hollows and rounds, so buy some. You know you're going to need a variety of bead planes, so put together a series of side beads and center beads and astragals. Thumbnail planes are always useful. So, too, are ovolos and quarter rounds—so, when you see them at good prices, buy them.

And you'll surely find a place to use some complex molders, so when you see them, buy some of those, too. For a while, the planes may go largely unused, but gradually, as you gain skill by profiling pieces of scrap wood, you'll begin to think of places to put that 1/4" side bead or that handsome Grecian ogee, and in a couple of years, you'll realize you have more molding planes than router bits or shaper knives. About that same time, you'll notice your router bits a getting are little dusty because it's been so long since you had them out. You may even forget where you stashed your router.

But there's no point in buying junk molding planes, so be sure those you purchase are usable—unless of course, you're a collector. Specifically, perform the following checks on potential new purchases:

 • Make sure the iron is the right one for the plane. (Some sellers think any iron that fits the throat will do.)

 • Be sure that the iron profile and the sole profile are near-perfect matches. While it is possible to reshape an iron, it's time consuming work.

 • Check to make sure the iron is restorable. Surface rust is no problem, but if the rust has eaten through the steel of the cutting edge, it may be impossible to restore the profile.

 • Be sure that the wedge fits its mortise along its full length.

 • Be sure that the sole isn't crooked. This, I think, is the most common reason I find for rejecting molding planes. While I have straightened the soles of molders I really liked, by the time I've reshaped the sole and re-shaped the iron to match, I'm typically left with a profile I don't like nearly as well as I liked the original.

 • Check to see that the iron hasn't worn a groove in the left side of the throat just above the mouth. Planes that have seen heavy use sometimes have worn a little slop in that location, enough to make it difficult to keep the iron where you want it during use. While I have fixed that problem by wedging a piece of veneer on the left side of the iron, it's an inconvenience.

Part 5: Where to buy

In the Midwest where I live, molding planes are available at every antique mall of any size, but sometimes the inventories are pretty thoroughly picked over. Nevertheless, many of my first molding planes were acquired in these malls at prices ranging from $12 to $50, with the lower prices assigned to hollows and rounds and the higher prices to complex molders. In fact, in my years of haunting area antique malls, I've found two dealers, one in Springfield, Ohio, and one in Zanesville, Ohio, who frequently replenish their stock with newly acquired molding planes. In addition, antique tool dealers sometimes show up at antique shows in my home state. These individuals typically offer cleaned and—unfortunately—refinished planes at slightly higher prices, but I have purchased planes from those dealers that I couldn't find anywhere else. But the best local sources are tool meets sponsored by tool collectors. The Ohio Tool Collectors Association sponsors several meetings each year at which members offer tools for sale. In fact, this is where I purchased my favorite complex molder, a plane I've used to produce moldings for a half dozen pieces of furniture

In addition, whenever I travel, I search out antique malls, and—particularly on trips to the East Coast—I've found antique dealers with pretty extensive inventories of molding planes, and if the dealers aren't tool specialists, they can sometimes be receptive to dickering over price.

But there are also sources available to anyone, no matter where they live. The internet is home to auction sites and many tool dealers as well. I acquired a fair number of my molding planes on eBay, and I would still be buying there, if the company hadn't changed the rules. Now, buyers can no longer pay with checks of any kind. They're required to surrender access to their checking or credit card accounts in order to conduct business on this auction site.

There are also a few companies offering a narrow range of new molding planes. Clark and Williams, a small firm in Eureka Springs, Arkansas, devoted exclusively to the construction of wooden planes, offers a half set of 18 matching hollows and rounds for $2455. In addition, they'll make custom molding planes to suit your specific needs. Lee Valley Tools also is now selling what it calls Asian hollows and rounds. These planes are made from a variety of rosewood known as *shungee*. Although the sizes are based on metrically measured circles, these Asian planes could be put to work in any shop. A set of 12 is priced at $229. They're also priced individually.

Molding Planes: Restoring a Molding Plane and Sharpening a Molding Plane Iron

Early on in my exploration of molding plane use, I bought every complex molder I could find, no matter how badly damaged. I figured that if I invested enough time and effort, I could make the plane work. And I was able to make moldings with every plane I restored, but sometimes, the outcome wasn't worth the effort. In some cases, this was because the restoration process involved completely reshaping the sole of a plane that had bowed—and then reshaping the iron to match, which ultimately resulted in a profile I liked much less than the plane's original profile. In other cases, it was because a half a day spent refurbishing a plane with an ordinary profile seemed wasted when there are so many planes out there with really interesting profiles and no significant defects. Now, I'm much more particular about what I buy: no more bowed plane bodies, no more missing irons, no more torn up throats, and no more plain profiles. I don't mind a plane that's dirty or one that shows superficial battering at the hands of a clumsy user, but I'm no longer willing to invest an entire day in the resurrection of a molding plane worth less than $50. Now, I'll take the time to restore a molder only if the profile is appealing, and only if it's one I don't already own and only if it doesn't involve major reconstructive surgery.

I bought this J. T. Brown (Baltimore 1824-1843) ovolo and cove complex molder in an antique mall in Zanesville, Ohio. The sole was straight, the iron matched up nicely with the sole, and there was no wear on the left side of the throat above the mouth, so despite an overall battered appearance, I knew the plane would restore easily.

You can free a stuck wedge by holding the plane against your body with your thumb and forefinger looped around the wedge. A few blows with a wooden mallet should free the wedge. If not, you can clamp the wedge in a vise, then strike the heel of the plane with your mallet.

Part 1: Restoring the iron

The most important aspect of molding plane restoration is the work done on the iron. Sometimes that involves nothing more than sharpening, but sometimes, it involves rust removal and reshaping. In fact, if the iron for a molding plane is missing, it's possible to make one from—for example—a rabbet plane iron of sufficient width, but more often, all that's needed is some fussy work at a grinder or with a file to remove minor profile defects. (* Lie-Nielsen Toolworks also sells blank molding plane irons in widths up to 1-5/8".)

If the iron needs major surgery, coat the back side of the iron with layout fluid, install the iron in the plane and mark the sole profile on the back of the coated iron with an awl. Then remove the iron and—on your grinder—rough in the profile, which you then finish with files. When you're doing this work you need to be sure that the new bevels you're creating are shallow enough so that the heel of each these bevels doesn't strike the surface of the work before the cutting edge does when the iron is bedded in the plane.

This rime of rust did little damage to the iron underneath.

2

I quickly cleaned off the rust on the iron with a sheet of 150 grit paper. Next, I lapped the back flat on a 250 grit diamond plate, then polished it on #600 and #1200 grit lapping plates.

3

Once the rust had been cleaned off, I saw that there was a small hollow on the tip of the iron. To eliminate this hollow, I had to remove metal all across the cutting edge until I'd gone past the low spot of the hollow.

4

I used a grinding wheel where I could.

5

I then switched to a round file on the concave areas and a flat file—here—on the convex areas.

6

This is the tip of the finished iron, which is wedged into the plane. Although the iron closely follows the contour of the sole, it isn't an absolutely perfect match; nevertheless, the plane works just fine. I mention this because these planes are more forgiving of slight differences between sole and iron profile than you might think.

7

In about an hour of easy restoration work, this molder was up and running.

Sometimes a problem that appears to require iron reshaping turns out, instead, to be the result of a worn throat. If a plane has seen heavy, careless use, the left side of the throat can be abraded by the left side of the iron. In such a case, the iron may appear—at first glance—to be in need of reshaping when, in fact, it's simply shifted too far to the left. It is possible to fix this by grafting new wood onto the left side of the throat. That side can also be shimmed. Sometimes the iron of a wide molder can be shifted too far to the right as well, even when it's snugged up against the left side of the throat. This is a result of the plane's wood body shrinking across its width. The solution to this problem is relieving some of the width from the left side of the iron (and the tang) on the grinder until the profile can be properly aligned in the plane.

Part 2: The wood

Sometimes you'll find a plane with a wedge that doesn't fit tightly against the front of the throat and/or the front of the iron. A tight fit here all along the length of the wedge is imperative if the iron is to be stable during use. A poor fit can be corrected by carefully removing shavings from the front of the wedge with a block plane while the wedge is fixed in a vise. This is fussy work, work that will give you renewed respect for the skills of the craftsmen who made these planes.

Planes that cut quirks have strips of boxing at the quirk locations (and sometimes at other wear locations as well). Boxing consists of strips of box-wood inlaid into a plane's wear points. The grain in these strips is oriented at a 45 degree angle, leaning back toward the heel of the plane. When the plane is in use, this angle creates an end grain presentation which allows the boxwood to resist wear and to resist breaking off if the plane is subjected to lateral stresses. Sometimes, the hide glue that holds these strips of boxing in place loosens over time, allowing the strips to fall out. These strips can be reinstalled with fresh hide glue. At other times, however, the boxing is still tight but misaligned, with a high spot or two along its length. This can be corrected with a block plane. And sometimes, part, or all, of the strip may be missing. You can scavenge boxing strips from parts planes, although the boxing thicknesses aren't universal, so this may require a little shimming or a little thicknessing. And sometimes, if only a short section of boxing is missing, the plane can be used in that condition. One of my favorite molders is a thumbnail plane missing a 2" section of boxing, and I've been using the plane that way for years.

The J. T. Brown molder didn't have any boxing strips because it doesn't cut a quirk, the location of most molding plane boxing. This molder, however, has a strip of boxing that—over time—had become uneven, although it wasn't loose. A couple of light passes with a block plane corrected that unevenness.

The left side of the throat on this side bead is badly worn. When the iron is wedged up tight against that left side, the iron is misaligned. Because these side beads are so common, I wouldn't recommend putting any restoration effort into this plane.

Part 3: Sharpening the iron

Fortunately, most molding plane irons require nothing more significant than a cutting edge tune up. If the bevel is clean, untouched by rust, that sharpening can consist of nothing more than lapping and polishing the back. This is done exactly like the lapping and polishing of bench plane irons. When the back is reasonably flat, I start with a 250 grit diamond lapping plate, following by polishing on 600 grit and 1200 grit lapping plates. If the back is not flat or if it's degraded with rust, I begin lapping with coarse sandpaper on a flat surface, then proceed through the diamond lapping plates.

You may feel an urge to work the bevel as well, but if that bevel is clean and undamaged by time, there is no reason to do anything more than polish it. The cutting edge consists of the intersection of two planes—the back and the bevel—and you can create sharpness at that intersection by working one of those planes, the back. Any work you do on the bevel will remove material from the profile, actually creating problems, rather than solving them.

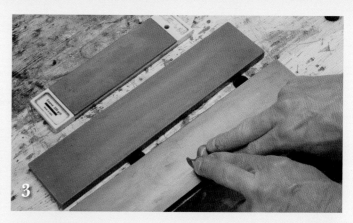

I then switched to my diamond lapping plate sequence: 250 grit, 600 grit, 1200 grit.

I then sanded the bevel with 120 paper, followed by 150, 220, and 320.

The bevel of this ogee iron was badly degraded by rust, so I ground past the rust into the good steel and—with various files—created new bevels.

The cutting edge then consisted of a polished back and a polished bevel.

I lapped away the rust on the back of the iron with 120 grit paper.

The polished back of the iron should reflect the sole of the plane.

Molding Planes: Using Molding Planes

There are few woodshop teaching experiences that can match that moment when a novice first puts a molding plane to work. These simple tools are steeped in such mystery that many craftsmen—even those accomplished in other woodworking genres—view mastering a molding plane as somehow beyond their skills, and when that first shaving squirts out the side escapement, even the most grizzled and experienced woodworker breaks into a smile. It happens every time. Magic.

Part1: Shaping planes

Dedicated molding planes with a sole shaped to a specific profile and an iron cut to match make it simple to produce moldings. You position the plane on the work at the angle indicated by the spring lines, crowd the fence against the edge of the work, and push.

However, the same work can be done without a dedicated molder if you have a few shaping planes and a willingness to invest some time and effort into the project. The shaping plane group includes the hollows, the rounds, and the snipe bills, but historically, the groundwork for these planes involved the use of other tools in the craftsman's kit. A period craftsman might first have sunk several rabbets across the width of the planned molding with a moving filletster or a rabbet plane. This accomplished two things. First, it removed some of the waste in a controlled fashion, and second the walls left by the rabbet planes provided battens for guiding an unfenced shaping plane. If, for example, he was going to use a round to create a concave shape on the molding, he could guide that round by pressing it against the wall left by a rabbet plane during his roughing in of that concave shape.

Craftsmen working with shaping planes today are more likely to prepare the work with a tablesaw, cutting away bevels, establishing fillets and quirks, before introducing the shaping planes. In fact, almost any shape can be roughed in with a series of saw kerfs. Once this preliminary work is done, the final shape can be created with shaping planes.

I've found that—although traditional rounds work perfectly well in many situations—the fact that the soles of these planes comprises only 1/6 of an circle makes it difficult to work them into tight spots. In such a place, I substitute a round that comprises 1/2 of a circle, a plane sometimes called a half round. This allows me to work into tight spots without the edges of the plane iron digging into the adjacent shape. Technically speaking, such a plane isn't a round. Instead, it likely was built for a dedicated purpose, perhaps as one half of a pair of table planes or maybe to work the concave trench into which a gun barrel would be installed.

Before you apply a shaping plane to the work, you need to set the iron. First, push the tang of the iron up into the throat, holding the cutting edge in place with the finger of one hand. With the other hand, push the wedge into its mortise. Then, tap the wedge finial once or twice with a wood mallet,

snugging the wedge and the iron into place. Check the cutting edge exposure by sighting along the sole from the toe and by rubbing your thumb across the mouth. Your eyes should see the tiniest bit of cutting edge above the sole and mirroring its shape. You thumb should feel just a whisker of the cutting edge dragging against your skin. (Remember: Never drag a finger *along* a cutting edge, only across a cutting edge.) If the setting isn't correct, free the iron and wedge and reset. When you think you have it set correctly, try it on the work.

At first, setting the iron will be a frustrating process. In the first months I spent with molding planes, I would typically need a half-dozen settings to get a single cutting edge exposure just right. Now, it's a much simpler process. More often than not, I get it right the first time.

You should also give the molding stock a close examination to establish the best direction of work before you put your plane to the molding stock. While the tablesaw doesn't care which way the grain runs, your planes do, so it's important to lay out the work so that when you begin to shape with planes you're working either in the direction of rising grain (see page 56) or along a straight grain. It's very hard to work a molding plane against rising grain because the shavings it takes are thicker than those taken by most other planes, making them particularly susceptible to tearout.

Once the iron is properly set, once you've determined the best direction in which to work, rest the toe of the plane on that part of the emerging profile that particular plane best fits. Then with your left hand bearing down on the plane just ahead of the iron and the right hand pushing at the heel, begin to work the profile. (If you're left-handed like me, this is going to seem backwards, but you have no choice. Although a very few left-handed planes were made, you're not likely to see any in your lifetime, so you may as well embrace this backward way of life.)

No molding plane work can begin until the iron is properly set. Too much iron (a condition indicated by the adjective "rank") will cause heavy shavings to choke the throat. Too little iron prevents the cutting edge from taking a shaving.

Be sure to clear the throat at the end of every stroke. If you don't, the shavings will bunch up there, bringing your work to a halt. When I first began to use molding planes (and occasionally even now), I found myself unconsciously placing my right forefinger in a position that interfered with the shaving's passage out of the throat, causing wood to pile up there. Even if you are scrupulous about your hand position, once in a while, the throat will become clogged. When that happens, I've found that a pair of tweezers is the best tool for pulling out impacted shavings, and if the tweezers can't remove them, you don't have any choice but to pull the iron, clear the throat, and reset the cutting edge.

Never widen a throat by cutting away wood from the plane's body. This practice doesn't address the cause of the problem, which is either an iron set too rank or a failure to clear the throat after every pass, and it can impair the performance of the plane.

These are the planes I used to shape an ogee molding for the colonial-era plate rack shown below. I used the shoulder planes to clean up the fillet. The shaping planes, the hollows and the half-round, faired the ogee shape. *Courtesy of Popular Woodworking* magazine

Period craftsmen roughed in moldings with moving filletsters and rabbet planes. Contemporary craftsmen are more likely to rough in these shapes on a tablesaw. *Courtesy of* Popular Woodworking *magazine.*

This is a detail of the plate rack's finished cornice molding. *Courtesy of* Popular Woodworking *magazine, Al Parrish photo.*

I faired the hump in the ogee with my hollows. I then used the half round on the concave section. *Courtesy of* Popular Woodworking *magazine.*

This plate rack is a reproduction of an original found in Old Sturbridge Village in Massachusetts. *Courtesy of* Popular Woodworking *magazine, Al Parrish photo.*

Part 2: Vertically aligned planes

Bead planes were designed to be used in a vertical alignment. The side beads and astragals have to be used at the edge of the stock because of their fences. They create their shapes on the edge of the work or on the face adjacent to the edge with their fences crowded against the surface adjacent to and 90 degrees from the surface being worked. Because they lack fences, center beads can be used anywhere across the width of a board. Usually, these are used against a batten clamped or nailed to the work. But some period craftsmen drilled a pair of holes through the bodies of their center bead and then pushed the arms of a screw arm plow through these holes, aligning the plane with the fence from the plow. Of course, used this way, they were limited to the reach of the screw arm fence.

The side beads and astragals are the easiest molding planes to use. When I want to demonstrate to anyone how easy it is to work a molding plane, I always reach for one of these simple molders.

Place the plane's fence against the edge of the work with the toe resting on the work. Align the plane so that its body is perpendicular to the surface being worked. Then push the plane forward until the cutting edge engages the surface. Continue pushing the plane forward with your right hand against the heel, keeping the plane snugged down against the work, and your left hand on the left side of the plane, ahead of the iron, pressing the plane's fence against the edge of the work. Maintain a consistent downward pressure with the right hand and a consistent lateral pressure with the left. Move the plane in a continuous motion along the full length of the work, and a shaving will jet out of the escapement on the right side of the plane. Then repeat.

Molding planes remove much more material in each pass than do smoothing planes. Otherwise it might take an hour to sink a molding profile 3/4" of an inch into the molding stock. Still, it does take multiple passes to form even a small profile.

Bead planes, like the small astragal I'm using here, are worked with the plane body in an upright position. *Courtesy of* The Journal of American Period Furniture.

This work is best done with a rhythm. You place the toe on the work. You crowd the fence against the edge. You push the plane through the stroke. You clear the shaving. You repeat these steps, moving through them the same way every time. In the beginning when you're building muscle memory, you'll need to consciously review the list of steps, but it won't be long until your body falls into the rhythm naturally: toe on work, fence crowded tight, push, clear shaving. Over and over.

Muscle memory will make it less likely that you'll start a stroke with the fence not against the edge but against some feature of the profile (which is easy to do because the fence is less than 1/8" high on most planes). It also makes it less likely that you'll forget to clear the throat each time and allow shavings to pile up filling the mouth with impacted wood. Nevertheless, you will probably make both of these mistakes from time to time as you develop your muscle memory.

This detail shows the emerging astragal. *Courtesy of* The Journal of American Period Furniture.

Part 3: Planes with Spring Lines

Most molders, including most complex molding planes, have a pair of lines—called spring lines—etched onto the toe, one marking the plane's vertical alignment and the other marking the plane's horizontal alignment. These lines—90 degrees apart—are extensions of the plane's fence and its depth stop. When the plane is held so that the line extending from the depth stop is parallel to true horizontal and the line extending up from the fence is parallel to true vertical (which, of course, it must be if the other line is vertical), the plane is in the correct alignment for work, the alignment that permits the most efficient cutting of the plane's profile. Holding the plane at this angle during use may seem awkward at first, but it will quickly begin to feel natural.

The first few passes taken by a complex molder are very much like passes taken by one of the simple planes, but as the complex molder begins to sink deeper into the molding stock, as a wider section of the profile is worked, you'll notice that it takes more effort to push the plane through its stroke. In part, this is because molding planes take heavier shavings than most other planes. In addition, the cumulative width of all the elements cut by a complex molder can total several inches. This width is greater than the straight-line width of the cutting edge because it consists of a line tracing all the beads, ogees, quirks, etc. the plane is forming. This means you're taking a heavy shaving across a fairly wide span. In fact when you're cutting a wide, complicated profile in hardwood, you'll notice that it takes considerable effort to power the plane through its stroke, and that's when the plane is most likely to go off the rails.

This head-on shot of the plane in the previous photos shows the plane working a nearly complete profile. Notice that the fence on the right side of the image is crowded against the edge of the work. Notice that the depth stop on the left side of the image is nearly touching the surface of the work. When that bottoms out, the profile is complete. *Courtesy of* Woodwork *magazine.*

This is an example of a sprung plane. My left thumb (right side of image) sits just above the plane's fence. My right thumb (left side of image) is brushing the side of the depth stop. *Courtesy of* Woodwork *magazine.*

This detail of a wider complex molder shows the spring lines etched onto the toe. Notice that the plane is aligned according to those spring lines. *Courtesy of* Woodwork *magazine.*

This is the correct working position for the little molder in the photo at the top left of the next page. Notice the angle at which I'm holding it. Notice, too, the little curl of shaving escaping from the side of the plane. *Courtesy of* Woodwork *magazine.*

Because it's difficult to hold a narrow strip during the molding process, I cut the molding on the edge of a wide board and then rip the molding from that board. *Courtesy of* Woodwork *magazine.*

The molding being cut in the two preceding photos was used on the waist of this colonial-era desk reproduction. *Courtesy of* Woodwork *magazine. Photo:* Brian Kellet.

The fence on a molding plane is very low. This means that if you make a brief false move with your hands while pushing the plane through its stroke, the fence can jump up over the edge of the work, causing the cutting edge to dig into the features it's creating. This isn't much of a problem when you're taking the first few strokes because the damage a slip causes at that point will likely be removed by subsequent passes of the cutting edge, but it's frustrating to have the plane jump its fence and slash across a nearly complete profile, and of course, that's when a jump is most likely because that's when you're pushing hardest to drive the plane through a cumulatively wide cut.

Most fence jumping is a result of inexperience. As you build muscle memory, you'll find your plane staying where it belongs more and more often, but there will always be some planes that continue to jump. Usually, this will be a result of the fact that some planes have very low fences, but sometimes planes with normal-sized fences will continue to jump even when your hands have grown comfortable operating a molding plane.

My experience is that planes with wider, more complicated profiles are most likely to jump, and for these planes, the only answer is an add-on fence, something I've installed on several of my complex molders.

The ogee plane on the bottom came to me without a fence. I assume it was originally used against a batten or maybe the edge of a rabbet. The quirk bead and cove molder on top did have a fence when I bought it, but it was prone to jumping that fence as I neared the completion of its profile. I added fences to both planes, making them much easier to operate.

Molding Planes: Cornice Planes

Cornice molders are the most impressive tools in the molding plane field. Unlike other complex molders, these behemoths were designed to create profiles across the whole surface of the board being worked in an orientation generally parallel to that surface. The moldings were then mounted, outside, under a roof overhang or, inside, at the intersection of a wall and ceiling, usually at a 45 degree angle. This gave the appearance of a large stack of moldings, an appearance not accompanied by the actual weight of that large stack. This is an approach still favored today by mills making cornice moldings, which are cut on the board's flat surface to be installed at 45 degree angles.

Cornice molders are fenced planes, with bodies often 4-6 inches in width. Even though few of these planes have irons more than four inches wide, the actual cutting width could be considerably greater than the iron width because the cutting width consists of a line following every contour of the plane's cutting edge.

Because it's difficult to cut such a wide profile with a single plane, the surface was usually prepared with hollows, rounds, moving filletsters, etc., to rough in the shape before the cornice molder was applied to the surface. In fact, it's possible to create cornice molding through the use of these shaping planes alone, and it's likely that many period craftsmen, who couldn't afford dedicated cornice molders, did just that.

Some large cornice planes have a hole drilled crosswise through the plane's body behind the nose. Ropes or wood dowels could be threaded through these holes making it possible for the efforts of the master to be augmented by the efforts of apprentices. The master would guide the plane, using his weight transmitted through one hand to hold the plane down while the other hand crowded the plane's fence against the edge of the work. The apprentices then supplied the forward thrust by pulling on the ropes or the wood dowel, in this manner powering the cutting edge through the work.

Often these planes were sold in pairs with one plane to be used in one direction on one side of the board being worked, with the other plane in the pair being used in the other direction on the other side of the board. This made it possible to create a five or six inch wide molding without a five or six inch wide iron that would have been difficult to push through the work.

Only those craftsmen building homes for the moneyed elite would have owned cornice molders because they were quite expensive. In the 1872 catalog for the Greenfield Tool Company, a pair of cornice planes wide enough to produce a 5-1/2" molding were priced at $5.50, more than the aggregate cost, in that same catalog, of a full set of bench planes: a smoother, a jack, a fore plane, and a jointer. And today, the relative cost of these planes is even greater. While a usable complex molder of ordinary width can be purchased for $40, a usable cornice molder might run $500 or more. For this reason, I have never owned such a plane, and even if I did, I would be afraid to use it. Instead, when I make cornice moldings, I make them by stacking narrower profiles together to create wide moldings.

John Sleeper (1754-1834), the maker of this double-iron cornice plane, also served in the army during the Revolutionary War, fighting in the Battle of Bunker Hill. He later followed Brigadier General Richard Montgomery on the brutal march through the woods to Quebec. After Montgomery's death in the attack on that Canadian city, John Sleeper was captured and spent the next nine months in prison. *Lee Richmond photo.*

This single-iron cornice plane is the work of John Lindenberger (1754-1817) who spent most of his working life as a planemaker in Providence, Rhode Island, after resigning from the army in 1779. He had seen action during the Revolutionary War at the battles of Brandywine, Germantown, Trenton, and Princeton. *Lee Richmond photo.*

Part 1: Designing a cornice stack

When I design a cornice molding, I try to think of that molding as consisting of three parts: a bottom, middle, and top. I like the bottom section to be a profile cut by a relatively narrow plane, one creating a small clutter of shadow lines. I think it's important that at least one of these lines should be hard-edged enough to mark clearly the division between the casepiece and the molding that crowns it. I like the middle section of the cornice to be cut by a plane with a simpler but wider profile, usually a wide ogee or a wide cove. Here, there will be fewer but wider shadow lines, creating a gradual transition between the cornice's top and bottom. For the top section, I select another relatively narrow plane, one creating a second small clutter of shadow lines. The most important duty for this profile is to cap the molding, so I like this section to have a modest overhang. Taken together, these three sections should be arranged so that they lead the viewer down into the piece below the cornice. This can be achieved by arranging the elements so that they form a reasonably straight line angling down toward the piece, or they can form a wide concave or ogee line, leading down toward the piece.

The middle shelf in this plane cabinet contains a variety of molding planes. Beside each of them is a short sample of the profile cut by that plane.

If you're interested in historical accuracy, you could choose your planes only from among those made in the same era as an original of the piece you're building, but I'm not interested in strict historical accuracy, even if I'm building a period piece. Instead, I'm trying only to create a piece of period-inspired furniture that will look appealing now, in the 21st century, so I sometimes mix and match molding planes from several different eras all in the same cornice. Plus, I don't have a wide enough selection of profiles from each of the periods in which I work to assemble my cornices.

In my molding plane cupboards, shelved beside each plane, I keep a short sample of the profile cut by that plane. When I'm planning a cornice molding (or any other kind of molding), I'll pull out some of these samples and begin trying them together in an effort to achieve a combination that will look right on the piece I'm building.

Sometimes, during this process, it's useful to change the orientation of a profile. If the sample is cut on the face of a board, I'll cut another sample with the same plane on the edge of a board. That change can sometimes suggest new ways of combining the profiles. Also, you can change the look of a cornice stack by changing the width of the individual boards making up the stack. For example, if I'm looking at a potential stack that leads the eye down to piece in a straight line, I can change that to a concave or convex line simply by changing the width of the middle board in the stack.

Also, I sometimes repeat a molding shape in more than one location on a piece, using a profile as one element in the cornice stack and then maybe as one element in the waist stack. This can have the effect of unifying the moldings, making them look like they all belong on the same piece.

The cornice molding on this Queen Anne highboy consists of a stack of three different profiles, each created with a different plane

111

In this photo, I'm cutting the cove which makes up the middle section of the highboy's cornice. *Courtesy of* The Woodworker's Journal.

The plane on the left cut the top section of this cornice. The plane in the middle cut the cove, and the plane on the right cut the bottom section. *Courtesy of* The Woodworker's Journal.

Dozens of feet of molding went into the creation of this kas, a Dutch form imported very early to the American colonies. Each of the raised panels is surrounded by a bolection molding. The skirt molding consists of two different profiles, and the cornice molding consists of four profiles: three cut with molding planes and the fourth—a simple radius—with a bench plane. *Courtesy of* Woodwork *magazine.*

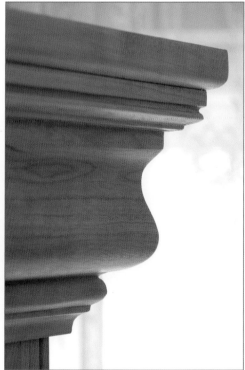

This detail of the kas cornice is made up of a top and bottom, each of which includes several shadow lines, and a wider, simpler ogee in the middle. *Courtesy of* Woodwork *magazine.*

Part 2: Attaching the cornice stack

A wide cornice molding can be tricky to install because on the sides of many cases—highboys, for example—the grain direction of the molding runs perpendicular to the grain direction of the material to which it's attached. If you glue a cornice molding directly to the side of the case, one of two things will happen when the humidity in the home drops: either the molding will pop off or the case to which it is glued will crack. I've seen both occur, not— thank heavens—on casepieces I built. While moldings can be nailed to the case—in that manner avoiding the perils of cross-grain gluing—nails holes are unsightly. Instead, I use a different method of attachment, one that allows me to sidestep cross-grain gluing without the filled holes indicating set nails, without, also, the risk inherent in swinging a hammer at finished moldings.

Underneath the cornice molding I attach a thin (about 1/4" thick) piece of primary wood wide enough to provide a backing for the entire width of the cornice molding. The grain of this backing material runs in the same direction as the grain of the molding I'll later apply, that is perpendicular to the grain direction of the case side. At the front of the case, where the miters in the molding will meet, I'll glue this thin strip to the case side, but along the rest of the backing material's length, I'll tack it to the side of the case with 10-15 small nails. I then glue (press fitting for a 60 count) the elements of the cornice molding to this backing material.

The glue under the front 2-3 inches of the backing material keeps this material (and the moldings glued to its face) in place at the front of the case where the miters meet, while the nails fastening the rest of the backing material's length allow cross-grain movement.

Sometimes I hide the full width of this backing material under the cornice molding. At other times, I cut the bottom profile on the bottom edge of this backing strip, incorporating it into the cornice molding.

Molding Planes: Joining Hand-Made Moldings

Modern woodshop technology has produced molding machines of incredible speed and power, and while machines can't match molding planes for richness of profile variety, they do produce moldings of astonishing consistency. You can be sure that the 100th stick of molding created on such a machine will be the same size as the first.

Moldings made with hand planes aren't quite so uniform, but the only place this is noticeable to the unaided eye is where two pieces of hand-made molding come together, for example at a miter joint.

Fortunately, the fix is quite simple. After you've cut the miter in your miter box, clean up the sawn edge with a couple of passes of a good miter plane. Then assemble the joint keeping the mitered surfaces tightly together, ignoring, for the moment, the surface discontinuities resulting from the molding's hand-made origins.

After the glue has dried, use whatever planes you need to work the high side of each discontinuity until the joint is nicely faired together. No one will ever see the error, and it won't take long for you to forget it was ever there.

The planes that fabricated the waist moldings for this highboy (seen from the back) are shown here. Two samples of the waist molding elements stand to the right of the planes. I made the half bead with my LN #60-1/2. I then used the complex molder you see here to create the rest of the molding, although I did alter the profile cut by that plane in two ways. First, I ripped off half of the molding's bead. Then with my #60-1/2, I put a radius on that molding's top outside corner.

After sawing the miters, I cleaned up the saw marks with this Lie-Nielsen #9 and a shooting board.

With a shoulder plane, I faired the top of the bead. I then used a half round to clean up the concave area below the bead.

My pencil is pointing at one of the shaping errors at this joint.

Here is the final—very tight—miter, along with the two planes I used to fair the joint.

Molding Planes:
Molding Plane Value

Today, you can purchase a 1-5/8" wide molding plane blank from Lie-Nielsen Toolworks for $27. Enough 10/4 beech for the body and wedge of a simple molding plane taking an iron of that size would be another $10-$15. Add a couple of dollars for material to box the wear points on the sole, and that brings the total materials price for a simple molder to about $39.

And—unless you're interested in a plane produced by a historically important planemaker—that's more than what you have to pay for such a plane on the antique tool market. Less than $39 for a plane produced by a master craftsman who spent years acquiring his skills. Less than $39 for a plane he signed, a plane already carrying a century or two of age. It's remarkable. In an age when a single machine-printed baseball card can bring over $1,000,000 at auction, the work of a 19th century master crafts-

User-grade hollows and rounds like these can be picked up for less than $30 each, often much less.

man adds exactly zero value to the materials cost of a superbly wrought molding plane.

I think we may be the last generation able to purchase these magnificent tools so cheaply. The current flood of antique planes being picked from basements and barns all across the Eastern U.S.

114

will end at some point, drained by the pull of tool auctions and internet sales, and nobody is making any more molding planes, at least not in numbers sufficient to keep the prices anywhere near the current levels.

During the months I worked on this book, I tracked the selling prices of over 100 planes on the online auction site eBay so that I could make some useful statement about the real value of these tools. To make the comparisons as meaningful as possible, I confined myself to those planes accompanied by a thorough enough photo record to make it possible to assign some kind of condition to each plane based on the condition standards enumerated by *The Fine Tool Journal.*

A dozen of those planes were user-grade hollows and rounds—much the most common planes in the molding plane genre—and those planes sold for very reasonable prices, between $12.50 and $29.00. The $29.00 selling price was for an Ohio Tool 1-1/4" round in what I guessed was Good condition. The next plane in the eBay listing was an Ohio Tool 1-1/4" hollow in Fine condition that sold for $15.00, so I suspect the $29.00 price was paid by someone determined to get both halves of the matching pair.

In addition, there was a Jo Fuller 1-3/16" round that sold for $213. Obviously, the purchaser of this plane had no intention of using the plane. Jo Fuller molders are highly collectible, despite the fact that the turn up fairly often on eBay.

Bead planes were similarly common, with selling prices ranging from $5.50 to $33.00. The $33.00 plane surprised me. It was a Mathieson and Son 1/8" bead drilled to accept a screw-arm fence, a modification I would have expected to result in a lower price. Plus, the body was too badly bowed to ever put into use.

Complex molders are becoming harder and harder to sell on eBay. Six years ago, when I began buying on the auction site, complex molders were selling for little more than shaping planes, but in the last couple of years, most of the user-grade complex molding planes I've seen have been listed with starting bids in the $39.00- $59.00 range. I suspect sellers have become more cognizant

Planes made by important planemakers—particularly large planes like this cornice molder—command very high prices. This plane was built by J. Sleeper, who fought in the Revolutionary War.

of the values of these tools and are pricing them accordingly. But they aren't selling, at least they weren't when I was watching. Of the half dozen complex molders I tracked, only one sold, an Ohio Tool quirk ogee which went for $49.00. The others—listed with starting bids of $49.00-$59.00—went unsold.

However, it's still possible to buy user-grade complex molders at antique malls for incredibly low prices. A couple of years ago, I picked up a 3" wide Quirk ogee with bevel with two irons for $25.00 in an antique mall in Findlay, Ohio, and in the past year, I've picked up four complex molders, each for less than $40.00 from the same booth in an antique mall in Zanesville, Ohio. Near the East Coast, plane buying is even easier. On a recent trip to Adamstown, Pennsylvania (outside Philadelphia), I picked up two complex molders for $29 and $35.00.

Each of these complex molding planes was acquired for less than $40, but I did invest many hours of searching through antique shops and malls to purchase at those prices.

Chapter 5
Block Planes

These three planes represent early American versions of metal planes small enough to be used one handed.

Assembling a Collection of Block Planes

There is general agreement in the woodworking community that the term "block plane" identifies a bevel-up plane, small enough to be used effectively with one hand. Although this use of the term is consistent with the spoken vernacular of most plane users and the advertising literature of most plane sellers, Lie-Nielsen Toolworks has a different perspective, identifying any bevel-up plane as a block plane, regardless of size. In the Lie-Nielsen catalog, the block plane class includes a half-dozen one-handers (planes almost any contemporary woodworker would identify as block planes), as well as four planes clearly intended to be used with two hands, including a 22" bevel-up jointer.

There is also general agreement within the woodworking community that a block plane is *not* any plane made from a block of wood, this despite the tendency of countless antiques dealers to list every plane made in such a way as a block plane. In fact, in R. A. Salaman's *Dictionary of Woodworking Tools"* he limits the block plane class to only planes made of metal.

Although there is general agreement about what a block plane is and what it is not, there is less agreement about the origin of this name. Long-standing tradition says that the term "block plane" is a nod to the fact that these planes were originally designed to level the end-grain surfaces of butcher-block tables. However, the 1926 Stanley Tools catalog offers another explanation. That catalog says that block planes were designed to smooth "the ends of boards," work the catalog says was described by carpenters as "blocking in."

Part 1: What kinds of new block planes make good users?

My first block plane was a little red and blue Corsair given to me by my dad in the late 1950s or early 1960s. I still have the plane, although I can't remember ever having used it in the construction of any piece of furniture. It lacks a depth-of-cut adjuster, and there is no adjustable mouth plate. The iron is bedded on two small surfaces: the top of a slender post cast onto the plane body midway along the length of the iron and a narrow band of roughly ground metal just behind the mouth. The iron is held in place by tension supplied by a wheel centered on a threaded rod installed above the iron at the location of the bedding post underneath. The threaded rod is turned into a tapped hole in a boss cast on the underside of the cap. When the wheel is turned one way, the threaded rod moves out of the boss, applying pressure to the iron. When the wheel is turned the other way, the threaded rod moves into the boss, removing pressure from the iron.

Though it's a simple, almost crude, tool, it could nevertheless be made to do useful work, but only by a craftsman skilled enough to tune it well and skilled enough to set the iron accurately without an adjuster. Unfortunately, its rough manufacture suggests that it was built to sell cheap to buyers who lacked the knowledge to note its deficiencies. Similar planes are still being marketed by Stanley and by other makers, priced between $15-$20. My guess is that these tools are being purchased, not by craftsmen, but by homeowners hoping to use them for one specific purpose, for example, to fit a stuck entrance door.

This may be why hand planes are so often regarded with exasperation by inexperienced craftsmen. They're the individuals most in need of the top-quality, ready-to-use-right-out-of-the-box Lie-Nielsen and Veritas planes, but they are also the individuals least likely to buy these more expensive tools. All too often, the result is a lifelong distrust of hand planes.

The block planes on the bottom end of the Stanley price range should be ignored, but those at the top* of the Stanley price range—the Contractor Grade block planes—can be made to perform reasonably well, and their price is certainly appealing.

These planes have the two features that most of us have come to expect in our block planes: a depth-of-cut adjustment knob and an adjustable mouth plate. The depth-of-cut adjustment knob is attached to a stamped metal component. A tiny nub on that component fits into one of the three slots cut laterally through the iron near its back end. When the knob is turned, the metal nub either pushes the iron forward or drags it backward. The lateral adjuster on this plane is another stamped metal component with a pair of metal tabs pointed downward beneath the rear of the iron. These tabs are part of a component that includes a pair of low shoulders fitting into the iron's wide lengthwise slot. When your fingertips rack the tabs back and forth, the iron moves in response. The adjustable

In the lower left, you can see the Veritas block plane in nickel-resist ductile iron. Moving right, the next plane is a Lie-Nielsen #60-1/2. Next is a Stanley Contractor Grade. In the upper right is a cheap little Corsair painted blue and red.

Each of these planes could serve as a good user. The Veritas and Lie-Nielsen were good right out of the box. The Stanley on the top left required some tuning.

The bottom iron from a Stanley Contractor Grade is 3/32" thick. The middle iron from a Li-Nielsen #60-1/2 measures 1/8" thick. The Veritas iron on top is 9/64" thick.

mouth plate is locked in place with a knurled knob rising from the toe of the plane. The actual adjuster is a chromed lever underneath that knob. Except for the ground sole and sides, the entire body of the plane is protected by a thick layer of japanning.

The biggest objection I have to this plane is its lack of an adequate bed for the iron. Instead of the broad accurately machined beds found on better quality block planes, the iron in this plane rests on a small bump of stamped metal on one end and a narrow band of coarsely machined iron just behind the mouth. In fact, when you look at how poorly the iron is bedded, you wonder how this plane can function at all.

Stanley Contractor Grade block planes usually sell for $50-$55, and the tuning process is demonstrated a little later in this chapter.

(When this book was being written in 2009, I made repeated attempts to get review examples of Stanley's new "Premium" planes, including examples of their new block plane, the Sweetheart #60-1/2, priced at $100. Unfortunately, every company representative I spoke to elected to pass on this opportunity to compare these new Stanleys to the other planes appearing in this book.)

The only Lie-Nielsen block plane I have used is the #60-1/2. This plane has a simpler and more robust adjustment mechanism than the one on its antique Stanley namesake. One end of a threaded rod is locked in a squat post cast onto the plane's body. A knurled knob with a metal collar is threaded onto that rod. The collar engages a single groove milled into the underside of the iron taking the iron with it as the knob is turned. When I first acquired this plane, I was surprised that there was no mechanism for lateral adjustment, but then I realized the plane doesn't need any. There is enough play in the groove milled onto the underside of the iron to make any necessary side-to-side adjustment by simply shifting the back of the iron with my fingertips. The adjustable mouth plate is similar in operation to the one in the Contractor Grade plane described above.

This plane has two very important advantages over the Stanley. First, the iron is much thicker than the iron on the Stanley. Second, this block plane has an enormous bearing surface for that iron. The machined bed at the rear of the mouth is 1-1/2" long. That's six times the length of the bed on the Stanley. In addition, the Lie-Nielsen has a second machined bed supporting the back end of the iron at the top of the squat post into which the adjustment rod is fitted. These two elements provide a rock-solid bearing surface for the iron, making it capable of wading through tough end grain without any stuttering of the cutting edge. In addition, every element of this plane is heavier, more accurately machined than the equivalent elements in the Stanley plane. But it is more expensive. At $165, it's a little more than three times the price of the Stanley.

When I started work on this book, I believed the Lie-Nielsen #60-1/2 that I was then using was about as good as a block plane could get. That plane has every feature I think a block plane should have in a simple, robust package. Then Wally Wilson of Lee Valley Tools sent me one of their new Veritas block planes.

I'm not sure this Veritas performs any better than my #60-1/2. Any useful measure of performance differences between these two superb tools is beyond my ability to devise. However based on its appearance as well as its high level of performance, the people at Lee Valley Tools can make a strong argument that their new plane is the best block plane ever manufactured. With its sweeping art deco design, it's as much a work of art as it is a tool. And it is very much a tool.

The quality begins with an iron that is thicker, even, than the iron in the Lie-Nielsen #60-1/2. That iron rests on a machined bed only slightly smaller than the bed on the #60-1/2. At the rear, the iron is supported by the turret in the Veritas adjuster, a confluence of components that must have been difficult to achieve. And, of course, like most of the planes in the Veritas line, at the heart of this block

The iron in the Stanley Contractor Grade (left) makes contact with a bed in two places: the narrow band of ground metal just behind the mouth and the tiny shoulders on either side of the control nub below the depth-of-cut adjustment knob. The iron on the Lie-Nielsen #60-1/2 is bedded on the large rectangle of ground metal behind the mouth, as well as the ground metal at the top of the cast post into which the depth-of-cut adjustment is fastened. The iron of the Veritas (right) is also bedded in two places: the area of ground metal behind the mouth and the top of the adjuster turret at the rear of the plane.

plane is the Veritas adjuster, which is simpler and sturdier than the Norris adjuster it vaguely resembles. The price of the Veritas block plane is high, at least when compared to the prices of Stanley block planes. The ductile iron version is $179, and the nickel-resist ductile iron of the example they sent me is $279.

Part 2: Antique block planes

Although I've seen hundreds of bench and molding planes in restorable condition at antique malls and flea markets, I've seen very few block planes in a similar condition. The irons on the antique block planes I've seen were often encrusted with thick rust, ground almost to the slot, with cutting edges slanting to one side or the other, serrated by repeated attacks on nails. The adjusters are often rust frozen or broken or missing parts. Sometimes the plane body is cracked or broken, probably as a result of being dropped on concrete garage or basement floors. Sometimes the sole is furrowed as a result of working materials too hard for a hand plane. In general, these are tools that have seen decades of abuse.

I think there is a reason for this higher mortality rate among block planes. Because they are so familiar, even to people who have never entered a woodshop, these are the planes an amateur might pick from a box of antique tools left him by an ancestor. That amateur might have used that block plane to remove a paint-saturated 1/16" from the width of a cupboard door in his home, to even up an edge on a sheet of plastic laminate or plexiglass.

Because so few antique block planes are found in good condition, I think the antique tool market may not be the best option for a contemporary woodworker assembling a group of users. I think in this instance the best course is to buy block planes new. And the good news is block planes are much cheaper new than bench planes.

Block Planes: Tuning a Stanley Block Plane

I check the sole of any new bench plane with a straightedge and a pair of winding sticks to identify any errors in flatness. Because of the diminutive size of a block plane, it's difficult to make the same checks—although I do try. I then lap those areas flat using a variety of abrasives. I also disassemble the plane to see if there are any mating parts that don't come together the way they should. Sometimes japanning or paint has seeped into contact areas. At other times, metal burrs may interfere. I clean up these surfaces with a file and/or sandpaper. The iron, too, frequently needs attention on diamond lapping plates.

Remove the brass knob at the front of the plane. This releases the adjustable mouth plate. Sometimes this part remains stuck even after the knob has been removed. In such a case, you can free the mouth plate by tapping on the top of the threaded rod the knob turns onto. Examine the top surface of the mouth plate. Make sure no gunk appears in the narrow bands on both sides that make contact with the plane body when the plate is tightened into place with the brass knob. Also, examine the bottom surfaces of the plane body where that body contacts the mouth plate. Remove any gunk in either of these locations with a file or sandpaper, as I'm doing here.

Stanley applies a thick layer of japanning to all surfaces of the lever cap. As a result, you need to sand off that japanning on the underside of the lever-cap lip, the point at which lever cap and iron meet. It's important to have clean metal-to-metal contact here all across the width of the iron. Otherwise, the cutting edge may not be supported well enough to remain stable during end-grain work.

Replace the mouth plate and turn the brass knob down tight. Then with the iron in place but the cutting edge raised up above the sole, flatten the sole by working it back and forth on a flat abrasive surface, like the marble slab I'm using here. Before I began to work the sole, I attached several sheets of 120 grit sandpaper to the marble using a spray adhesive.

As the worn areas testify, there is a section near the toe and another at the heel that are perceptibly lower than the rest of this block plane's sole. Continue working the sole, until all or nearly all of the high spots have been reduced to the level of those low areas.

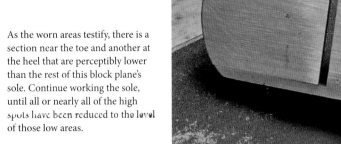

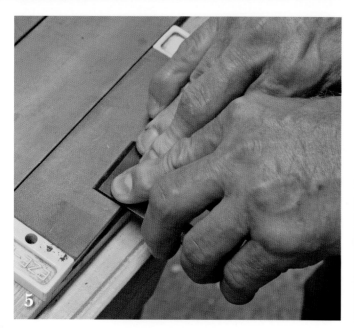

I flatten and polish the back of every iron that comes into my shop. New Lie-Nielsen and Veritas irons are flat, but not perhaps polished. The irons from new Stanleys and from all antique planes need more work. The back of the iron from the new Stanley Contractor Grade block plane I'm tuning in this chapter was in poor condition, although the bevel on the front was nicely ground. I first lapped the back of the iron with 120 grit paper, and within 15 minutes, it was flat. Then I polished the flattened area by working my way through two coarse grits: first 150 grit paper, then a 250 grit diamond plate (the one I'm using in this photo). I finished by polishing on 600 and 1200 grit diamond lapping plates.

When the tuning was finished, this little block plane performed very nicely.

Block Planes: Using a Block Plane

My guess is that you'll find at least one block plane in every woodworking shop in America, even in shops without a single bench plane. This is because these little one-handers are so good at so many miscellaneous woodshop tasks.

For example:

• Is there a bristling comb of splinters on the bottom of a plywood crosscut? In a single stroke, your block plane can cut a skewed bevel on that bristly edge, making the comb disappear.

• Want to check the color and figure of the wood underneath a rough-cut, weather-stained surface? Set the iron of your block plane to lift a rank shaving, and then take a few strokes on that rough surface. The wood underneath will appear.

• Is there a surface discontinuity where the rails and stiles of a frame-and-panel construction come together? Take a few shavings with a block plane to lower the surface of the high component until it's flush with the low component.

• Want to create perfect fit of a too-tight shelf into a pair of dadoes? Set your block plane to take whispery thin shavings and reduce the thickness at the ends of that shelf a few thousandths at a time until you achieve a perfect fit.

A block plane is the tool of choice for each of these situations—and about a thousand more known to every woodworker. One of the hallmarks of good furniture work is the absence of gaps at the intersections of parts. At least in my shop, that absence is

achieved not so much through perfect execution with the saws that cut parts initially to size but through the ability of planes (and some other tools as well) to reduce a part's dimensions one shaving at a time. Jointing and miter planes are the tools of choice for many fitting situations, but for some jobs a one-hander, like the block plane, is the best possible tool.

This Veritas block plane, made of nickel-resist ductile iron, is not only a solid workshop performer; it is also a singularly beautiful tool.

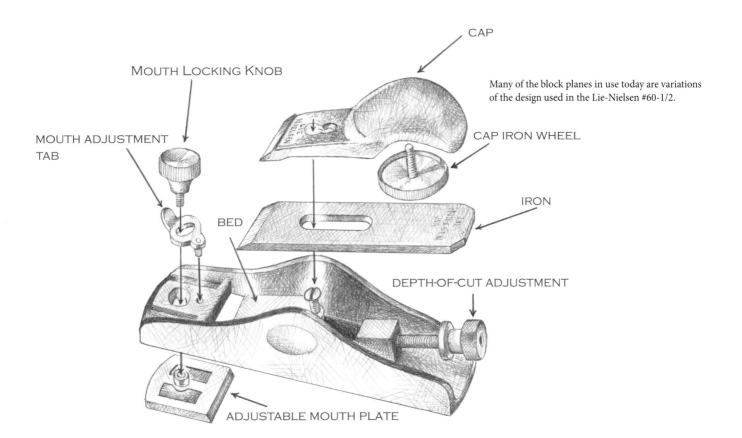

MOUTH LOCKING KNOB

MOUTH ADJUSTMENT TAB

CAP

Many of the block planes in use today are variations of the design used in the Lie-Nielsen #60-1/2.

CAP IRON WHEEL

IRON

BED

DEPTH-OF-CUT ADJUSTMENT

ADJUSTABLE MOUTH PLATE

Good workshop technique begins by matching tool to task. The long edge of this shelf-unit end is best smoothed and straightened with a moderately long plane like the Stanley #5 shown here. The shorter section at the bottom of this part is better worked with a shorter tool, like the Lie-Nielsen #60-1/2. A block plane is particularly appropriate here because that short section is end grain. Also note the direction the block plane is headed. If it worked in the other direction, the plane would pull long fibers from the back of the shelf at the end of every stroke. Working in the direction it's headed, there is no danger of breaking out long wood fibers because of the bevel at the end of the stroke.

Often the intersection of a board's top and edge will be relieved either to reduce the damage a bump can cause or simply to give that part a more pleasing appearance and feel. This can be done on a power jointer, but it's awkward to handle parts on a jointer when the fence is titled 45 degrees from the vertical. A plane—in particular a block plane—can quickly create bevels without requiring any machine set-up time and without the awkward (and possible dangerous) practice of feeding work past jointer knives at a steep angle.

When I cut out the back of this small cupboard, I made it slightly wider than the cupboard. Then, after nailing the back in place, I planed the sides of that back until I'd achieved a perfect fit.

The dadoes into which the ends of this shelf will be fit were deliberately cut slightly narrow so I could reduce the thickness of the shelf ends a bit at a time in order to arrive at a perfect fit.

The cross piece on this cupboard front was cut a bit long so I could pare down the ends until they matched the uprights perfectly.

This model-maker's block plane—the Lie-Nielsen #100—was small enough to allow me to work between the nail heads when I leveled this cupboard front.

A good block plane—like the Veritas I'm using here—makes it possible to quickly and accurately level a cabinet front.

A block plane can also be used to create bevels where surfaces intersect.

Chapter 6

Scrapers

When you're faced with a patch of grain too twisted and stubborn for your favorite smoothing plane, don't reach for a belt sander. Reach, instead, for a good scraper.

(The material in this chapter originally ran in Woodwork magazine.)

A good scraper can't replace a good plane, but in a craftsman's arsenal of wood-surfacing tools, there should be room for at least a few scrapers because there are things scrapers can do that can't be done as efficiently, or as well, by any other tools.

Although there are dozens of different kinds of scrapers for applications as disparate as scraping paint and scraping the labels from boxes (believe it or not, the Stanley #70 was designed for this singular use), for the purposes of this chapter, I'm going to look only at three categories of scrapers used in the process of preparing wood for finishing.

The first category includes those card scrapers that are nothing more than thin pieces of springy steel. This group includes those scrapers which were traditionally made from old hand saw blades, and—although some craftsmen still make their card scrapers in

this fashion—most of us buy these tools pre-cut from tool vendors in a variety of shapes. The second group includes those scrapers built around bits of springy steel which are mounted in metal bodies with mouths and soles much like planes. These bodies make it easier to control the scrapers' depth of cut, as well as to protect the user's hands from the not-inconsiderable heat generated by the friction of steel against wood. The Stanley #80 is the most prominent example of this type. The final group—the Cadillac division of the scraper universe, at least in my judgment—includes those scrapers built around inflexible pieces of steel mounted in bodies having not only mouths and soles like planes but also wooden knobs and totes. This group includes the Stanley #112, considered by many to be the tool of choice for surfacing large areas of swirling eccentric grain, and the Stanley #85 with a blade the full width of the plane body. It also includes the petite #212, which—like the #85 and despite its diminutive size—commands significant prices in the collector's market.

Part 1: How a scraper works

The cutting action of a plane is a little like the cutting action of a farmer's plow, lifting, separating, and turning aside a neatly sheared layer of wood. A scraper, on the other hand, is more like a snow blade mounted on the front end of a pick-up truck which scoots its cutting edge along the pavement, pushing ahead of it a bubbling froth of snow and ice.

Although a properly sharpened scraper will produce loose rolls of shavings similar to those produced by a plane, it does not always leave behind the clean surface of sheared wood fibers left by a plane. Even a well-tuned scraper sometimes leaves behind a faintly disturbed surface that require a bit of sanding before the application of the first coat of finish.

Some scrapers push shavings from the surface being worked with the extremely sharp and un-burred edge of an iron drawn along the grain in an approximately vertical posture. This is the kind of scraping action you get when you take a sharp butt chisel and—with the bevel facing away—drag it toward you to remove a pencil line from a wood surface. This is also the kind of scraping action Tom Lie-Nielsen recommends people try when using his trio of scraping planes: the #85, #112, and the #212.

Scrapers can also lift shavings through the use of a metal burr formed when the scraper iron's sharp edge is slightly rolled by a smooth tool of hardened steel called a burnisher. This is the method of cutting performed by hand-held scrapers and by the Stanley #80. It can also be employed with scraper planes, both those of modern manufacture and the classic Stanleys on which those modern equivalents are based.

In order to make it easier to roll a burr, scraper irons are typically made of softer steel than that used for plane irons. Many scraper irons, for example, are made from steel rated RC 55 as opposed to the steel in plane irons which are often hardened to RC 60-62.

An iron with a burr is pushed across the wood surface being smoothed with the burr on the leading edge of the iron, pushing its way across the surface. A heavy, crudely formed burr will lift a good deal of material from the wood, but will leave a disturbed surface that will require some fairly serious sanding. Such a burr is very easy to make. A smaller, more carefully formed burr will take a less aggressive cut and leave behind a cleaner surface, one requiring only the lightest sanding. In fact, if a craftsman is scrupulous about jointing, honing, and rolling the burr, a scraper iron will lift neat little rolls of shavings and leave behind a remarkably clean surface, even when working difficult species. And this is the great virtue of scrapers. When used to smooth panels composed of figured wood, they leave behind a relatively clean surface with little of the tearout that even a finely tuned smoothing plane might cause on that same figured wood.

Part 2: What to buy

Both Lee Valley Tools and Lie-Nielsen Toolworks offer good quality plane-style scrapers at reasonable prices. Plus, the internet has opened up the antique tool market so that any craftsman anywhere can find classic Stanley scrapers on many sites, including eBay.

Also, irons for the Stanley #80, as well as irons for the scraper planes, the #12, #112 and burnishers can be purchased from Hock Tools (www.hocktools.com). My Stanley #12 and my Stanley #112 are both equipped with Hock irons and both irons have performed very nicely.

I would recommend that someone with little experience with this genre of tool first consider card scrapers. A set can be purchased for as little as $15. And although you can use any smooth, rounded piece of hardened steel as a burnisher—I used to use the polished shank of a Phillips screwdriver—I think the best results are had with a dedicated burnisher, and I would recommend that tool as the second purchase. For several years I've used a vaguely-ovoid-in-cross-section burnisher I believe to be an antique Stanley (it's unmarked) that I picked up at an antique mall, and in preparing this chapter, I used a round burnisher Ron Hock sent me, a tool that produced excellent results.

The next purchase should be a Stanley #80. These antiques are still available at, it seems, every antique mall in the country for less than $50, and since there's almost nothing to get broken or out of alignment in this very simple tool, it would be hard to find one that couldn't be used, although they're often seen without irons. For many years, I've said that the #80 was my favorite tool because it gave me a way to surface cranky material without turning to my least favorite tool: the belt sander. However, in recent years, I've come to learn that the #80's smarter older brothers, the #12 and the #112, are even better at this work (so too is a card scraper, I think).

The #12 is still relatively easy to find on the antique market. There are two or three or more available almost every day on eBay for less than $80. The #112 is even better because it has a familiar, plane-like feel in operation, with a knob and tote very much like those on a smoothing plane. It is a bit pricey, however. Good user-quality #112s run in the $175-$200 range. Collector quality scrapers are, of course, much higher. For just a bit more than the user-quality Stanley #112, you can buy the Lie-Nielsen #112 which is just like the Stanley, only better, with a heavier iron and a beefier adjustment mechanism. In addition, Veritas has a scraping plane much like the #112 priced below teh Lie-Nielsen #112. Although I've never used this particular tool, I've never yet been disappointed by a Veritas product.

The #85—both the original Stanley and the Lie-Nielsen equivalent—are exceptional tools. The iron in the #85 is T-shaped so that it runs the full width of the sole, allowing you to work right up to a perpendicular surface. Plus, the knob and tote are mounted on pivots so that you can cock them to one side to protect your knuckles from that perpendicular surface.

The #212 is another matter, however—at least for me. Because of its rarity, this tool commands extraordinary prices on the antique tool market, so I've never had the opportunity to use an original, but Tom Lie-Nielsen sent me his bronze version to try, and, while it works beautifully and it's made beautifully, it's not a tool I would consider buying because—due to its size—it wouldn't get much use in my shop. The designated market of the Stanley original, I understand, consisted primarily of makers of musical instruments and makers of flyrods.

Part 3: Rolling a burr

Before I joint a scraper, I clean up the back. In the case of flexible scrapers, this means enough light sanding with 320 paper to clean off any rust or crud that might have collected there. In the case of rigid irons like those for the #112, I flatten the back on a diamond lapping plate in the same way I flatten the back of a plane iron.

A card scraper should be jointed so that its edge is 90 degrees from the front and back of the scraper, while the edges of cabinet scrapers like the #80, the #12, and the #112 are jointed so that their edges are approximately 45 degrees from the fronts of the irons. This will already be done for you if you purchase the tools new, but if you buy an antique you may need to reform the bevel.

While the bevels on the irons for the #12 and the #112 can be cleaned up on a grinding wheel just like the bevels on plane irons, the bevel on the iron for a #80 is best shaped using a file. This is because this particular (flexible) iron typically has a permanent bow across its width as a result of being bowed during use. This makes it difficult to handle the iron on a wheel. You can work the iron between your hands to take out most of the bow, but it's still very tricky to get the iron flat enough to grind it the way you would a plane iron.

I used to joint hand-held scrapers with a metal file, holding the scraper between two pieces of wood in a vise. I then worked the file back and forth along the edge, taking care to hold it so that it was perpendicular to the front and back of the scraper. I then finished up the edge by passing a stone back and forth to remove any marks the file left behind.

Now, however, I have a different arrangement. My file is mounted in a groove milled into a block of wood so that the face of the file is 90 degrees from the surface of the wood block. I then work the scraper back and forth while it's laid flat on the block of wood, pressing the scraper's edge against the file.

Once the edge is jointed, work it on the surface of a stone (I use a 1200 grit diamond lapping plate) until you've eliminated any file marks, leaving a clean crisp surface.

The next step is "work hardening/drawing" the edge. Lay the iron on the edge of your bench. Lubricate the edge you're going to work with a drop of oil. Then firmly and slowly strop the iron with the side of your burnisher, sliding the burnisher slightly toward you with each pass.

Once you've jointed and work hardened the edge, use your burnisher to roll that edge over in order to create a burr. I used to do this with the iron held between blocks of wood in a vise, but several years ago in *The Hand Plane Book*, I saw Garret Hack rolling the burr with the iron held in his hand. I tried that method and liked it, so that's the approach I now use.

To roll the burr, take several firm—but not strenuous—passes along the jointed edge with your burnisher, moving it simultaneously along the length of the edge and—fractionally—in the direction of the burr you're forming. The first pass should take place with the side of the burnisher laid flat on the jointed edge of the iron. With each successive pass, elevate by a few degrees the hand in which you're holding the burnisher.

After maybe the third pass, you should have a usable burr.

A good burr will be a tight, compact presence just below the jointed edge of your scraper, a presence you can feel with your

My scraper-iron jointer is a length of wood into which I've plowed a groove just wide enough to hold a file 90 degrees from the board. A handle allows me to hold this securely while I joint a card scraper. *Courtesy of* Woodwork *magazine.*

I push a drop of oil along the edge, then "draw" that edge with several strokes of my burnisher to prep the scraper for raising a burr. *Courtesy of* Woodwork *magazine.*

With the scraper in one hand, I push the burnisher along the prepped edge, while I'm simultaneously pushing it fractionally in the direction of the burr I'm forming. Courtesy of *Woodwork* magazine

thumb. If the burr is jagged and serrated—which will register on your thumb—it's too coarse, and you need to joint, work harden, and burnish again.

(It is possible to do work with a coarse burr, although it leaves a rough surface. Because of that, I have sometimes used a coarsely formed burr to create a texture on a wood surface.)

The formation of a proper burr is the part of the scraping process that confounds many users. Fortunately, it's a process anyone can master if they're willing to spend some time practicing the formation and use of new burrs. It you devote even a single afternoon to the process of creating one new burr after another, you will acquire a skill that will provide you with a lifetime of woodshop benefits.

Part 4: Using a card scraper

Once you've established a working burr, a card scraper is very simple to operate. Grasp it between your hands, one on either end. Impose a slight forward bow with your thumbs pushing against the center and push the scraper along the surface being smoothed. The photo illustrates the use of a burr about halfway through its useful life when it's pushing shavings mixed in with a little dust. A sharp new burr will push shavings with very little dust. An exhausted burr will push only dust.

With my thumbs pushing against the middle of the scraper, I flex the scraper and push it forward to lift shavings from the surface. *Courtesy of* Woodwork *magazine.*

Be careful. That part of the scraper you're cutting with will heat up with astonishing speed. Some Windsor chair-makers I know wear gloves when they use a card scraper on chair seats because of this heat.

If your scraper doesn't push a shaving from the surface, change the angle at which you're holding the scraper. Every burr has a slightly different angle at which it will work best, and until you find the right angle for the burr you've just made, it won't perform as it should. It helps, I think, to think of the burr—in cross section—as a fishhook, and your goal is to find the angle that will cause the tip of the hook to just barely engage the wood. Too far, and the hook digs in and stalls. Not far enough, and the rounded bottom of the hook rubs on the surface.

If, at its best angle, your scraper pushes dust rather than shavings, your burr isn't sharp enough, and you'll need to repeat the work hardening and burnishing steps in order to form a new burr.

Because of the way we hold these scrapers, there is a natural tendency to use only that part of the burr in the middle, directly below the thumbs. However, by shifting the scraper from side to side in your hands, you can take advantage of the whole width of the burr, in that way getting more mileage from a single burnishing.

Some burrs last longer than others. I've had some that cut long enough to surface a small table top. Others require replenishing more often. The good news is you don't have to repeat the jointing process each time the burr is exhausted. When the burr begins to push dust rather than shavings, simply repeat the work hardening/drawing and burnishing processes to reform the burr. Eventually, however, that won't work, and you'll have to go back all the way back to the jointing process in order to form a completely new burr.

The set of card scrapers I bought twenty years ago included one gooseneck scraper with a range of curves along its perimeter, and while I rarely use this tool, there are circumstances in which nothing else will do. For example, I sometimes cut wide cove moldings by feeding stock past a tablesaw blade at an angle. This produces a very rough cut, and there always seems to be one section of the gooseneck scraper's curves that's just right for cleaning up that cove.

The #80 is a hybrid, halfway between the card scraper and the plane-style scraper. It has a mouth and a sole like the plane-style tools, but unlike them, it is used with a bow sprung in the flexible iron.

This is a close-up of the top side of the iron in an #80. It has been given a burr which shows up as the faint dark line just at the wave crest of the bevel. Notice also the slight bow in the iron imparted by the adjustment screw. *Courtesy of* Woodwork *magazine.*

Once a burr has been rolled on the iron's 45 degree angle, slip the iron into its holder very carefully so that the burr isn't disturbed by contact with the scraper body. Then slide a sheet of computer paper under the leading edge of the sole. With the burr resting on the work, snug up the thumb screws on either side of the iron so that it's firmly locked in place at that depth. Finally, turn the adjustment just enough to give the iron a slight bow across its width. Too much bow and the tool will plow a furrow in your work.

If the tool begins to cut less well, you can increase the depth of cut by tightening the adjustment thumbscrew just a bit to increase the bow. When that fails to produce the desired result, it's time to pull the iron and reform the burr.

The #80 can quickly level a board showing curly figure, but mine, at least, tends to leave a fairly disturbed surface, more so than a card scraper with a nice tight burr. *Courtesy of* Woodwork *magazine.*

Part 5: Using the #112

Tom Lie-Nielsen recommends that purchasers of his plane-style scrapers (the #112, the #212, and the #85) try them without a burr before they roll a burr on their irons, and they will work very nicely in this way. In fact, the three I tested all produced shavings right out of the box. All I had to do was set the depth on the iron, a process accomplished by placing a sheet of paper under the front half of the tool's sole as illustrated in the photo at the top left of the next page.

You may, however, choose to put a burr on your plane-style scrapers, and many users think they work better this way.

The depth of cut can be fine-tuned by changing the pitch of the irons on these plane-style scrapers. This is accomplished by loosening the wheels on the threaded adjustment shaft, moving one into the new position and then tightening the other nut until the iron and holder are trapped between the wheels. Tilt the iron forward and you increase the depth of cut. Tilt it back and you decrease the depth of cut.

There is a potential problem, however, with using the pitch change to adjust depth. If you're using your scraper with an unburred iron, that method is pretty foolproof. If, however, you're using a burred iron, you may find that changing the pitch changes the effectiveness of the burr's cutting edge. While tilting the iron forward will increase the depth of cut, it may also interfere with the burr's ability to engage the work surface at the proper angle. Scrapers don't work well on soft woods, tending to fragment those surfaces instead of lifting neat shavings. But scrapers work well on hard woods like cherry, maple, and walnut, and they leave behind remarkably clean surfaces. (I would assume scrapers work equally well on tropical hardwoods, although I don't work with those species.)

While scrapers will work against the grain and even across the grain, the best results are achieved when they're pushed in the direction of the rising grain.

Photo 3 on the next page illustrates the kind of work a well-tuned scraper can manage. I set up the shot by carefully lifting my #112 from the surface in mid-stroke. This left a portion of a shaving still attached to the surface. If you take a look at the surfaces around that shaving—all of which have been treated by the iron on the #112—you'll see that they're quite smooth. Yes, you will almost certainly have to do a little sanding to remove the faint marks left by the scraper iron and slightly roughened areas where the grain might have gotten a little swirly, but you can almost certainly eliminate the need for the coarser grits in most situations.

And in my shop, anything that allows me to reduce the amount of time I spend sanding is a good thing.

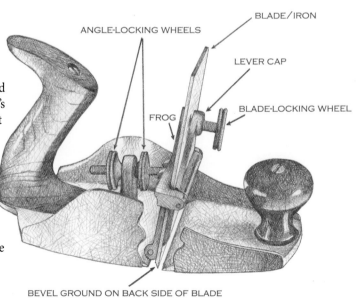

ANGLE-LOCKING WHEELS
BLADE/IRON
LEVER CAP
BLADE-LOCKING WHEEL
FROG
BEVEL GROUND ON BACK SIDE OF BLADE

This cutaway view of a #112 shows the scraper's key components.

128

To set the iron on a #112, I place a sheet of copy paper under the front half of the sole, then lower the iron until it meets the wood, then tighten the adjustment wheels. *Courtesy of* Woodwork *magazine.*

You operate a #112 just like a smoothing plane. *Courtesy of* Woodwork *magazine.*

The #112 leaves behind a surface requiring little sanding. *Courtesy of* Woodwork *magazine.*

The T-shaped iron on the #85 makes it possible to use this tool right up against perpendicular surfaces. *Courtesy of* Woodwork *magazine.*

The thin iron on the top is a hand-held scraper designed to be flexed in use. The slightly thicker iron below it is the iron for a Stanley #80. It too is flexed in use. The black iron below that is the Hock replacement iron I have not yet sharpened for my Stanley #12. The massive iron at the bottom is the iron for a Lie-Nielsen #112. *Courtesy of* Woodwork *magazine.*

Lie-Nielsen Toolworks offers high-quality cabinet scrapers in three configurations: the #112 in the rear, the #85 in the middle, and #212 in the front.

The tiny Stanley #212 is one of the pricier tools in the antique plane market. *Collection of Max Stebelton.*

Veritas Redefines the Way a Card Scraper Can Be Prepped and Used

Two years ago, I was teaching a chairmaking class at the Marc Adams School south of Indianapolis. On the first day, we were preparing slats for the steamer, and as I walked past the bench of one of the men taking the class, I noticed an odd-looking black plastic device about the size of an open wallet. I asked him about it.

"Veritas," he said. He offered it to me and stepped back so I could try it on the chair slat he was cleaning up. "It's a holder for a card scraper."

I tried it. "Incredible," I said. "No hot thumbs." I didn't want to put the scraper down because it was such a pleasure to use a good card scraper without worrying about burning the tips of my thumbs.

So several months ago, I asked Wally Wilson of Lee Valley Tools if I could try out his card-scraper holder to use for this book. Not only did he send me the holder I'd requested but also the Veritas jointer and the Veritas burnisher.

It took just one afternoon to convert me. The jointer quickly and accurately establishes the basis for a good burr, and the burnisher rolls that burr just as easily. In fact, the burnisher has a dial on it that allows you to set the carbide burnisher for the creation of burrs of from 0-15 degrees.

The Veritas scraper holder is priced at $39.50 and the burnisher, $32.50, and the jointer, $19.50.

The Veritas scraper jointer has two fences: one for 90 degree jointing and another for 45 degree jointing. In this photo, I'm jointing a 90 degree edge on a card scraper.

The Veritas burnisher consists of a short carbide rod in a holder that allows you to easily create accurate burrs at a variety of angles.

The Veritas card-scraper holder holds a card scraper for you, imposing a bow with a screw, similar to the screw on the #80. Because your thumbs don't contact the metal at the bow, they're protected from the considerable heat built up at that point of the scraper.

Drawing the Iron: Science or Fiction?

We can perform meaningful assessments of a burr in three ways. First, we can feel the burr's presence when we drag a thumb across the cutting edge of a scraper iron (and an experienced thumb can even distinguish between a coarse burr likely to leave behind a coarse surface and a finer burr likely to produce an almost-ready-for-finish surface). Second, we can assess the quality of the burr by looking at the shavings it produces. A sharp burr rolls up neat little shavings. A dull burr generates only dust. And of course we can make a final assessment by examining the surface that our burr leaves behind. If that surface is smooth and clean, free of whatever defect we intended to remove with the scraper, the burr can be deemed a good one. But because the actual metal-to-metal process of creating a burr takes place on the near-microscopic level where the unaided eye struggles to see exactly what's taking place, that process is the subject of debate among woodworkers.

Take, for example, the "work-hardening/drawing" step in the process. This is something I've always done, although I'm not entirely sure why.

If you see this as a "work-hardening" process, you might think that stroking the iron with a burnisher in the presence of an oily film causes a change in the iron on the molecular level. I have no idea if this is true or even possible, under the slight pressure and heat that can be generated in this way.

If you see this as a drawing process, you may think that the steel in a scraper iron is elastic enough for a useful extension to be pulled from it when a burnisher is dragged along its wide surface. But I'm not convinced. I do know that I can "draw" a used burr prior to rolling it for a second round of scraping. That "drawing" can be confirmed with my thumb. My thumb is not, however, a sensitive enough instrument to confirm the results of "work-hardening/drawing" on a freshly jointed and honed edge. If that process does, in fact, draw out an extension, that extension is a very, very slight one.

It makes sense to me that when the full force of a burnisher's pressure is applied to the very thin side of a scraper iron, that side will quickly deform and produce a burr (which is very easy to assess with your thumb, if not with your eyes). It makes less sense to me that a similar deformation can occur when that same burnishing pressure is spread across the much greater width of steel that is effected during the "work-hardening/drawing" process.

But I'm a creature of habit, and because I've always taken a few seconds to "work harden/draw" the iron before I roll a new burr, I'll continue to do it until somebody smarter than I am tells me to stop.

Chapter 7

Routers

For a 21st century craftsman, a "router" is something tethered to the wall with a black power cord, a tool best used with hearing protection and a chip collector. But in the latter part of the 19th century and the early 20th century, a "router" was a tool like the one you see here: cordless and silent, something that removed material in neat shavings, instead of fragmenting it into dust ejected into the air.

I'll have to admit that these little tools haven't seen much use in my shop. In the last 40 years, I've grown accustomed to cutting hardware mortises with a mallet and chisels, and I don't do any inlay work. The result is that, even though I own two Stanley #71-1/2 s and even though I have used both, I don't have a proper appreciation for the range of applications other craftsmen have found for these clever tools. In fact, with rare exceptions, the only task to which I have ever put my routers is clearing out the mortises for mouth patches on the worn soles of antique wooden planes.

The noisy, dirty routers sold today in every home-improvement superstore are descendants of much earlier tools that produced no air-borne dirt and virtually no noise. The oldest of these descendants were small wooden planes which held a narrow iron at a prescribed depth to excavate mortises, usually in the direction of the grain. These wooden routers are typically known by one of several politically incorrect names: hag's tooth, granny's tooth, old-woman's tooth. In each case, the name is a reference to the single cutter/iron that hangs—like a single tooth in an otherwise toothless woman's upper jaw—below the body of the router.

The oldest version fixed that cutter with a wedge, much like the tiny wedges that fix the slitter in wooden moving filletster planes. Later wooden routers had a metal thumbscrew that held the cutter at the correct depth.

Then in the mid-1880s Stanley Tools introduced their metal version, the #71, which holds the cutter at the prescribed depth through the use of a metal collar equipped with a thumb screw that wraps around both the cutter and a stationary metal post which rises from the router body. These—and their descendants, the #71-1/2 s—are the hand routers we see in fairly significant numbers on the antique tool market. Originally, the #71s had a pair of cutters—1/4" and 1/2" — each with a straight cutting edge. Then, in 1917, Stanley added a third cutter, a V-shaped plow. Also early in the 20th century, Stanley added a small wheel on a threaded post that could raise and lower the cutter incrementally. Later improvements included a depth stop, as well as a fence that could be attached to the bottom of the sole. By the 1890s Stanley was producing a router with an arched sole ahead of the cutter that was different than the original #71, so in 1896, they added the #71-1/2, which is essentially the same as the original #71.

The #71-1/2, like its forerunner the #71, is a simple tool with a wide sole and a cutter that projects below that sole.

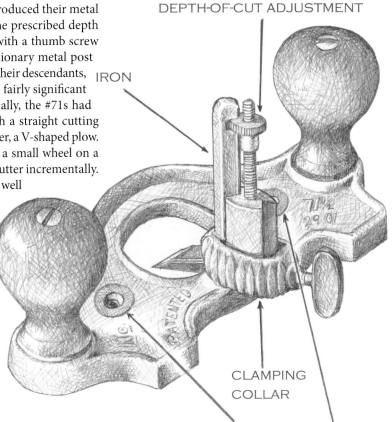

DEPTH-OF-CUT ADJUSTMENT

IRON

CLAMPING COLLAR

SCREW HOLES FOR ATTACHING WOOD SOLE OR FENCE

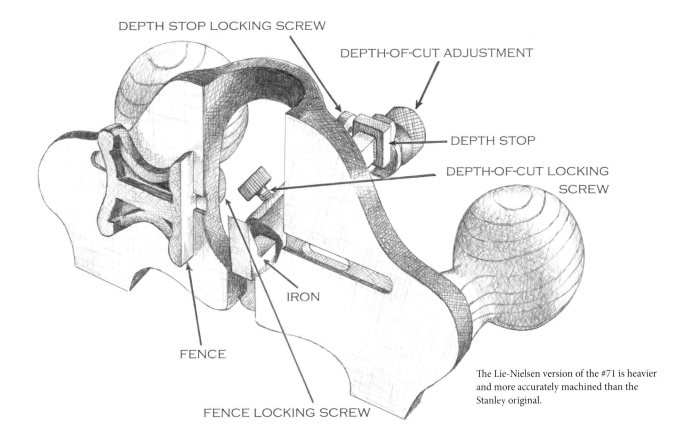

DEPTH STOP LOCKING SCREW

DEPTH-OF-CUT ADJUSTMENT

DEPTH STOP

DEPTH-OF-CUT LOCKING SCREW

IRON

FENCE

FENCE LOCKING SCREW

The Lie-Nielsen version of the #71 is heavier and more accurately machined than the Stanley original.

These tools work best when the depth of cut is increased a very small measure at a time. I excavated the mortise for this plane-sole patch in four incremental steps.

These antique routers can be found in good shape for as little as $40—that is, equipped with only a single cutter—but it might cost as much again to buy the two missing cutters. And a complete Stanley router with depth stop and fence, with a full complement of cutters, might cost $100 or more on the antique tool market. Lie-Nielsen makes an improved version of the Stanley #71, also known by the same number. The Lie-Nielsen router has every feature associated with the Stanley router in a heavier, more accurately machined package. That router is priced at $140 with a single cutter and fence. Veritas also makes a vastly improved version of the Stanley #71 which sells for $149 with three cutters and a fence.

In 1926, Stanley added a much smaller, more stripped down router, the #271. This is a plane that some of my router-using friends prefer to the heavier, bulkier #71. The Stanley #271 is less often seen on the antique tool market than the #71-1/2, and—perhaps as a result—commands a price almost as high as the #71 and #71-1/2, despite the diminutive size of the #271. Lie-Nielsen sells a small router based on the #271, priced at $80. The Veritas version of this small router is priced at $55.

Apparently, at some point, Stanley offered a router package, including the #71, with a full set of accessories, plus the #271. I've seen these antiques priced at $200.

The router leaves behind a clean-bottomed mortise.

Chapter 8

Shop-Made Planes

Making your own hand planes is a powerfully instructive process, allowing you to see more deeply into the ways the elements of a hand plane work together to produce good performance.

In the last six years, I've made probably a dozen planes. Some were more usable than others, but most ended up in the back of a shop cabinet, never taking any shavings once I'd learned what I could from the construction of those planes. But two did turn out well enough to earn spots on the racks above my bench. One—a small coffin-shaped wooden miter plane—is rarely taken down now, but that's only because I recently purchased a Lie-Nielsen #9 to use for shooting board work. If I didn't have the #9, this little wooden plane would see a lot of use. My other successful build is an infill jointer made from a Gerd Fritsche kit. This plane performs

beautifully, although its enormous weight makes it pretty tiring to use for long periods of work. Still, though, this jointer is my most successful shop-built plane. Of course, I can't take credit for that success. The quality was built into the parts Gerd sent me and into the instruction he supplied when I got stuck.

(If you're interested in tackling one of Gerd's plane kits, please visit his website at www.tradtional-handplanes.com. Gerd also sells completed planes.)

In the following photos sequences, I'll take you through the process of building each of these planes.

Infill Jointer

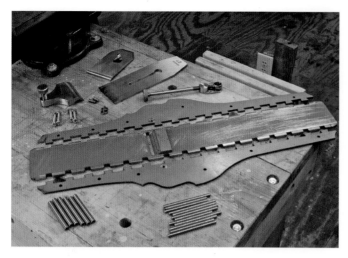

The kit Gerd Fritsche sent me contained all the metal parts necessary to build an infill jointer. This kit is also available with roughed in wood components, but I decided to use some local walnut for the wood parts of my jointer.

First, I applied a bevel to the top edges of the front and back sections of each sidewall. I left the top edges of the middle sections square, although I did clean up the marks left behind by the cutting process in those middle sections. In this photo, you can see the difference between a sidewall with a beveled edge (bottom) and one without (top).

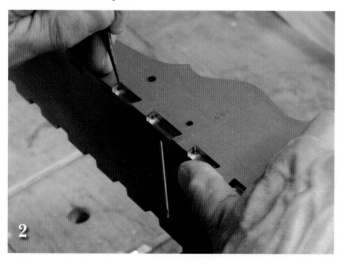

Although the tails on the sidewalls required only a little touch-up filing, the pins still had perpendicular sides when the kit arrived at my shop, so I held the sidewalls in their final positions with one hand and, with the other, marked the pin angles with a sharp stylus.

In this photo, I'm pointing to a tail socket in which the sides have been filed to the proper angles. Notice that the sockets to the left have not yet been filed to those angles.

You can see the filing work better in this close-up.

In this photo, I'm filing bevels on each side of each dovetail, a step I found difficult to visualize during my preparation for the plane build. These bevels will later be filled with metal driven into them during the peening process. At this point, the object is simply to create space for that metal.

This close-up shows the bevels on the sides of each tail.

My wood buck (the block of wood with which the shell is supported during peening) is a length of scrap walnut heart I'd planed to the exact dimensions of the cavity inside the completed shell. I then ran temporary rivets through all the rivet holes to hold the shell in the proper position on that buck. I also used C-clamps and scraps of wood screwed to the buck to assist in holding the shell components in the right alignment while I beat on the shell with a ball peen hammer. In this photo, I'm peening the ends of the tails.

The ends of the pins on the lower left have been peened which caused the metal in the extra length of each pin to flow into the bevels filed on each side of each tail. The pins in the upper right have not yet been peened. (The peened rivet is the rivet holding the throat plate. None of the other rivets should be peened at this point in the build.)

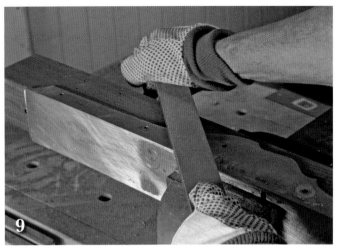

Once the pins and tails have been peened enough to push metal into the bevels on the sides of the tails and into any gaps, I began the slow work of filing the sole and the sidewalls smooth and level.

After making paper patterns for each of the three wood components—tote, bun, rear infill—I traced those onto a piece of walnut.

I resawed and planed the material for the tote, then roughed in the shape on the bandsaw and with a Forstner bit.

137

Using the tote of a Spiers panel plane as my guide, I shaped the tote with carving chisels.

The adjacent plane of the bun shape was formed with planes, chisels, rasps, and sandpaper.

I chopped out the cap screw slot in the rear infill.

I glued the tote mortise and pressed the tote into position.

After bandsawing the bun shape in one plane, I placed the bun into position and traced the sidewalls of the adjacent plane onto the bun.

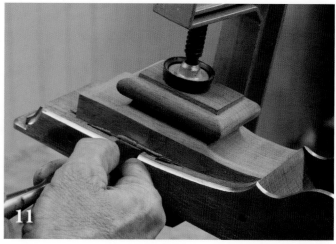

I placed the bun in the shell and fine-tuned the bun shape to match the shell.

I had some slight gaps at the front and rear of the plane (the sidewalls slipped a few thousandths during peening) so I used a punch to push metal from the sidewalls into these gaps. I then filed the bevels smooth.

With a reamer mounted in my drill press, I cut tapers for each of the rivet holes.

With the infill clamped into place, I drilled the rivet holes through the infills.

I removed the wood from the plane shell and—using the rivet holes as my guide—I drilled the larger bushing holes.

The bushings were a tight fit, so I pressed each into its hole in a wood vise.

With the rear infill permanently in place, I did a final filing of the mouth, throat plate, and wood bed.

139

After the rivets have been pushed through their bushings, the ends are driven down into the taper around each rivet hole. The surplus material is then filed off.

At this point, the plane required a lot of cosmetic work with various sandpaper grits.

With the iron/cap iron assembly in place, plus a couple of 1/8" thick spacers, I marked the side of the lever cap on the sidewalls and measured down from those marks to the locations of the holes for the lever cap screws.

With the lever cap held in place with duct tape, I drilled through the sidewalls and into the sides of the brass lever cap.

I then tapped each of the holes in the sides of the lever cap.

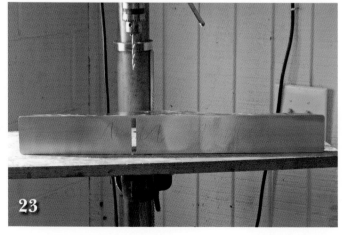

After installing the lever cap, I started the tedious process of lapping flat the enormous sole of this jointer. First, I scribbled on the sole to give me a measure of the lapping progress. The partially worn away lines you see here indicate low spots ahead of and behind the mouth.

24

25

The lapping task was more difficult than it should have been because of a slippage of the sole during peening. If I had done a better job of restraining the sidewalls during that process, my lapping would have gone much faster. As it was, I spent almost a day sliding this heavy plane back and forth on my lapping plate. I began with 60 grit abrasives. Then when the sole was flat, I switched to 120 grit, finishing up with 150 grit. The last step in the construction of this plane was sanding every metal surface with 220 grit paper, followed by 320 grit paper.

I don't know that I've ever experienced more pleasure in the construction of anything made in my shop. This jointer is not only an excellent tool; it is also an engaging piece of shop-made sculpture.

Wooden Miter Plane

You need an iron, preferably one tapering in thickness from maybe 1/8" at the top to 7/32" at the business end. Fortunately old tapered irons can be picked up cheap in nearly any flea market or antique mall. Just find a wood smoother long past its prime and scavenge the iron. Because you're making a single-iron miter plane, you can discard the cap iron that came with the smoother, but you may want to hang onto the worn-out plane body and wedge to refer to as you make your miter plane because the miter plane you make will be very much like the smoother from which you took your iron. The only significant differences will the shallower bedding angle and the absence of a cap iron on your miter plane. Before you discard the body of your worn-out flea market wood smoother, you might want to check a reference like *American Wooden Planes* to ensure that the plane you're junking doesn't have any value as a collectible.

The wood you select should be a dense, stable hardwood like the beech or birch preferred by 19th century planemakers. I choose a piece of hard maple because I had it on hand. Traditionally, the grain was aligned so that the wood that was closest to the bark on the living tree formed the sole. This doesn't mean that your plane blank must come from wood that grew near the bark. It just means that when you select a face to be the sole of your plane you should select that face that was closest to the bark in the standing tree. Also,

1

it was aligned so that—when the blank is viewed from the side—the grain lines slope from front to back. This reduces the likelihood of fibers tearing out when the plane is in use. Nevertheless, it is possible to construct a completely usable plane without the scrupulous observance of these rules. In other words, if your wood isn't perfect, go ahead and make your plane. You need to design your plane around the iron you've selected. Mine came from a fairly narrow plane so the tool I designed around it was fairly narrow, but most smoothers have wider

irons than the one I used, so design your plane to suit your iron. Remember that your design must include enough material on the outside of your wedge slots to give the plane body strength. You should have at least 3/16" of thickness at these critical places. Bandsaw the plane to shape. I opted for a coffin-shaped plane, like the worn-out miter plane from which I took my iron. Clean up your bandsaw marks with a plane, making frequent checks with a machinist's square to ensure the perpendicular relationship of side and sole.

Lay out the mortise on the top of the plane. Then indicate the bedding angle on either side. These bedding-angle lines will help you locate the mouth, the back edge of which lies on a line across the sole connecting the two bedding angle lines you made on the sides of the plane. Typically the mouth is placed about 1/3 of the way back from the toe of the plane.

Before you start to work on the excavation, take a few minutes to study the interior of an old wood smoother. While the specific details of the interior—the bedding angle, for example—will be different for different kinds of planes, the essential features of wood bench-style planes are usually the same. Most have a mouth, a throat, abutments, and wedge slots in the same approximate configuration.

Carefully, keeping your tools above the bedding slope, begin to excavate the mortise with paring and mortise chisels.

When the excavation in the top of the plane body has descended to within 3/4" of the sole, turn the plane over and begin to open the mouth. Keep the opening quite narrow at first. (And remember to stay away from the bedding slope.) I recommend a 1/8" mortise chisel for this purpose. You'll find it easier to work this mouth if you have the plane fixed in your vise at an angle that allows you to work approximately straight down into the mouth parallel to the bedding slope.

When the mortise you're chopping from the bottom of the plane meets the mortise you chopped from the top, you're ready to begin defining the bedding slope. This was traditionally done with a wide paring chisel wielded by a master planemaker. For those of us lacking the skill of that master planemaker, it's better to use a narrower paring chisel and level the bedding slope a bit at a time. A planemaker's "float" can then be used to finish the bedding slope. A float is a specialized file with oversized teeth running across its full width. This tool quickly removes irregularities in the surface, making it possible for those of us without extraordinary skill with a paring chisel to produce a perfectly flat and level bedding slope. The Clark and Williams Company (www.planemaker.com) offers for sale a variety of floats manufactured by the Lie-Nielsen Toolworks. These floats are also available direct from Lie-Nielsen Toolworks. When you're defining the bedding slope, make frequent checks of your angle by laying a small straight edge on the bed and sighting the angle from the side to see that it aligns with the layout lines you drew on the sides of the plane.

When the bedding slope is just the way you want it, you're ready to saw out the wedge slots. I use a detail trim saw sold by Woodcraft. (To produce a cleaner cut, I first tapped out the saw's set using as hammer on the sides of the saw teeth which I had rested on my tablesaw top.

The bottom cut for each slot should be made a bit above the bedding slope so you can pare the bottom of the slot down to the proper level. The top cut should be made far enough above the bottom to allow both the iron and a wedge to fit between the two cuts. I used a bevel square to mark the top cuts to ensure that each would be approximately the same distance above the bottom. With a narrow chisel, tap out the waste between the two saw cuts. Pare—or rasp—the outside edges of the wedge slots flat and smooth.

Saw out the wedge on your bandsaw. Because I like the way it looks on the wedges of some antique planes, I sawed the top curve of the wedge at a shallower angle than I used for the rest of the wedge. When I finished the cut I'm making in Photo 6, I reset the table on my bandsaw to cut 90 degrees. Then I cut the wedge blank to length. Then, before I cut out the legs on the wedge, I stood the blank on its side and cut the wedge taper on the bandsaw. It's important that you leave extra thickness when you're sawing the taper because you have to fit it later to the wedge slots. Mark the legs of the wedge and saw them out. Test-fit the wedge in the plane with the iron in place. Study the way the wedge meets the tops of the wedge slots. A tight fit here is imperative because any looseness will result in the iron chattering as it pares tough end-grain material. Pare each leg, a shaving at a time, until it fits its slot perfectly. This is the fussiest part of the planemaking process, so take your time.

Set the iron so that the cutting edge is just a bit above the sole. Tap the wedge in place with a wood mallet. Then, carefully tap the top of the iron until it just peeks through the mouth. Tap the wedge more firmly in place to fix the iron and take a test shaving. If there isn't enough iron showing, tap the top of the iron again and take another test shaving. If the shaving is too thick, hold the plane against your chest with the heel facing front and the thumb and forefinger of the hand holding the plane wrapped around the wedge and iron, then rap the heel of the plane with your wood mallet. The iron and wedge should come loose in your hand and can then be reset. The business of setting an iron in a wood plane requires "feel" which can only be achieved with practice. Take your time. Enjoy.

Chapter 9
Modern Planemakers

In the 21st century, the woodworking field is graced by a number of dedicated and talented men who are committed to the goal of raising the craft of planemaking to levels equal to or superior to anything seen in the past. This photo taken in the shop of Lie-Nielsen Toolworks near Warren, Maine, shows a completed Lie-Nielsen #4 standing in front of a half dozen #4 bodies in various stages of completion.

Planemaking is alive and well—in fact, flourishing—in the 21st century. You can see it in the high-quality manufactured planes like those sold by Lie-Nielsen Toolworks and Lee Valley Tools. You can see it also in the planes crafted by individual planemakers like Konrad Sauer and Jim Leamy. In fact, you could argue that the state of planemaking has never before reached the heights it enjoys today.

This first half of this chapter looks at planemaking as it practiced in Jim Leamy's one-off shop outside Philadelphia. The second half of the chapter looks at planemaking as it's practiced in the small factory that produces the Lie-Nielsen line near Warren, Maine.

(Variations of these two profiles appeared earlier in Woodcraft *magazine.)*

Jim Leamy:
Toolmaker Extraordinaire

When I open the door to Jim Leamy's shop and step down from the kitchen of the comfortable two-story home he shares with his wife Becky, I step into a working environment that's a little different than any other woodshop I've ever visited.

First, Jim has an elephant tusk. A real one. It's three feet long, standing on end, arcing up from a base about four inches across to a rounded tip. And then, right beside the elephant tusk, there's a supply of brass bar stock in a variety of sizes, including one monster cylinder 2-1/2" in diameter. Next to the bar stock is his supply of wood, but here, too, Jim's shop confounds expectations. Instead of the neat pile of 4/4 material I find in the shops of most of the woodworking craftsmen I've visited, Jim has short lengths and random widths of 8/4 material, which he stores standing on end leaning against one wall of the shop. There's boxwood, several kinds of rosewood (including cocobolo), aboyna burl, figured mahogany, bubinga, ebony.

Some of his machinery is recognizably intended for wood-working. For example, a big Jet tablesaw sits in the middle of the room, and a Jet thickness planer is crowded against one wall. But the room also contains equipment that would be more at home in a machine shop. His tool collection includes a milling machine, a metal lathe, and a small metal tapping machine.

Then I remind myself that this is not the shop of a craftsman who reproduces period furniture. This is the shop of a craftsman who reproduces period tools.

Even furniture makers accustomed to the high cost of good-quality hardwood will be astonished by the prices of the materials with which Jim works. The last time he found Brazilian rosewood in large enough pieces for planemaking he paid $125 a board foot, and each of the planes Jim made from that material consumed

Jim Leamy spends his workdays crafting plow planes which some plane enthusiasts believe are the finest ever made.

$350 to $400 worth of rosewood. Even the bar stock is expensive. The 18" length of 2-1/2" brass came to $140. And of course, those numbers are insignificant when they're compared to the cost of ivory. Each of the five Sandusky presentation plows Jim has under construction on the day of my visit requires the use of almost $2300 worth of ivory.

Jim's shop comfortably fills the 2-1/2-car garage in which it's housed. One wall is lined floor-to-ceiling with 19th and early 20th century plow planes, all neatly stowed parallel to the wall with the fences out. Another floor-to-ceiling rack on the adjacent wall houses his collection of wooden molding and joinery planes. Next to the molders, there's a third rack for patented metal planes, specifically the collection of Stanleys that started Jim on his hand-plane odyssey over 25 years ago.

Leamy stands at the tablesaw with five partially built Sandusky presentation plows. The five ebony bodies are aligned with their noses to the viewer. In front of each body is a nearly completed fence and a pair of nearly completed ivory arms.

Part 1: A dream job

Jim Leamy is a solidly built man in his early sixties, a man who favors blue jeans and flannel shirts worn over white t-shirts. His hair is thin but still retains the ghost of its original sandy color. His eyebrows and eyelashes are pale almost to the point of invisibility. His hands are thick-fingered, strong, and dexterous, capable of the subtlest manipulation of tools and material.

His voice is soft, uninflected, but prone to sudden staccato bursts of laughter. Although his face, like his voice, reveals little in the way of expression, it's clear that he cares passionately about his work. This isn't something he does in order to pick up a few extra bucks to supplement his military pension. (Twelve years ago, he retired after thirty years in the Air Force.) This is work that matters, not only to Jim but also to his clientele, who often pay thousands of dollars for a single Jim Leamy plane.

The truth is, this is work Jim would do even if nobody paid him to do it.

His love affair with the hand plane began over 25 years ago when—while stationed in the Seattle area—Jim began to collect antique planes. On the West Coast, there are very few wooden planes available to collectors, so at first he focused his attentions on those planes that were available: the ubiquitous Stanleys.

Not long after he began to collect planes, he began to sell them, motivated—at least in part—by the desire to make his plane-collecting hobby pay for itself. This buying and selling of antique tools is an interest he continues today. Often, when he sets up a table at a tool show to present the plows he's made, he sets up a second table on which he presents antique planes he's offering for sale.

As his collecting expanded into wooden planes, he realized there were many he wanted badly but would never be able to afford. That's when he began to look seriously at the possibility of making his own.

At that time, there was little in the way of published information about how 19th-century plane makers practiced their craft. Kenneth D. Roberts's work, *Wooden Planes in 19th-Century America,* was in print, but in the pre-Amazon era, the simple fact of a book's existence did not mean it would be known to everyone who might have an interest. And Donald Rosebook's lavish homage to the plow-plane maker's craft—*Wooden Plow Planes*—was decades away from existence.

Fortunately, by the time he had decided to make plows, Jim was an accomplished woodworker. Today, some of his antique tools are stored in meticulously executed wooden chests Jim made before his career as a planemaker had taken off. So despite the absence of

Leamy stands between two sections of his antique plane display. His collection of plow planes is shelved on the right. His collection of molding and joinery planes is shelved behind him.

historical information about the craft, Jim began his work armed, at least, with a knowledge of tools and materials.

These traits—although essential—aren't enough to launch a career as a planemaker. Just as important is a marketing plan that will put the product in front of those relatively few individuals who have the resources to buy the work, as well as the desire to commit those resources to such a purchase.

The tools Jim makes couldn't be sold at a Wal-Mart or even at a very pricey tool store. The truth is—Jim acknowledges—that except for his modest line of infill smoothing and mitre planes, none of the planes he makes will ever be used in the day-to-day operations of a woodworking shop. These plows aren't purchased by users; they're purchased by the same collectors who pay $10,000 for an antique Ohio Tool Co. plow in ebony and rosewood. This is a fate Jim's tools share with the work of other top-level tool makers. No one who lays down $6000 for a Karl Holtey smoother would ever use it to surface a table top because there are plenty of good planes under a grand for that kind of work, planes on which a scratched sole would be an irritation but not a catastrophe.

This circumstance is both good and bad. It's good because it pays men like Jim Leamy and karl Holtey enough money so that they can extract every last bit of quality from their material. It's bad because Jim's plows will never have the opportunity to do what they've been so carefully crafted to do.

Jim's marketing plan is pretty basic. He simply shows his tools at top-level antique tool shows and lets the work speak for itself. "The Midwest Tool Collectors have two big shows every year, and that's where I get most of my business, from there and the Brown auctions," he explains. "I also go up to Nashua (New Hampshire) for the two shows (the Live Free or Die Antique Tool Auctions) there every year."

Part 2: Keeping up

By now, Jim reckons that he's working at a pace comparable to that of 19th century plow plane makers like Solon Rust. "There's a lot of little things I've learned over the years to improve my production, but I'm sure it took those guys as long to make a plane as it does me." He hesitates, then adds: "They might have been a little quicker because they weren't as conscientious about quality as I think I am. A lot of them—well, they were banging them out to sell."

Typically Jim works with production runs of only three or four copies, although last year he did a run of ten: four centerwheel and six Montgomery plows. "That's just ridiculous," he says ruefully. "I had parts everywhere, and you got to keep track of them because they're not interchangeable."

On the day of my visit, Jim's working on an edition of five copies of the Sandusky presentation plow in ebony and ivory that several years ago sold at auction for a record price. These five plows are all made with authentic ivory (legally acquired from reputable dealers), although Jim does offer the same plow made with artificial ivory. With artificial ivory, the plow runs about $3000. The price is higher with the real stuff, how much higher depends on the current price of ivory.

After assembling the photos, drawings, special tools, and materials that a run of plows requires, Jim starts work by cutting out the bodies. "I'll rough-shape the handles, put the throats through, then finish the bodies off."

He next mills the blanks for the molded fences. Ironically, instead of using a plow plane to do this rough work, Jim removes the bulk of the waste with a tablesaw. And then, instead of using molding planes—as Solon Rust and his contemporaries did (according to Kenneth Roberts)—Jim creates the final profiles using scrapers. Only the tiny beads are cut in the manner of Jim's 19th century antecedents, using molding planes Jim designed and built for this purpose.

Jim estimates he can profile a fence in an hour or an hour-and-a-half, once the rough work has been done on the tablesaw.

This plane is a reproduction of a plow plane made by George Strode, the Ohio planemaker discussed in Chapter 11.

He then turns his attention to the metal work. All of his plows have metal parts which he fabricates from bar stock, but some plows—like these presentation planes—have more than others. For instance—in addition to the normal complement of thumbscrews and depth stop—this plow requires a nickel-plated brass centerwheel. Each of these parts is made one at a time, on either a milling machine or a metal-working lathe.

The centerwheels are turned from a chunk of 2-1/2" brass bar stock. The bar he's currently working from is about 18" long. He expects to get eighteen centerwheels from that bar, each of which will take an hour to turn.

He doesn't turn large lots of metal parts in advance. Instead he makes up only what he needs for the run of plows currently underway.

Construction information for the Montgomery plow—on the counter in the middle of this photo—is laid out here below the window: photos on the left, paper patterns and drawings in front of the plow, specialized tooling in the box.

Leamy spends months—and in some cases years—preparing for the reproduction of a particular model. First, he acquires good photography of the plane he intends to reproduce, shooting the plane from all angles, recording the top and bottom as well as all four sides. Whenever possible, Leamy takes those photos himself, but he has built plow planes using a photographic record supplied by a friend if Leamy didn't have access to the original plane. If he does have access, he will also take measurements. This meticulous study results in a wealth of information he stores in the form of photos, paper patterns, measurements, and special tooling associated with each of the plows he makes.

The wall of planes in his shop is not merely a decorative testament to his hobby of collecting old planes; it's also his reference encyclopedia. When he's tooling up for the fabrication of a new plow, he takes down plows made by the same maker from the same time period to study how they were put together. Even though the high-end plows Leamy reproduces are made of materials not found in the craftsman-grade plows sold by a particular maker, the manufacturing processes are often the same.

After the metal work is done for the Sandusky presentation plows, Jim focuses on the ivory. Parts are first sawn out, then—in the case of the arms—turned on a lathe. On the day of my visit, the ivory arms for these planes were turned and ready for the next step: polishing. This process removes only a negligible amount of material—perhaps a couple of thousandths—and brings the surface of the ivory to the soft sheen buyers want to see.

"The next step is to inlay the diamonds on the arms," Jim explains. After the diamonds are inlaid, he will go to work on the ivory bridges that sit between the arms atop the fence. These bridges are dovetailed into the arms in the same way the bridges on other Sandusky centerwheels are dovetailed in place.

Jim started this run of five planes in mid-December and expects to have them finished by mid-May. "I usually work 6-8 hours a day, six days a week. And sometimes, I'll come out here on Sunday for a few hours."

Part 3: A most unlikely career

Each of the plow planes produced in Jim Leamy's shop is a tangible expression of his creative drive. Some of those plows require the creation of processes not part of the shop repertoire of most 21st century woodworkers. Some require the design and fabrication of new tooling. Some require both.

But none of these plow planes constitute Jim's greatest creative accomplishment. That distinction is reserved for the career he's invented.

As a result of twelve years of unrelenting effort, Jim has moved from part-time plow-plane maker to a full-time professional in the field. This is a career he couldn't have imagined as a child, a career no high-school guidance counselor would have recommended to a young Jim Leamy.

Jim Leamy isn't the first man to make a living as a maker of plow planes. There were many who worked in the field in the 19th and early 20th centuries, but Jim Leamy is the first full-time 21st century maker of plow planes. He is also the first man of any century to make a living producing only the very best plows, from all of the very best plow-plane designers.

That's a claim even Solon Rust* couldn't make.

* Solon Rust was the master plow plane maker at H. Chapin's Son's Union Factory during the last third of the 19th century. He is credited with several important technical innovations and is possibly the best known individual in the field.

Note: Jim's full line of planes can be seen at www.jimleamyplanes.com.

In August of 2004 at the Brown 25th International Tool Auction in Harrisburg, Pennsylvania, the original on which this reproduction is based, a one-of-a-kind Sandusky presentation plow plane, sold for $114,400. That price was a record for an American tool, and it's fitting that this high-water mark was attained by a premier example of the plow plane. While a smoother was the plane a 19th-century craftsman most often pulled from his tool chest, it was the plow plane that best represented the craftsman's status. Journeymen owned simple plows in beech and boxwood with a few brass accents, while a master craftsman owned a rosewood or ebony plow with ivory details. A plow plane performs a very simple task. It "plows" grooves of varying widths and varying depths at varying distances from the edges of boards.

Grooves of different widths are accomplished through the use of irons of different widths. Traditionally, a plow plane came with a set of eight, ranging in width from 1/8" to 5/8". These irons are bedded against a metal "skate" which the iron bisects on the bottom of the plow. Depth of cut is established by a—usually—brass depth stop. The distance between the edge of the board and the groove is determined by the placement of the plow's fence which rides on a pair of arms each of which penetrates the plow plane's body. Early in the 19th-century, planemakers redesigned this tool, changing it from something strictly utilitarian into something having the visual presence of a work of art. The fence was changed from a simple slab of wood to a complicated molding requiring a number of different planes to produce. Brass was substituted for the boxwood thumbscrews and depth stop on earlier examples. And instead of the beech or birch bodies common in the early American plows, these new plows were often made of rosewood or ebony, sometimes accented with ivory and even—in some cases—bits of silver.

Miracle in Maine:
The Lie-Nielsen Toolworks

(An edited version of this chapter was published in Woodcraft magazine, January 2007)

When your name is on a sign on the front of the building and on every letterhead and every tool and every piece of packaging wrapped around every tool, you have to be "on" all the time. The man who started the company, who still conceives every product the company offers, whose presence is felt everywhere in the manufacturing plant and the company's small office area—that man can't have an off day. He has to be there, fully involved in the moment, when he greets a customer or a company employee or even a writer/woodworker like me.

Tom Lie-Nielsen—the founder, president, and head tool designer of Lie-Nielsen Toolworks—has mastered this demanding life. Our paths have crossed several times in the last five or six years, and every time I have found him to be the same, a remarkably consistent personality: patient, personable, articulate, and profoundly knowledgeable about the tool-making world.

After I tour his plant and meet some of the employees who work there each day to produce some of the most highly respected tools in the woodworking field, Tom and I walk up the stairs in the oldest building on the Lie-Nielsen campus to his second-floor office.

Well, I walk. Tom sprints, three steps at a time. At the top, Tom looks back at me—not yet halfway up—and says with an apologetic shrug, "Well, you had all that camera gear to carry."

His office is large, cluttered and unfinished. Like the Lie-Nielsen Toolworks itself, it is a work in progress. The floor is awash with boxes spilling parts, with books, with tools. One box is a wooden crate filled with perhaps a dozen very dusty LN #9s in a style he no longer makes, a style distinguished by bronze bodies and wood stuffing. I recognize the plane from a recent eBay auction in which the plane eventually sold for considerably more than its original purchase price. The crateful now in Tom's office had been in storage for several years, and the contents are waiting to be cleaned up and sold to buyers on a waiting list.

Tom's desk is not what you expect to find in the office of one of the leading figures in American craftwork. A panel of laminated hardwood has been thrown casually across three two-drawer OfficeMax-style filing cabinets with a kneehole space between two of the cabinets. Scattered across the desk top are stacks of paperwork, a phone, a laptop, and of course, tools.

Just beyond his desk is an open door leading into another large, empty, and even less finished space. That area, he later explains, will be either a shop or an employee lounge or perhaps some combination of the two.

He offers me a chair and he sits in the one behind his desk, one foot folded underneath him in a posture I could maintain only with a grimace. He seems comfortable.

"Do you mind if I smoke?" he asks.

Tom Lie-Nielsen stands in the showroom of his Warren, Maine, factory with a low-angle jack plane.

Tom Lie-Nielsen of Lie-Nielsen Toolworks, sits in his then-unfinished office in the company's manufacturing facility near Warren, Maine.

The buildings of the Lie-Nielsen campus are well integrated into the Maine landscape that surrounds them.

148

Part 1: A measured growth

Tom Lie-Nielsen has succeeded in a field which has consumed some of his competitors. The demise of the Shepherd Tool Company, despite the appeal of their product, points to the difficulty of succeeding as a maker of high-quality hand tools. It is, Tom explains, a lot like furniture making, a "very hard way to make a living." How, I ask, has he done it?

"A single-minded obsession for twenty-five years," he answers with a grin. "And when I started, I had a lot of time, and I didn't have any financial commitments—no children, no mortgage—so I was able to spend a lot of time learning how to make things."

"Plus I didn't have the internet. (Without it) I was able to pursue what I wanted to do in obscurity. Slowly, as I felt more and more capable, I exposed myself to a bigger market. In those days, when you brought out a new tool, it wasn't like everybody in the world knew like that." He snaps his fingers. "Slowly people would find out about it in catalogs and magazines. "Today the exposure a tool maker has is both a blessing and a curse. If you're in business and you're on the internet and people order something, they want it right now, and they want it perfect. That's a very hard thing to achieve immediately, right out of the gate."

"I've tried to do things slowly and methodically and deliberately."

His speech, too, is slow and methodical and deliberate. He weighs each word before releasing it. He speaks in complete, carefully composed sentences, offering each with the easy and urbane delivery of a professor at a small New England college.

At the same time he was building his product line—which began with a single tool, a variation of the Stanley #95—Tom Lie-Nielsen was also building his business skills. He realized early on that it wasn't enough simply to manufacture tools. He must also manufacture them in a way that ensured consistent quality, and he must develop mechanisms for maintaining customer satisfaction after the tools were in the hands of those customers. Plus, he has made an effort throughout his career to restrain the natural impulse to add to his catalog too many new products too quickly, an impulse he believes may have contributed to the struggles of some other contemporary tool makers.

The #95 was followed by a skew block plane and a 1/2" infill shoulder plane offered as a kit. He then turned his attention to the Lie-Nielsen version of the Stanley #1, a tool prized by collectors because of its rarity. Although it wasn't his original intention to produce Lie-Nielsen versions of the entire Stanley numbered sequence of bench planes, at some point after the appearance of the #1, Tom realized he had solved many of the technological problems in bench plane manufacture and that expanding his line to include the whole Stanley #1-#8 sequence would be a natural extension of work he had already done.

Each of the Lie-Nielsen bench planes is based on the Bed Rock line of Stanley planes, the style widely considered to be the best of the antique bench planes offered by the Stanley Company. The Bed Rock line offered the ease of adjustment Bailey-style users had previously enjoyed. Plus it added a larger area of machined metal at the frog/plane body interface, making irons bedded in a Bed Rock slightly more stable than those bedded in the other bench planes Stanley offered. These classic Bed Rocks are the tools of choice for both modern users and collectors of Stanley antique

planes. To the many functional virtues of the classic Stanley Bed Rock, Tom added improved metallurgy in the plane's five castings, thicker irons, higher machining tolerances (in particular flatness), and an improved breaker.

He also made an early and continuing commitment to aesthetics. He realized that when a craftsman spends $300-$400 on a bench plane, he wants more than efficient operation; he also wants something that appeals to the soul. As a result, Tom focuses considerable attention on his tools' aesthetics, on the way each one looks on the shelf and feels in the hand. The Lie-Nielsen bench planes, for example, include the distinctive flat-topped sidewalls consumers have come to associate with the Bed Rock line. But unlike the rosewood knobs and totes on the original Bed Rocks, the Lie-Nielsen planes feature American cherry, and many of his bench planes have bodies cast from bronze, not the iron of the Stanley original. Also every part of every Lie-Nielsen plane—even the head of every screw—is buffed and polished to a soft inviting sheen. The result is a tool that evokes the classic Stanley Bed Rock while simultaneously asserting its identity as a product of the Lie-Nielsen Toolworks.

Part 2: The ebb and flow of business

Every owner of every successful woodworking shop I've ever interviewed has confessed that there have been periods of financial struggle, periods when it was necessary to commit often borrowed financial resources in the hope that somewhere in the unseen future a planned expansion of space or manpower or product line would somehow work out.

Chris Gamage is one of three LN employees who produce scrub planes. Here, he's filing the mouth on a copy of the LN version of the Stanley #40-1/2.

The Lie-Nielsen Toolworks has experienced several such periods. "Right now, " Tom explains, "is a case in point. We've grown a great deal in the last two years physically and in terms of numbers of employees." (They currently have 80.)

The company recently completed the construction of a large building on their site in Warren, Maine. This new building was essential in order to tame the chaos that had developed in the

149

These crates of bronze frogs for #4s rest near the base of a row of Grizzly drill presses Louis Natale uses to drill holes in the frogs.

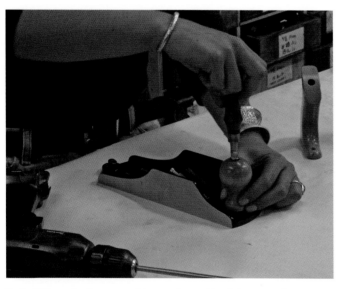

Becka Libbey, who does most of the actual assembly of planes, attaches a cherry knob to the iron body of a bench plane in the plant's assembly area.

company's manufacturing areas in recent years. This chaos was the inevitable result of trying to pack a #8-sized product line into a #4-sized manufacturing space. With the recent addition of saws and chisels to the Lie-Nielsen catalog, there simply wasn't room for the company's employees to work efficiently.

The management of Lie-Nielsen Toolworks—in particular Tom Lie-Nielsen himself and his company VP, Joe Butler—has looked for unconventional solutions to the problem of manufacturing high-quality tools at reasonable prices. For example, while you will find some high-tech (and expensive) tooling on the shop floor, particularly in the new chisel area, more often you will find either reconditioned antique machinery experiencing a second life or consumer-grade machinery employed unexpectedly in a manufacturing setting. In the bench plane area—for instance—

machinist Louis Natale drills the holes in the bronze frogs for various LN bench planes on a row of Grizzly drill presses stabilized by a few 2 x 4s. The construction is distinctly—and refreshingly—old school. It's production work the way you would sketch it out on the back of an envelope over a cup of coffee.

The company has applied this brand of unconventional thinking even to the task of adding shop space. The new manufacturing building was erected by Lie-Nielsen Toolworks employees—borrowed from their work as tool makers—in a kind of 21st century barn raising. The interior work—the drywall, the wiring, the plumbing—was then done over a period of months by a small team of LN employees on long-term loan from their regular jobs.

The company's unconventional approach to tooling and the expansion of the physical plant has been done in order to keep costs down. Plus, they don't have, in Tom's words, "a lot of managers running around." Also, the company's decision to adopt a Japanese operating style called "lean manufacturing" has allowed them to reduce materials inventory and to reduce, therefore, the need for expensive space to store that inventory. Instead of ordering—and then warehousing—large amounts of raw materials, they have standing orders at their suppliers for frequent deliveries of small batches of these materials.

The small-batch concept also extends to the way things happen on the shop floor. Instead of making 500 #7 jointers over a period of several weeks, the bench-plane group will complete a small batch on, for example, Monday, and then Tuesday switch to #8s and on Wednesday to something else. This means it isn't necessary to find storage space for large numbers, for example, of #7 frogs waiting for the next step in the manufacturing process.

Part 3: Keeping up

Although unconventional operating methods can reduce a negative cash flow, by themselves these methods won't turn red ink black. When a business expands its product line, work force, or physical plant, there is an inevitable gap between the time these expansions are funded and the time the added revenue generated by these expansions is enjoyed by the company.

For example, at the time of my visit (September of 2006), Tom is several months into the planning of three new products, the two routers and a new shoulder plane. During the months the company's design team —consisting primarily of Tom and the pattern maker Mark Swanson—works on these new tools, their efforts generate no income. During the weeks in which new shop procedures are designed and put in place to make possible the manufacture of these new tools, the efforts of the people on the shop floor involved in this process generate no income. The same is true for those employees involved in crafting catalog and website entries for these new tools. All of this effort takes place long before the company receives any income resulting from the introduction of these new products.

While the time spent developing three new products might have only a modest effect on the company's bottom line, the construction of a large new manufacturing facility—like the one LN employees recently erected—has a much more consequential effect. And when your name is on the front of the building and on every tool that goes out the door that effect is not just an abstraction on the company's balance sheets, it's also a powerful force in your emotional life.

I ask Tom how he handles those periods when his business seems to be hemorrhaging cash through every door.

"That's been one of the hardest things," he says. "I've got a commitment to my employees (he's never laid anyone off) and their families, who are relying on me—not to mention my own family. It's particularly scary in the context of the outside world.

"When the first Gulf War happened, the phones just stopped ringing. The same thing happened on 9/11."

He then makes a reference to the sleepless nights his competitors might occasionally experience, a reference that causes me to wonder how Tom sleeps during those times when much is at risk. "Larger companies in the field can afford to make mistakes I can't afford to make. I'm not saying my competitors don't have sleepless nights, but this (Lie-Nielsen Toolworks) is a small business that has gotten big but in many ways remains a small business."

Tammy O'Donnell packs and ships every product that goes out the door. Notice the racks of boxed planes on the shelves behind her. Stacks of instructional DVDs can be seen in the right foreground.

Part 4: The miracle in Maine

On the long drive to Warren, Maine, from my home in Lancaster, Ohio, as I prepped myself for my interview with Tom, the question I kept picking at was this: How has he made it work? How has he managed to conceive and then bring to maturity a business that has not only won the respect of everyone in the woodworking field but has also succeeded as a business?

I've profiled other successful tool makers, for example Jim Leamy in the previous chapter, but what Jim has created is a legacy of individual craftsmanship, of objects made by his own hands. I've never seen a work of craftsmanship from the hands of Tom Lie-Nielsen. Although I imagine him to be a first-rate workman, when you step back to take an appreciative look at what he has created, the skillful manipulation of woodworking or metal-working tools is irrelevant. What Tom has crafted isn't an object, but a company, a brand known and respected by virtually everyone in the woodworking field.

Last weekend, I was in Louisville, Kentucky, meeting with furniture maker Woode Hannah. When the subject turned to tools, Woode crossed the room, pulled open a drawer on his bench and revealed a small collection of Lie-Nielsen planes. Earlier this month—in fact the same week I visited the Lie-Nielsen Toolworks—I visited Maine furniture maker Charlie Durfee and at one point, Charlie gestured proudly at a small grouping of Lie-Nielsen planes on a shelf. Several months before that, I was in Canal-Winchester, Ohio, meeting with yet another craftsman, Charles Murray, who pulled open drawer after drawer of Lie-Nielsen bench planes and shoulder planes and block planes.

What's remarkable to me is not so much the quality of those tools—which is self evident—it's the esteem with which Lie-Nielsen Toolworks is regarded everywhere in the woodworking field, not only by Lie-Nielsen customers but even by toolmakers who are in competition with Lie-Nielsen Toolworks. Larry Williams, one of the owner/operators of Clark and Williams, a company in Eureka Springs, Arkansas, which makes high-quality wooden planes in the 19th century manner, offers this assessment of his competitor, Tom Lie-Nielsen: "Thomas is as solid and honest as his tools. Contemporary woodworkers and tool makers are indebted to his leadership in building and improving a mature woodworking technology."

On the long drive home from Warren, Maine, I think about the issue of leadership. For twenty-five years, Tom Lie-Nielsen has been in the forefront of the tool-making field. He was the first to demonstrate—for those of us working with wood in the closing decades of the 20th century—that it was possible to *manufacture* hand tools built to a high standard. When other toolmakers were unable or unwilling to take the risks that would have moved them from their garage workshops into the dedicated facilities that permit the manufacture of tools in the numbers required by a national market, Tom took those risks.

And that, I think, is the miracle in Maine. It isn't a miracle of craftsmanship; it's a miracle of risk taking in the pursuit of craftsmanship, and it's in that context that Tom's leadership has asserted itself. When his willingness to take risks was joined to the honesty Larry Williams identifies in Tom's character (and you mix in just enough luck to miss the birth of the tell-all internet), what has resulted is an iconic business that produces some of the finest woodworking tools being made in the 21st century.

At least, that's what I think, but if you're not yet convinced, try this: Head east on Highway 1 through Waldoboro, Maine. You'll pass Moody's Diner on the outside of town. Tom's place is about five miles north of the diner on the right. Look for a group of buildings painted white with red, metal roofs. There's a sign out front that says: "Lie-Nielsen Toolworks." Park your car, step into the showroom, and ask if you can test drive a couple of planes. I think you'll be impressed.

Chapter 10
Restoring Antique Planes Responsibly

Some of these antique bench plane irons have been restored to near showroom-brilliance; others have been ground and sharpened only. While some antique irons—and the planes in which they're housed—can be restored with little regard for good conservation practice, other irons and other planes—because of age or rarity or historical importance—should be given only minimal restoration. In fact, some should not be touched by anything but a dust cloth.

(The material in this chapter originally ran in Woodwork *magazine.)*

None of the antique planes I own have significant financial or historical value, so—at least in my mind—there's never been a good reason to avoid modifications that would make them more suitable for my day-to-day workshop activities. I've installed new irons and cap irons. I've replaced missing or badly damaged wedges. In several cases, I glued on fence extensions to planes I simply couldn't tame otherwise. And of course, the irons in all my antique planes have been reground and honed to suit my tastes

In short, I have treated these tools the same way I believe their original owners likely treated them, as working tools, not museum pieces, with respect but not reverence. I have always told myself this approach didn't violate their historical significance, that these modifications actually enhanced that significance by adding other chapters to the tools' history. But this is a position I've never made the effort to defend, even to myself.

Then in the February 2006 issue of *Woodwork* magazine, I wrote a story about restoring to use a Greenfield plow plane which has—like my other antique planes—little historical or financial value. In that story, I described the process of stripping off an awful coat of red paint applied by some earlier owner, of opening up the wedge mortise a bit so the wedge wouldn't stick, of sanding away rust, and of applying a coat of Waterlox to the tool's wooden parts.

That story prompted several reader letters. One of those letters—which I answered in the April 2006 issue of the magazine—asked for some guidelines on the subject of tool refinishing. I answered the question to the best of my ability, but as I answered it, I realized that I didn't know as much about this subject as I should in order to be offering advice to others.

I then asked John LaVine, the editor of *Woodwork*, if I could research and write a follow-up story for which I would develop a few very simple guidelines for myself and for anyone else who might see them as useful. This chapter—which originally ran in *Woodwork* magazine—contains the results of that research.

152

Part1: What to restore?

There's nothing insightful about the three-tiered classification system that follows. Experienced collectors have been regarding their tools in this way for many years, but for someone like me, who has never thought of himself as a collector, seeing these principles spelled out in this way has been helpful.

1. Tools that should not be used at all.

These are tools with significant historical and/or financial value. Maybe they aren't one of a kind, but they are extremely rare. These are tools which represent important parts of our craft's historical record.

Any tool made by an important (and especially infrequently seen) tool maker and any tool that comes from the tool box of an important furniture maker would fit in this category. For example, any plane made by Cesar Chelor belongs here. So too would any tool that can be linked to the tool chest of Duncan Phyfe, even if the tool is of a type that would otherwise have little value.

In addition, even undocumented tools of great age, particularly those which might represent transitions in the evolution of a class of tools should be protected under this umbrella.

These are tools which should be given a gentle cleaning and set aside.

2. Tools that may be gently used.

Although these tools are genuine antiques, they are not sufficiently rare to be revered.

For example, into this category I would fit a moving filletster I have, a plane made by Enos Baldwin (or his son Elbridge) early in the 19th century. This is a 160+-year-old-antique with an authentic maker mark. Nevertheless, it has little financial value—maybe $60-$70—and probably less historical value. This is because moving filletsters of this type are quite common. This is a plane I cleaned up, sharpened, and have since used maybe once every couple of weeks.

3. Tools that may be used—and modified—to suit your workshop needs.

These two nearly identical Strode sash planes are owned by Max Stebelton, a collector in Lancaster, Ohio. The tool on the left is encrusted with 100+ years of grime. The tool on the right has been carefully wiped with a rag soaked in denatured alcohol.

These are tools which—despite their age—are quite common and have little financial and virtually no historical value.

Although I don't know much about the manufacturing history of other kinds of tools, I do know that molding planes were churned out by the tens of thousands during the 19th century. This means that even little-used examples are still abundant—except, of course, in the case of unusual and/or large profiles.

Here, in the Midwest, on almost any day, in almost any antique mall, you can find a number of rounds, hollows and beads. And some of these are likely to be in good shape.

These are tools that can be used—I believe—with little regard for history. If, for example, you wish to bore a couple of holes through the body of an Ohio Tool Company center bead plane so that it can be used with the fence of a screw-arm plow, there really isn't any good reason not to, and the addition of such a fence can make the center bead a more useful tool.

Max Stebelton, of Lancaster, Ohio, displays his collection of wooden planes on a series of shelves and workbenches.

Part 2: Which tool fits in which category?

Deciding—at least in general terms—how to treat the tools in each category is relatively easy. It's much more difficult to figure out into which of the three categories you should place an individual tool, and unfortunately, there is no simple solution to this problem.

If I purchased a simple molder—(a hollow or round) a side bead, for example—made by any of the large companies in the field, like Ohio Tool, I would place that tool in Category 3, and I wouldn't hesitate to modify that molder as I saw fit. That's because the side bead type and the Ohio Tool brand are both very common. But in the case of a molder with an unfamiliar mark, I wouldn't even clean it until I'd done enough research to establish its rarity and value.

In the case of a molder with an unfamiliar mark, my research would begin with Emil and Martyl Pollack's *American Wooden Planes*, a comprehensive study of the makers in the field. If the mark didn't show up there, I would try references on English wooden planes. If the mark still hadn't shown up, I would temporarily assign the plane to Category 1, and hope that somewhere down the line I might learn enough about the tool's maker and its value to assign it to one of my categories.

Although I know little about the history of tools other than planes, I do know that there are respected references about many of the most commonly collected tool types. Plus Clarence Blanchard's magazine, *The Fine Tool Journal*, is an excellent source of information about many types of antique woodworking tools.

But in the case of those planes for which a maker can be identified, the identification of mark is just the first step in the process of assigning the tool to a category. Once you've identified a maker, then you need to establish rarity.

Pollack's book is helpful in this regard because it rates each of the marks associated with each maker, giving it a 1-5 "star" rating. Five stars indicates fewer than ten examples are known to possess that mark and one star indicates that 250-500 examples are known to possess that mark. In addition, the UR (unrated) designation indicates marks too rare to rate and FF (found frequently) indicates marks known to exist in very high numbers.

These stars are helpful, but they don't tell the whole story.

First, *American Wooden Planes* is an amazing piece of scholarship used by every collector of wooden planes I know, but Pollack was working with spotty and sometimes contradictory historical records, so it's important to be open to the possibility that some of the book's details could be wrong.

For example, Max Stebelton, whose collection of antique planes can be seen all through this book, developed information that the Strode listed in Pollack's book was likely not the Strode who had made the planes attributed to his hand. Pollack's book identifies the maker of the Strode planes as J. Strode from Pennsylvania, information Pollack obtained from the 1840 census. Stebelton, however, has done research that indicates the known Strode planes can be traced to a father/son pair—John and George Strode—who lived in Fairfield County, Ohio.

Second, rarity is not the only measure of value. There is also a quality Pollack identifies as the "charisma" of the maker. For example, there are Francis Nicholson marks to which Pollack assigns only two stars, indicating between 100-250 examples are known to exist, but a Francis Nicholson plane with a two-star marked is worth much, much more than almost any other two-star-mark plane in Pollack's book. This reflects the importance of Nicholson's work in the history of American plane-making.

The bun (knob) on this early Spiers panel plane exhibits the kind of transparent restoration New York City collector, Joel Moskowitz, prefers. The restorer made no attempt to conceal the repair. *Joel Moskowitz photo. Collection of Joel Moskowitz.*

These three Robert Towell infill planes from the collection of Joel Moskowitz exhibit the kind of untouched splendor most modern collectors desire. *Joel Moskowitz photo. Collection of Joel Moskowitz.*

Joel Moskowitz' favorite "user" planes—a #7 Norris shoulder plane, a post-War Norris panel plane, and a pre-War Norris A-5 smoother—are also unrestored, although he did replace the original iron in the panel plane with a Holtey replacement. *Joel Moskowitz photo. Collection of Joel Moskowitz.*

In addition, to "charisma" there is yet another quality that can influence a tool's value to both historians and collectors: beauty. And while this term is even more subjective than "charisma," there are some tools which almost every collector views as beautiful. For instance, I think there is close to unanimous agreement among modern furniture makers that the work of top-flight contemporary plane makers—like Karl Holtey, Konrad Sauer, Wayne Andersen, or Jim Leamy—meets every conceivable criterion of beauty, this despite the fact that a stunning Wayne Andersen mitre plane can be purchased for less than a collector might pay for a battered Robert Towell antique plane of the same type.

It's not easy to assign a tool to one of the three categories listed above. The collector must simultaneously juggle issues of rarity, charisma, and beauty, balancing one against another until the collector arrives at a single classification. While this is relatively easy to do with tools on either end of the value spectrum, it's much more difficult to make assignments of those tools nearer the middle of the spectrum. Is it a 1 or 2? Is it a 2 or a 3?

My advice is to err on the side of caution. You can always put that John Denison plow plane to work someday in the future, but once you've refit the wedge, you can't put that shaving back.

Part 3: How much is too much?

For tools that fit into Category 1, that is tools that should not be used under any circumstances, I would recommend no cleaning at all, except, of course, for dusting. This is because any chemical cleaning agent—regardless how mild—will remove some of the tool's surface, and in the eyes of historians, that surface is an important element of the tool's history. If, for example, you owned a carving gouge once used by Duncan Phyffe, would you really want to obliterate the mark of his hand?

In the case of valuable tools, Joel Moskowitz, a collector of British infill planes and the owner of Tools for Working Wood (a vendor of high-quality modern tools), abhors any cleaning beyond wiping with an oily rag. He points out that the best dealers do no substantial cleaning or any polishing whatsoever: "None—I repeat none of the better dealers polish up their stuff. Clarence (Blanchard) doesn't, Pat Leach doesn't, I doubt Martin Donnelly does."

Most of the experts I consulted agreed that tools in Category 1 should only be dusted and set aside, preferably in an environment protected from fluctuations in temperature and humidity which can cause rust, as well as strong light which can both degrade surfaces and wash out color.

Many collectors and collector/users believe, however, that tools fitting into Category 2 may be cleaned with some fairly aggressive cleaning agents—although not everyone agrees on what those cleaning agents might properly be.

The Fairfield County, Ohio, collector Max Stebelton wants his tools to look clean. He rejects the notion that tools should be left untouched. "I want mine to look as if they were being used," he explains. To achieve this, he carefully wipes new acquisitions with denatured alcohol soaked into a rag. "That takes the dirt off, and it doesn't raise the grain."

Molding planes, which were given a coat of oil when they left the factory, are sometimes oiled by collectors, particularly if their surfaces look dry. In this situation, Stebelton uses a 50/50 mixture of turpentine and boiled linseed oil. "I put a coat of this on, leave it for 20-30

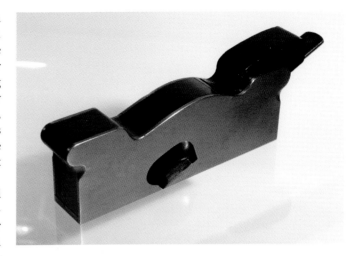

The metal on this Mathieson shoulder plane exhibits the over-zealous cleaning for which some British dealers are known. *Lee Richmond photo.*

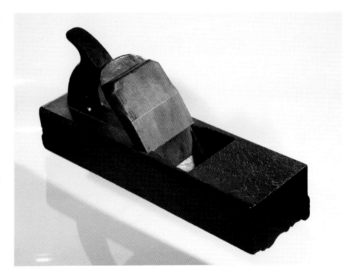

This 18th-century Lindenberger crown molder from the collection of Lee Richmond has the pristine but unrestored magnificence that all collectors wish to see in their tools. *Lee Richmond photo.*

This two-ironed crown molder from the collection of Lee Richmond has the normal array of bumps and dings and stains that are typically seen in a 200+-year-old wooden plane: however because of the importance of this plane (the maker J. Sleeper fought at Bunker Hill in the Revolutionary War) few collectors would wish to see any of these defects restored. *Lee Richmond photo.*

minutes, then wipe it off." This is something Stebelton does only once, and—according to Stebelton—this single light application of oil does not darken the wood. He observes that there are planes in his collection that he oiled 20 years ago which look as fresh today as they did on the day he initially cleaned them—without any additional attention other than occasional dusting. Stebelton also sometimes brightens his tools with a light coat of beeswax, carefully buffed out.**

Lee Richmond—a tool appraiser on the PBS series "Antiques Roadshow" and the owner of The Best Things, a company that sells antique woodworking tools, as well as high-quality modern woodworking tools—has a different approach to cleaning. He advocates the use of a mild cleanser "… like the Turtle Wax red rubbing compound, not the finer white polishing compound. It is best used sparingly on an old rag, like a sock. Work it into the fabric until it (the tool) has a burnished surface and then put more on in tiny dabs when needed."

Richmond believes it's best to apply no finishing materials more intrusive than a coat of paste wax. He recommends Behlen's Blue Label Wax.

Jim Leamy, the plow plane maker from Adamstown, Pennsylvania, is also an antique tool collector and dealer, and he, too, cleans his acquisitions: "I try to buy tools that are in excellent condition and only require minimal cleaning or restoration. But if they do (need cleaning), I normally clean with waterless hand cleaner to get the grunge off, then apply a coat of wax. Occasionally I will use 4-0 steel wool and paste wax to brighten a finish, and on very rare occasions I have wiped on a new coat of finish."

In the case of tools fitting into Category 3, I believe there is no reason to avoid any cleaning that will enhance the tool's performance and your pleasure in owning the tool. Most of my antique tools fit into this category, and I clean/restore/modify them as I see fit. And my restoration usually includes a light coat of finish. In my case, the finish I apply to my tools is the same as whatever it is I'm applying to the furniture I'm making with those tools.

Part 4: What constitutes "acceptable" restoration?

I think this question is easier for collectors to answer than it is for collector/users like me. When I buy an antique tool—while I am aware of and appreciate its history—my first thought is how I'm going to use it in my shop. I never buy a tool I can't use, no matter how interesting it might be. In fact, much of the pleasure I get from owning antique tools is the pleasure I get from using them. Yes, that Ohio Tool plow plane looks good on my shelf, but it looks even better in my hands with a shaving curling up from its iron.

I don't disparage the white-glove reverence many collectors have for the antique tools they've acquired. I think it's important that we have people who are committed to maintaining examples in untouched condition. Otherwise, we would lose an important part of our craft's historical record. I just think the world of tool collecting is wide enough to accommodate both those collectors who don't use and those collectors, like me, who do use.

This is a perspective shared by Michael Podmaniczky, the senior furniture conservator at the Winterthur Museum in Winterthur, Delaware, who offers this encouragement to users like myself: "…using something is a noble pursuit." To bolster his argument, he quotes the late John Gardner, curator at Mystic Seaport, a museum of maritime artifacts: "A boat is not a boat unless it's in the water." But then, to complicate matters, Podmaniczky adds this: "And it won't be a boat for very long if it is put in the water. Catch 22…Preservation in a dark nitrogen tank maximizes longevity, and daily use maximizes the soul and understanding of the object."

If we accept Podmaniczky's argument that antique tools—except for those in Category 1—can be (should be?) used, the next problem we users face is deciding how much "restoration" we can properly carry out in order to make that use happen.

Most experts would agree that—for tools in Category 2—it is "acceptable" to enact any reversible restoration. For example, if you want to produce a molding using a period plane, it would be "acceptable" for you to replace the plane's missing wedge in order to stick that molding. But if you need to straighten the sole of that same molder—a process that requires alteration of the plane—you would be crossing the line into "unacceptable" restoration because that bit of restoration could not be reversed.

Further, after you had used that plane to make your molding, most tool collectors believe you should either discard the replacement wedge you made or mark it in some way so that future collector/historians will know the wedge was not part of the original plane.

Replacing a part that can be removed without irreversibly altering the tool is one thing, but what about making an irreversible alteration in order to make the tool more usable? For instance, if you owned a Jacob Siegley plow plane worth maybe a grand and you wanted to use it to plow some grooves for drawer bottoms, should you reshape the wooden handle if doing so would make it better fit your hand?

The answer, I think, depends on a couple of things, one of which is the size of your wallet.

The Siegley plow has value, but it is not a one-of-a-kind plane. If you alter the one you own, there are others out there for historians to examine, so I think it would be "acceptable" for you to do it—as long as you're willing to bear the financial consequences of altering a 110-year-old antique to fit the idiosyncrasies of your hand. It's a little like lighting a cigar with a flaming $100 bill. I admire the boldness of the gesture—and I do think you should be free to make that gesture even if it makes others cringe—but I wonder about its wisdom. After all, there are other plow planes out there with little financial and historical value that you could shape to the contours of your hand.

Ideally after modifying the handle, you should note the alteration somewhere in the documentation accompanying the Siegley plow, but I think I'm talking about two different personalities here. The "you" that would alter the handle for such a reason is probably not the "you" that would note the alteration.

Part 5: Restoration "rules"?

I'm not an expert on tool restoration. I have restored to use some dozens of planes, and maybe 50 miscellaneous tools, and I'm not sure that I'd be willing to stand behind all the restoration techniques I've used. I now think that some of my restorations were excessive, even though none were enacted on valuable tools. In retrospect, I wish my approach had been more thoughtful.

In the months I've spent working on this story, I've read several books on this subject and spoken to several experts in the field, and while there is unanimity on some points—the need to preserve Category 1 tools untouched for example—there is considerable disagreement on others.

The suggestions that follow are my own. Unless specifically

noted, they don't represent the opinions of any of the experts I consulted. And of course, all of the suggestions apply only to Category 2 tools. Tools in Category 1 should not be restored at all, and tools in Category 3 may be restored with impunity.

1. Approach rust removal cautiously. Avoid wire brushes and particularly wire wheels because they leave irreversible marks on the metal.

It's possible to remove rust using electrolysis, using naval jelly, even—I've heard—using Coca-Cola, but these processes sometimes result in surfaces that look strangely barren, moonlike. I prefer metal that has been given a light sanding in order to remove the worst of the rust because—in my view—metal treated this way looks more like metal that might be found in a working shop. A light coat of wax or oil will then reduce the likelihood of the rust spreading.

Also, as Lee Richmond (and others) have noted, tool dealers in the UK are notorious for using power tools to scour away rust and to bring metal to a raging polish. Such treatment of metal is an abomination to most conservators.

Charles Murray, a furniture maker in Canal-Winchester, Ohio, who, like me, is a collector/user, removes and stores the irons of valuable bench planes in his collection. He then replaces those irons with good Hock irons which he sharpens and uses in his work. This is the kind of responsible tool stewardship I would like to practice more in my own shop.

2. I have come to believe "Less is more" in the area of wood restoration. If the tool is to be displayed, I would recommend no alteration of the wood. If there is a bit of wood missing, embrace the loss as part of the tool's history. If the tool is to be used, I would recommend only those alterations necessary to make the tool usable. Yes, to the addition of a missing molding plane wedge, properly marked, of course. No, to the reshaping of a chipped horn on a Stanley tote. Yes, to the replacement of missing boxing on the sole of a molding plane. No, to the widening of the throat.

One author in the field recommends placing wooden planes with stuck parts in an oven on low heat in order to achieve enough shrinkage to extract the stuck part. That does not seem, to me, to be good practice. First, the idea is theoretically flawed. If, for example, the intent is to shrink the width of a wedge in order to free it from a plane body, you have to remember that the plane body will be shrinking right along with the wedge that's trapped inside that body. Also, for several years, I routinely baked the rungs for my rocking chairs in an oven in order to achieve the smallest possible tenon diameter before assembling the chair, and I know that strange things can happen to wood in an oven. A part that goes in straight may come out looking like a pretzel.

I think it's best to avoid such extreme approaches.

Joel Moskowitz shared a story that I believe exemplifies the kind of responsible wood restoration I want to practice in my own shop. Several years ago, he bought a very early Spiers panel plane (See photo on page 154). The original plane—according to Moskowitz—would have had an "open" handle. This one—like many others from that period—had a very old replacement handle of the "closed" type. Fortunately, the individual who sold the plane to Moskowitz didn't replace the old replacement, which had itself become an important part of the plane's history. Second—and I think more to the point of "acceptable" wood restoration—Moskowitz notes that, at some point, part of the plane's bun (knob to us Americans) had broken off. Instead of removing that part of the original bun that remained and making an all new bun, the individual who restored this plane simply spliced in some new wood to replace only that part of the bun that had disappeared. Further, that individual didn't do what most of us would have done, that is he didn't attempt to use stain or dye to hide the fact that part of the bun had been replaced.

The tool that results from this responsible conservation is not only usable; it is also transparent. A modern collector can now see at a glance a good part of this tool's history.

3. Although most woodworking tools are made of wood and ferrous (rustable) metals, often you will find other materials used in secondary roles. For example, plow, dado, and filletster planes use brass (or brass and iron) depth stops. Ivory was often used to accent high-end tools, for example on the tips of plow plane arms, and in the case of presentation tools, like the Montgomery plow plane Jim Leamy reproduces, silver may also be found.

I have no experience restoring either ivory or silver, but I have lots of brass in my collection. At one point, I scrubbed this material relentlessly until I'd removed every bit of tarnish and, of course, patina. It turns out that brass can be sanded just like wood, and a brass thumbscrew rubbed out with 1000 grit paper looks pretty impressive and—I have to admit—out of place on a 19th century tool. So in the future, I'm going to give brass parts minimal cleaning and live with the results.

Part 6: Final thoughts

Before you clean/restore/modify any antique tools, you should take the time to place those tools into one of the three categories I've described here. Then, in the case of tools assigned to Category 2, you need to decide what philosophical approach you're going to take.

If you're a collector only, as opposed to a collector/user, you might choose to give those tools only a thorough cleaning using, perhaps, one of the cleaning techniques described in this article. If you're a collector/user, you may need to do a bit more in order to restore the tools to functionality.

This decision will require a bit of soul searching. Do you want to do a restoration in which you return those tools, as closely as possible, to showroom brilliance or do you want to retain the bumped and banged look they might have had in the tool chest of their original 18th or 19th century owners?

Obviously, if you've chosen to replicate showroom brilliance, you're going to attempt to hide the evidence of your work. In such a case, you might choose to dye replacement wood in order to better match pre-existing wood. You might choose to inflate bumps and dings with steam or hot water. If you decide to return your tools to the look they might have had in the tool kit of their original owner, you then have to decide whether to mark replacement parts as such on some hidden area or whether to indicate those repairs in whatever documentation you keep in regard to your collection.

Responsible tool ownership takes a bit of effort, but it is, I believe, better to make that effort than to deal with the regret of having done the work carelessly or thoughtlessly. I speak from experience.

Note: As I was finishing work on this chapter, two contributors expressed concern about the use of linseed oil. I was surprised by this because of the long tradition of using this product on wood tools. Michael Podmanizcky offered this comment: " It (linseed oil) polymerizes and thus changes character. Machine oil does not, and thus stays, well, oily. But that is only a problem on furniture. These are tools that want to be a little oily." In that same vein, Joel Moskowitz referred me to an internet post by Larry Williams of the planemaking firm Clark and Williams. In that post, Williams says that linseed oil will promote "fungal growth."

Chapter 11
Plane Collecting

In the 20th and 21st century, tool collectors in general, and plane collectors in particular, have assembled an important record of this country's woodworking past, identifying tools and practices that would otherwise have been lost to historians. Today, in the 21st century, I can make use of this group of 19th century wooden dado planes from my own collection because several generations of collectors before me kept alive the knowledge of a dado plane's function and operation.

Despite the fact that I own several hundred planes, I usually identify myself as a user, not a collector. To justify my position, I point to the fact that every plane I've ever purchased I bought with the intention of using in my shop. But the truth is that much of the appeal my planes have for me rests on my appreciation of them as sculptural objects with great aesthetic presence. So the truth is I am a collector, just as surely as those individuals who never sharpen the irons of their acquisitions. And I'm proud to be a collector, proud to be a part of that group of plane enthusiasts which—together in recent decades—has moved plane scholarship ahead by leaps and bounds, enabling user/collectors like me to identify the curious tools they find at auctions, in antique malls, in flea markets. Plane collectors have formed a bridge of knowledge that spans those decades in the 20th century when hand plane use was all but abandoned, reaching from the last era in which these

tools were fundamental elements of every woodworking craftsman's tool kit to the present era in which those tools are once again being given the respect they deserve.

I'm indebted to every collector who has ever added to the body of hand plane scholarship because without that scholarship, I might never have known how to use a moving filletster, what a snipe bill was designed to do, or even the intended function of hollows and rounds. In particular, I'm indebted to a collector in my hometown, a man who has collected hand planes for over forty years, a man who has worked diligently to acquire and to organize the finest collection of tools I have ever seen.

In fact the first thing I did after signing the contract for this book was to contact that collector, Max Stebelton, and ask for his help.

Max Stebelton:
Tool Collector

(This profile originally ran in The Fine Tool Journal.)

I first met Max Stebelton maybe ten years ago. A mutual friend thought he and I should meet, given my addiction to furniture making and Max's addiction to antique furniture-making tools.

But my life was busy, and so too was Max's, and we didn't meet again until the winter before last when—as part of a story I was writing for *Woodwork* magazine on tool restoration—I called him to see if I could come out and talk tools.

For me at least, this second visit was much more pleasurable than the first because—in the intervening years—I had made the decision to move away from power tools in the direction of hand tools which meant that I was then

Max Stebelton, of Fairfield County, Ohio, stands in the main room of his collection building. To the left, on the glass counter before him, is the George Strode, three-arm plow, which is the crown jewel of Stebelton's collection. Like many collectors, Stebelton began by purchasing every interesting tool he encountered. More recently, he has found himself focusing much of his attention on tools produced in his home county. One result of this focus is his discovery that planes marked J. Strode surrounded by starbursts are not the work of Joshua Strode of Chester County, Pennsylvania, as had previously been thought, but were in fact the work of John Strode, the elder in the father/son team of Fairfield County, Ohio, planemakers.

working—on a daily basis—with many antique tools. As a result, I found Max's collection and his knowledge of that collection to be much more meaningful. Despite the bitter cold of that January afternoon, he and I spent over an hour reviewing his many planes in the unheated building that houses his collection.

One of things I like best about Max's collection is its breadth. Unlike some other collectors, he doesn't specialize in a single kind of tool. Yes, he has over 800 specimens in my primary category of interest: planes. But he is an omnivorous collector, and the planes represent only a fraction of the items he has on display (and in storage). A quick turn around the main room of his collection brings you face to face with blacksmith tools, miller's tools, sawyer's tools, turner's tools, and in the collection's second room, he has a large—and very interesting—display of kitchen tools.

Part 1: The Georgian

In the early 1970s, the Fairfield (County) Heritage Association contacted Max's contracting firm about restoring a massive three-story brick Georgian near downtown Lancaster, Ohio. This enormous home was built in 1832 for the Samuel Maccracken family by Daniel Sifford using Asher Benjamin's 1830 volume *The Practical House Carpenter* as his guide. The restoration project involved much more than tidying up the paint and woodwork. Some parts of the home had to be completely rebuilt, including the 25-foot-tall columns on the west portico and the porch on the east side. In the process, Max found himself looking for antique molding planes with which he could make replacements for some of the missing architectural moldings.

His efforts to find the necessary planes were unsuccessful. In fact, he ended up having knives ground for his sticker to the required

specifications, and he produced the moldings in that way. But his search for the right molding planes had piqued his interest.

He had, in fact, already made his first two purchases of antique tools. In 1970, at a farm sale, he had purchased two very ordinary wood jack planes. These, together with a half dozen antique tools given to him by his dad, represented the extent of Max's collection at the time of his Georgian experience.

Part 2: The Strode connection

In the early years of his collecting life, Max found interesting tools everywhere he looked. There were farm sales and auctions almost every weekend; and at nearly every one, he found something that would fit into his collection. Also friends and business associates, knowing of Max's interest in antique tools, called to tell of him of tools about to go on sale, enabling him to have first choice at many local sales.

In fact, the most highly prized item in Max's collection—a George Strode plow plane decorated with ebony and ivory and brass—came to Max's attention in 2001 when a local auctioneer, Mike Clum, called to tell Max that the plane was about to come up for sale.

Realizing perhaps that it would whet Max's appetite for the plow, Clum offered to let him take the plane home for several weeks before the sale. Max accepted Clum's offer, shared the plow with his wife, Jean, and in the days leading up to the sale, carefully studied the plane. He realized that if he could acquire this masterpiece of the planemaker's craft, it would be the centerpiece of his collection, the culmination of decades of patient tool collecting.

He was concerned, however, about the price the plane might fetch at auction. He knew it was not an object he would be able to purchase for a few hundred dollars. He shared his concerns with Jean, who encouraged him to spend whatever he needed to spend in order to acquire this plane.

In the end, the plane went for much more even than Max had reckoned, but buoyed by Jean's encouragement, he offered a bid higher than any other he'd made in his career as a collector, and when the sale was over, he walked out with the Strode plow tucked under his arm.

The evening of the sale, when the plow was finally in Max's permanent possession, he received a phone call from a fellow collector who had bid against him for the Strode plow, and that collector told Max he had seen paperwork indicating that there was a Fairfield County, Ohio (Max's home county), connection to the Strode family.

Max had already demonstrated an interest in focusing his collecting on items that could be traced to Fairfield County. There are several pieces of ironwork in his collection bearing the Lancaster, Ohio, name.

When he bought the Strode plow, Max already had three planes marked J. Strode in his collection, but he had no idea these might have originated in Fairfield County. At that time, J. Strode was identified in *AWP* (*American Wooden Planes*) as a planemaker who had lived and worked in Chester County, Pennsylvania*.

Max called Mary Lou McCandlish, a secretary with the Fairfield Heritage Association. She provided him with enough information to contact a Strode descendant, Carolyn Tilley. "From her, I learned Wallace Barr had written the book *The Strode-Barr Descendancy* available at the Fairfield County Library," Max explains. "I had known Wally very well, having restored the early Barr homestead in Amanda Township (Fairfield County) for him and his wife, Doris. In his book, he stated John Strode was a furniture maker who lived in Hocking Township (also Fairfield County)." Combining this information with information from another Strode descendant, I was able to find John Strode in the 1850 census, listed as a planemaker. I also found George, John's oldest son, listed as a 'plain' maker, living in Greenfield Township, Fairfield County."

From that moment on, the acquisition of other Strode materials became a point of emphasis in Max's collecting life, and he has since purchased other Strode planes, including the spread you see before him in the photo on the previous page. His collection of Strodes now includes a pair of sash planes, a matched pair of table planes, some miscellaneous

molders, as well as the magnificent George Strode plow plane, which the modern plow plane maker Jim Leamy (profiled on Chapter 9 of this book) offers in his line of high-end reproduction plows.

Part 3: A collector's life

In 2004, Max retired after almost 50 years as a contractor and, his passion for collecting gradually came to fill up that part of his life once occupied by work.

Stebelton's collection is housed in this building which was originally the second story from a 19th-century Fairfield County inn, a building Stebelton dismantled and then reassembled on his property.

His hobby is one that now commands a large portion of his time and attention. Almost every day he is working on the collection itself or talking about it with other collectors or prowling the internet and the local library to research some of his more interesting acquisitions. Plus he travels several times a year to tool meets and sales throughout the Midwest and up and down the Eastern Seaboard, in company with good friend and fellow collector Dick Lawton. In addition, although he sees less and less in the way of collectible material at local sales and auctions, he still goes out most weekends, usually in the company of a fellow collector, to see what he can find.

He describes his interest as being first of all rooted in the tools themselves. He sees them as objects of intrinsic beauty and interest. As a man who has been involved with tools all his life Max has deep respect for the men (and sometimes women) who designed and created the objects he displays in his collection. Perhaps just as important in Max's mind are the connections he has formed with other collectors and tool enthusiasts. "I've met some really great people over the years at tool meetings," he explains. "I've made a lot of good friends."

One of his most highly prized recent acquisitions is this magnificent Type B, Stanley #41, complete with filletster bottom, a full set of irons, and—most important—the plane's original box

160

Chapter 12
Illustrated Glossary

This panel raiser from the Pleasant Hill Shaker community west of Lexington, Kentucky, was used to create the fields around raised panels.

This illustrated glossary is not intended to offer a representation of every plane being made today or every plane that can be found on the antique tool market. It is intended, instead, to provide images of some of those planes and plane components a 21st century user or collector is most likely to see. For a final identification of a particular 21st century plane, you should visit the websites of contemporary plane manufacturers or makers. The identification of antique planes may require more effort. Some types are represented by well researched websites, like the site Patrick Leach maintains for Stanley planes (www.supertool.com/StanleyBG) or the site David Lynch maintains for Record planes (www.recordhandplanes.com). In addition, there are several

wonderfully thorough books on various types of antique planes, the best example of which is John Whelan's *The Wooden Plane: Its History, Form, and Function*.

The glossary is arranged with numbered planes—like those in the Stanley sequence—occurring first. These are followed by an alphabetized listing of other planes and plane components.

(The photos in this chapter come from a variety of sources. Some were taken by photographers in the employ of the Lie-Nielsen Toolworks, others by photographers in the employ of Lee Valley Tools, others by photographers in the employ of Clark and Williams. Of the rest, most were taken by the author, a few by Joel Moskowitz.)

#1, Lie-Nielsen, Stanley: The smallest plane in the seminal Stanley sequence of bench planes, this little tyke (bottom right) resembles its bigger siblings in most details, but because of its diminutive size, it's hard for most users to manage in its theoretical two-hand configuration. *Collection of Max Stebelton.*

#4, Lie-Nielsen: This is the classic #4 size in the Lie-Nielsen line of bench planes. It's based on the Stanley #604.

#2, Lie-Nielsen: Midway between the #1 and the #3, this small bench plane is based on the Stanley #602.

#4, smoother, Veritas: Equivalent to the classic Stanley #4, this bevel-down smoother features the Veritas adjuster and a movable frog that permits users to change the width of the mouth.

#4-1/2 Lie-Nielsen, Stanley: Big brother to the #4, the #4-1/2 apparently made its first appearance in the Stanley line in 1885, offering customers a wider and heavier smoothing plane, perhaps—as Patrick Leach theorizes—to compete with the heavy English infills then being offered by Spiers, Norris, and others. This plane weighed in it at 4-3/4 pounds, a full pound heavier than the #4, according to the Stanley 1909 catalog. Lie-Nielsen currently offers a #4-1/2 (shown here on left) that is even heavier (5-1/2 pounds), although the Lie-Nielsen version is actually based on the Stanley #604 1/2 from the company's premium line of bench planes.

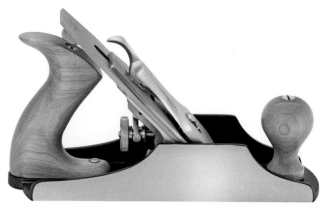

#3, Lie-Nielsen: In my view, this is the smallest bench plane that feels comfortable in the hands, a good choice for working in tight quarters.

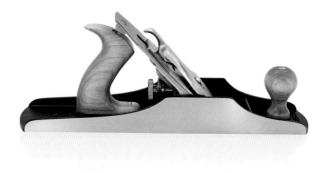

#5, Lie-Nielsen: An updated and improved version of the Stanley #5, which was the most popular jack plane in the history of metal planes.

#6, Fore plane, Veritas: This plane offers all the features of the Veritas #4 in a bigger size.

#6, Lie-Nielsen: This bench plane is the size of the traditional metal fore plane.

#5-1/4, Lie-Nielsen: This junior jack has an iron 1/4" narrower than the iron of the Lie-Nielsen #5.

#7, Lie-Nielsen: Although this is the smallest of the Lie-Nielsen jointers, it is still a heavy plane.

#5-1/4, Veritas: Built like the other bevel-downs in the Veritas line, this is the company's small jack plane.

#7-1/2, Lie-Nielsen: This plane is not based on any Stanley original. It is, instead, a Lie-Nielsen invention, a low-angle, bevel-up version of the #7.

#8, Lie-Nielsen: The largest of the Lie-Nielsen jointers, this behemoth may be too heavy for some users to handle comfortably.

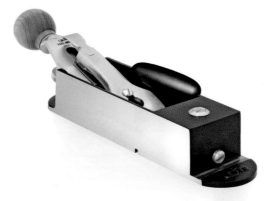

#9, Lie-Nielsen: This improved, updated version of the Stanley cabinetmaker's block plane is the miter tool of choice for many modern craftsmen.

#10-1/4", Lie-Nielsen: Based on the Stanley #10-1/4, this large rabbet plane is equipped with tilting knob and totes to enable a user to work right up to a vertical surface. It comes with slitters on both sides for work across the grain.

#10-1/2, Stanley: This carriage-maker's rabbet plane is the same size as the Stanley #4. *Collection of Max Stebelton.*

#12: The #12 is several steps up the quality ladder from the #80, Stanley's most popular scraper. Unlike the #80, the #12 is built around an inflexible iron. This iron can be adjusted to various pitches using a pair of nuts on a threaded rod attached to the pivoting blade-support assembly.

#20, Stanley: A compass plane, the #20 has a flexible steel sheet as its sole which can be adjusted to conform to round surfaces of various radii. *Collection of Max Stebelton.*

#39, Stanley: These planes—all identified with the number 39 and a width of cut—together constitute the most successful line of metal dado planes ever made.

#40, #40-1/2, Stanley: These are Stanley's scrub planes, with the #40-1/2 a bit larger than the #40. *Collection of Max Stebelton.*

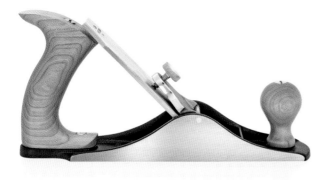

#40-1/2, Lie-Nielsen: This is a heavier modern version of the Stanley scrub plane.

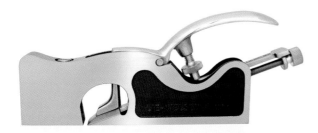

#041, Lie-Nielsen: Based on a Preston plane, this 5/8" wide tool, is the smallest of Lie-Nielsen's adjustable shoulder planes.

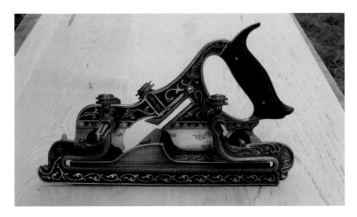

#41, Plow plane, Stanley: The Miller's patent plow is arguably the most beautiful metal plane ever manufactured. Introduced in 1871, this plane was designed to compete with the beautiful wooden plows then in widespread use. *Collection of Max Stebelton.*

#042, Lie-Nielsen: With its 3/4" wide iron, this is the medium size in Lie-Nielsen's line of adjustable shoulder planes. This plane is based on a Record original.

#45, combination plane, Stanley: When equipped with a full set of accessories, this mechanical marvel can do the work of dozens of different planes—that is, if the user is blessed with superhuman patience. An engineering and marketing masterpiece, this plane, nevertheless, is most often found with few signs of actual wear because it is extraordinarily complicated to set up and use. Plus, lacking a sole and a mouth, it isn't equipped to perform as well as the many wooden planes it was purported to replace. *Collection of Max Stebelton.*

#50, beading/combination plane, Stanley: First offered as a beading plane only, the #50 eventually became a sort of poor man's #45. *Collection of Max Stebelton.*

#51, #52, Chute board and plane, Stanley: This pairing of plane (#51) and shooting board (#52) constitutes one of most useful of the many offerings in Stanley's once enormous line. The plane, which is used on its side, fits neatly into the track on the shooting board, which is aligned in opposition to a movable fence. *Collection of Charles Murray.*

#55, Universal combination plane, Stanley: Even more complicated than the #45, this plane offers users a wide variety of potential applications obscured behind an almost impenetrable wall of instructions. Although I don't personally know anyone who has done any meaningful work with this tool, almost every tool collector I know has fantasized about owning this Victorian confection. *Collection of Max Stebelton.*

#62, low-angle jack plane, Stanley: This plane combines the end-grain cutting potential of a block plane with the size of a jack plane. Plus, it has an adjustable mouth. *Collection of Max Stebelton.*

#60-1/2, Lie-Nielsen: This well made block plane is ideal for one-handed use.

#71, Lie-Nielsen: This router is a beefier version of the Stanley #71.

#60-1/2R, Lie-Nielsen: This is the rabbeting version of the Lie-Nielsen #60-1/2.

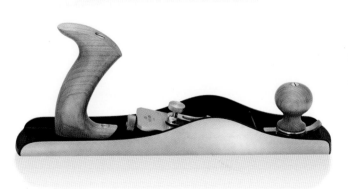

#62, Lie-Nielsen: The Lie-Nielsen #62 is an improved modern version of the Stanley #62.

#71-1/2: The #71-1/2 (shown here) and its predecessor, the #71, were the large format routers offered by Stanley. The #71-1/2 came into existence after the sole in front of the iron was arched on the #71 (in the same way as the big Lie-Nielsen router seen in this glossary in the previous photo). The #71-1/2 retained the flat sole all around the cutter. Today, these routers are typically found with only one cutter, the one fixed in the router, despite the fact that most were originally sold with a set of three: one 1/4" and one 1/2" ground straight across and a third cutter ground to a "V" shape.

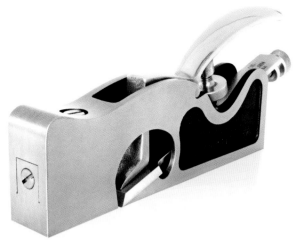

#73, Lie-Nielsen: With its 1-1/4" wide iron, this shoulder plane—based on a Record original—is the largest shoulder plane in the Lie-Nielsen catalog.

#78, Stanley: This is the most popular moving filletster (rabbet plane) ever made.

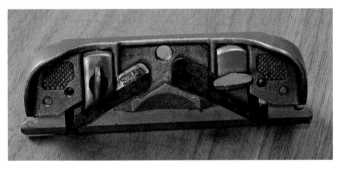

#79, Side rabbet plane, Stanley: This little plane is designed to widen rabbets, dados, and plowed grooves. *Collection of Max Stebelton.*

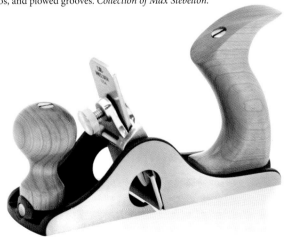

#85, Lie-Nielsen: The Lie-Nielsen #85, based on a Stanley scraper of the same number, has a T-shaped iron, which allows it to work up next to perpendicular surfaces.

#95, Lie-Nielsen: This is the Lie-Nielsen version of the Stanley of the same number.

#95, Edge trimming block plane, Stanley: The sole and fence are 90 degrees apart which makes it possible for this little plane to true up an edge that might be not quite square. *Collection of Max Stebelton.*

#98, #99, Lie-Nielsen: The right and left hand Lie-Nielsen versions of the Stanley planes of the same numbers. (See next entry.)

#99, Side rabbet plane, Stanley: This is the left hand member of a pair of side rabbet planes. They were designed to clean up or widen the sides of rabbets, dadoes, or plowed grooves in a controlled fashion. The #98 is the right hand member. *Collection of Max Stebelton.*

#100, Lie-Nielsen: A modern version of the Stanley #100, this model maker's block plane is designed to be used with the squirrel tail nestled in the palm.

#112, Lie-Nielsen: A heavyweight version of the Stanley #112, this Lie-Nielsen scraper has a more robust adjustment mechanism and a thicker iron than the Stanley original.

#100-1/2, Lie-Nielsen: This variation of the #100 has a sole radiused both across its width and from end to end, enabling it to work in concave environments.

#102, Lie-Nielsen: Based on the much lighter, Stanley #102, this block plane is the simplest in the Lie-Nielsen line of block planes.

#112, Stanley: This is the Cadillac of the Stanley line of cabinet scrapers because, in addition to all the features found on the #12, it has a plane-style knob and tote, which makes this tool as easy to operate as a plane.

#110, block plane, Stanley: This is a stripped-down, bare-bones plane, lacking the depth-of-cut adjustment and adjustable mouth of Stanley's better block planes. The handsome floral work cast into the shoe-buckle cap iron was eliminated on later versions. *Collection of Max Stebelton.*

#140, Lie-Nielsen: Based on the Stanley #140, this block plane has a skewed iron for improved cutting and a removable side so it can be used for rabbeting work.

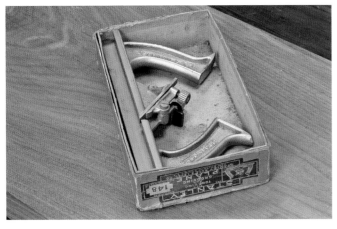

#148, Match plane, Stanley: The largest of three Stanley match planes, this plane is designed to cut a 1/4" tongue centered on 7/8" stock when aligned in one direction and a 1/4" groove centered on 7/8" stock when aligned in the other direction. *Collection of Max Stebelton.*

#164, Lie-Nielsen: This is the Lie-Nielsen version of the quite rare Stanley #164, a smoother-sized block plane.

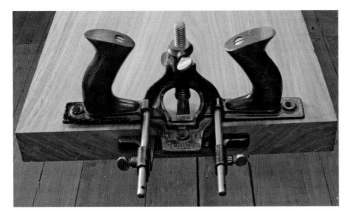

#171, Router, Stanley: This router is designed specifically to cut mortises for hardware installation, in particular for hinges. It has the capacity to cut mortise up to 3" in length and 5/16" in depth. *Collection of Max Stebelton.*

#193: Fiber board plane, Stanley: This curious plane was designed to work fiber board. *Collection of Max Stebelton.*

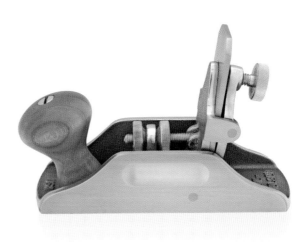

#212, Lie-Nielsen: A more robust version of the Stanley #212, this scraper is the smallest of the Lie-Nielsen scraping planes.

#212, Scraper, Stanley: This miniature scraper operates just like its bigger brothers, the #12 and the #112. In the words of the Stanley catalog, this scraper is "… designed to be used with one hand and well adapted for Violin Makers and all Mechanics requiring a light adjustable scraper." *Collection of Max Stebelton.*

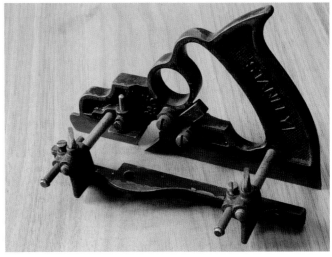

#230, Weather-strip plow plane: Designed to cut narrow grooves in window sash to receive weather-stripping. *Collection of Max Stebelton.*

169

#271: The Lie-Nielsen #271, which is based on the Stanley #271, is the smallest router Lie-Nielsen offers, just as the Stanley version was that company's smallest.

#278, Rabbet and filletster plane, Stanley: This plane can be set up to work on either the right or left side, unlike most other rabbet and filletster planes. *Collection of Max Stebelton.*

#340, Roughing plane, Stanley: This plane—intended to remove the coarse surface left behind after boards had been sawn from the log—featured an arched sole that makes contact with the surface it works only at the mouth and the heel. *Collection of Max Stebelton.*

#603, Stanley: The planes in the Stanley sequence numbered from #602-#608 were the Bedrock premium bench planes offered between 1898 and the years just prior to WWII (they didn't all disappear from the Stanley line in the same year). This photo pairs a #603 (left) with its equivalent in the Bailey-style line, the #3 (right).

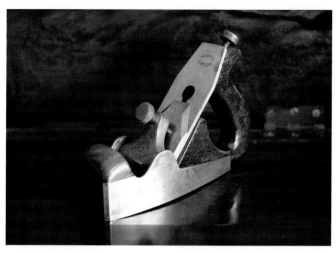

A5, Norris: This is/was the most popular of the Norris smoothers in large part because of the patented Norris adjuster.

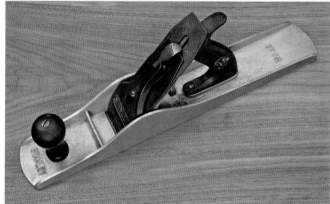

A6, Stanley: This short-lived experiment in plane metallurgy was Stanley's attempt to create a market for bench planes made from aluminum, rather than iron, bodies.

Astragal: An astragal is a bead bordered on two sides by a fillet (flat). The two molding planes shown here are designed to cut astragals.

Bailey-style bench planes: Bailey-style planes are those based on the design work of Leonard Bailey (1825-1905), in particular the design of his adjuster which allows incremental depth-of-cut movement of that cutting edge via the rotation of a knurled knob on the back of the frog. The sizes range from a #1, a smoother, the smallest, to a #8, a jointer, the largest.

In the photo, Stanley Bailey-style bench planes in sizes 3-8 are aligned behind a pair of Lie-Nielsen Bailey-style planes, a #1 and a # 4-1/2.

Bedrock planes, Stanley: Ranging from a #2 size—the #602—all the way to an #8 size—the #608—this was Stanley premium line of bench planes all featuring a large ground interface between the frog and the body of the plane. It also included a #604-1/2, a #605-1/4, and a #605-1/2. Pictured here is a #605.

Block planes: Block planes are single-iron planes (no cap iron) usually small enough to be used with one hand. The iron is bedded bevel-up at a low angle which enables the plane to excel in end grain work, for example the surfacing of butcher block tables. It's this ability that is the probable source of the name "block plane," even though many casual users of planes believe that block planes are those made from blocks of wood. Stanley literature offers a credible alternative explanation for the term "block plane." According to Stanley, these are planes designed to work end grain, a process Stanley says was once called "blocking." Because the irons in these planes are bedded bevel-up at low angles, the term is often enlarged to include a wide variety of single iron planes. Lie-Nielsen Tools, for example, lists a 22" low-angle, bevel-up jointer on its web listing of block planes.

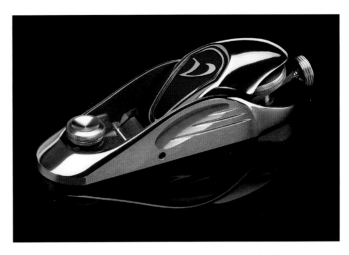

Block plane, premium, Veritas: The best in the Veritas line, this block plane has the Veritas single-knob adjuster which controls both depth of cut and lateral alignment. In addition, the plane has a moveable mouth plate that includes a set screw to "remember" a previous placement. The Lee Valley website points out that this plane is made of "a nickel-resist ductile iron."

Block plane, Veritas: This plane is exactly like the plane above except it isn't made from the same expensive material.

Bolection molding: A bolection molding bridges a joint between two different surfaces, one the framing element and the other, the framed element.

Boxing: Boxing strips are pieces of boxwood or—much less often—lignum vitae (third plane from left) inlaid in a wooden plane's sole in areas in which wear is most likely to occur, for example, the quirk beside a bead. By aligning the grain of the boxing material at an approximately 45 degree angle to the surface being worked—in this manner creating what was an essentially end-grain presentation—planemakers were able to maximize the durability of this inherently durable material.

Boxing is inlaid in many different patterns. Each of the three side beads in the middle (just to the left of the moving filletsters) represents a different boxing style. The leftmost side bead is fully boxed, the center side bead is single-boxed and the right side bead is double-boxed. Each of these variations of boxing was priced differently during the heyday of wooden molding planes. For example, in the Sandusky Tools catalog for 1925, a single-boxed 1/4 side bead was offered for $1.70. The same plane in a double-boxed configuration was $2.00, and a fully boxed 1/4" side bead was $2.20. The elaborate patterns in the two moving filletsters on the right and the two table planes on the left were even more expensive.

Bullnose, Veritas: By removing the brass toe locking knob and then upper frame, this bullnose can be converted to a chisel plane.

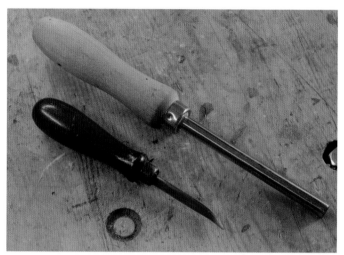

Boxwood thumb screws: Thumbscrews fashioned from boxwood—like those appearing on this Yankee plow—were used to fix the arms and depth stops on many early American plow planes.

Burnisher: These handled rods of smooth steel are used to raise a burr on a scraper. The larger burnisher in this image is a Ron Hock tool. The smaller is an antique, possibly a Stanley.

Bullnose plane: Because of the short length of sole ahead of the iron, bullnose planes can cut rabbets or mortises in tight corners. This particular example is an English infill bullnose with an ebony wedge. Much more commonly seen are the all-metal bullnoses like the Stanley #75.

Butt mortise plane: More like a router than a conventional plane, this tool is designed to cut square mortises for butt hinges.

Butt mortise, Lie-Nielsen: This is the Lie-Nielsen version of the plane described above.

172

Card scrapers: When properly jointed and burnished, card scrapers can smooth and clean up a surface too tangled to be smoothed and cleaned-up with a plane.

Cabinet pitch: The plane in the rear has its iron bedded at what is called "common pitch" (45 degrees) making it a good choice for soft woods. The plane in the foreground has its iron pitched at a much steeper angle, "cabinet pitch" (55 degrees) making it a good choice for hardwoods. "Cabinet pitch" is sometimes further broken down into three categories: "York pitch"= 50 degrees, "middle pitch"= 55 degrees, and "half pitch"= 60 degrees.

Center bead: A center-bead plane can place a bead bordered on both sides with a quirk anywhere across the width of a board or panel (only in the direction of the grain). They're usually used against a batten or plow-type fence.

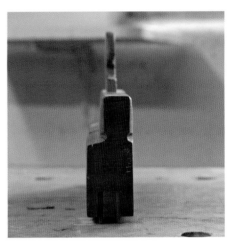

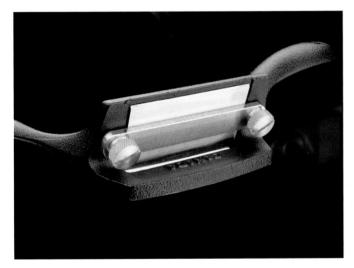

Cabinet scraper, Veritas: This is an improved and updated version of the Stanley #80.

Chairmaker's scraper, Veritas: Designed for chair work, this scraper can be used in any place its variously shaped irons might fit.

Chamfer plane: This plane is designed to cut chamfers of varying widths, the width being determined by the amount of exposed iron.

Cap irons: These secondary irons stabilize the cutting edge of primary irons and direct shavings up into the planes' throats.

Chariot plane: Forerunner of the modern block plane, these small-scale bevel-up planes are sized for one-handed work.

Chisel planes, Lie-Nielsen (#97 & #97-1/2): Tools like these are the only surfacing planes that work all the way up to a perpendicular component.

Clark and Williams is the only American company currently producing high-quality wooden planes. The planes in their line—like this single-iron smoother—are based on 18th century British originals.

Clifton planes: The British plane manufacturer Clifton produces a line of bench planes based on the Stanley series. Like the Lie-Nielsen line, these planes are characterized by heavier components and a finer degree of finish than that found on the original Stanleys.

Coffin-style plane: A form executed in both wood and metal, coffin planes are smoothers tapering slightly on both ends, with more taper toward the heel than toward the toe.

Combination plane: These planes—like the Stanley #45 pictured here—are equipped with multiple accessories to allow them to perform the work of many planes.

Complex molding plane: As opposed to a simple molding plane which cuts only one shape, a complex molding plane cuts a profile composed of several simple shapes.

Corebox plane: These clever tools were used primarily by patternmakers to cut rounded channels in the direction of the grain. *Collection of Max Stebelton.*

Cornice planes: Usually with an attached fence like the plane on the right, cornice planes were used to cut wide cornice moldings to be used where a room's walls meet the ceiling or—in exterior applications—where the walls meet the overhang of the roof. *Collection of Max Stebelton.*

Craftsman-made planes: Examples like this chisel plane were made, not by professional planemakers, but by woodworking craftsmen, who either couldn't find or couldn't afford a needed form.

Dado planes: These wooden planes, equipped with slitters on both sides, are used to sink trenches across the grain.

Depth stops: Used primarily on dado planes, plow planes, and filletster planes, these usually metal accessories establish the depth of cut.

Diamond lapping plates: A relatively recent product, these lapping plates have the distinction of being the only widely available lapping plates which will remain flat, even after many thousands of uses.

ECE bench planes: The German manufacturer, E. C. Emmerich offers a line of wooden bench planes—like the one seen here—with lignum vitae soles and a metal adjuster.

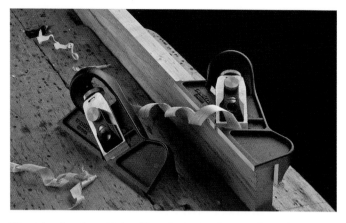

Edge-trimming planes, Veritas: These diminutive planes can be used to clean up and square up an edge.

Fence, Veritas: The Veritas fence is an updated version of an earlier Stanley fence. This attachment makes it possible for even inexperienced plane users to create edges truly perpendicular to a board's primary face.

Filletster bottom, Stanley: A filletster bottom converts a plow plane to a moving filletster. This particular bottom was designed for the Miller's Patent plow. *Collection of Max Stebelton.*

Filletster planes (moving filletster): These planes are designed to cut rabbets of varying widths both in the direction of the grain and across the grain. The plane at the top is a Stanley #78; the plane in the middle, a wooden moving filletster, and the plane in the foreground, the Veritas moving filletster.

Floats: Designed to level the throats of wooden planes, these specialized rasps have parallel rows of full-width teeth, each one perpendicular to the centerline of the rasps.

Flush plane, Veritas: Basically a plane iron with a handle (attached by a powerful magnet), the Veritas flush plane is designed to cut away anything projecting above the surface, for example, a line of glue squeeze-out.

Fore plane, wooden, Clark and Williams: In 18th and 19th century shops, the wooden fore plane did much of the rough preliminary work of surfacing boards and panels. This 21st century Clark-and Williams fore plane is equipped with a cambered iron to make rapid stock removal possible.

Fore plane, Stanley: This category of plane has produced a good bit of contradictory language in the hand-plane literature. According to Allen Sellens, author of *The Stanley Plane*, the sizes shown here—the #6 and the #606—are the fore planes in the Stanley metal bench plane sequences. This position is echoed by many British authorities. For example, Vic Taylor in *The Woodworker's Dictionary* identifies a fore plane as an "… adjustable metal bench plane, 18" long…." (Both the #6 and the #606 are 18" long.) However, the wooden fore planes listed in the Greenfield Tool Company's 1872 catalog are a good bit longer, measuring 21"-24" in length, the size of the Stanley #7 (22") and the Stanley #8 (24"). To further muddy the waters, the 17th century writer, Joseph Moxon identifies the classic wooden fore plane as one measuring 18", disagreeing with the wooden fore planes in the Greenfield catalog.

Frogs: These metal components provide beds for plane irons. Most can be detached from their planes like these shown here, through the use of screws or attachment pins.

Gage plane: Known as self-setting planes because of a unique iron-securing design, this brand was eventually purchased by Stanley which added the line to its catalog. Gage planes can be found with both wooden bodies (shown) and metal bodies.

High-angle frog, Lie-Nielsen: The bed of the Lie-Nielsen #4-1/2 in the background is 5 degrees steeper than the 45 degree bed of the Stanley in the foreground to enable the plane with the high-angle frog to more efficiently cut difficult species.

Half-inch shoulder plane, LN: The only wedged plane in the Lie-Nielsen line, it is also one of the smallest shoulder planes offered by any contemporary tool manufacturer.

Hollow and round pair: This matched hollow/round pair would have been one of a set of pairs in the tool kit of a 19th century craftsman, with the set consisting of up to 24 pairs.

Honing aides, Veritas: Each of these Veritas honing aides can enable inexperienced craftsmen to achieve sharply honed edges in a minimum of time.

Infill bench planes: These infill bench planes are much like a set that might have been used by a late 19th century British craftsman. This set consists of a Spiers smoother on the right, a pair of panel planes (Shepherd and Spiers) and a jointer (Fritsche) on the left.

Japanese planes: Japanese planes typically have their iron/cap iron assembly secured against an often metal bar. These planes are intended to be pulled toward the user, instead of being pushed away like Western planes.

Irons: The term "iron" is preferred by most plane enthusiasts when identifying the cutters/blades used in various planes.

Jointer, wooden, Clark and Williams: This single-iron 28" jointer is designed to true the edges of really long stock.

Jack plane, wooden, Clark and Williams: The single-iron Clark and Williams jack plane is designed to be used as a small-scale fore plane, managing the rough initial work on smaller boards and panels.

Jointers: The longest of the bench planes—typically over 20" in length—these tools are intended to level and true edges prior to glue up. They are also used to level large individual boards and large panels. The class is sometimes broken into two separate classes: fore or try planes in one class and jointers in the other. The fore or try planes are the shorter planes. These are used to for leveling work. Jointers comprise the longer group. These planes are used primarily for edge jointing. The wooden jointer in the rear measures 28"; the infill, 22-3/4"; the Veritas low-angle, 22"; the Stanley #7, 22"; and the Sargent VBM, 24".

Jack planes: These are intermediate bench plane sizes, halfway between smoothers and jointers. The jack in the rear is a wooden antique; the plane in the middle, a Stanley #5; the plane in the foreground, a Lie-Nielsen low-angle jack.

Lever caps: These plane components lock the iron/cap iron assembly into place. The Stanley lever caps shown here apply tension through the use of a cam under the small lever at the top of each lever cap.

178

Lignum boxing: Although most planemakers used boxwood boxing (top plane) to protect the wear points on the soles of the molding, filletster and plow planes they made, some planemakers used lignum vitae, like that seen on the bottom plane in this photo.

Low-angle jointer, Veritas: The iron in this plane is bedded at 12 degrees, making it essentially a really long block plane, but it is also a first-rate jointing plane.

Low-angle block plane, Veritas: The low-angle block plane in the rear has a bedding angle of 12 degrees, noticeably lower than the bedding angle of the standard block plane in the foreground, which has a bedding angle of 20 degrees.

Low-angle smoother, Veritas: This is essentially the same plane as the other Veritas low-angle smoother. The only functional difference is the 38 degree bevel grind which gives this plane a steeper cutting angle of 50 degrees which some users prefer for hardwoods.

Low-angle smoother, Veritas: With its iron bedded at 12 degrees like the low-angle block plane, this bigger brother is perfect for a wide variety of smoothing jobs, including end-grain work on butcher block tables.

Makers' marks: Nearly every wooden plane made in the last two centuries has a maker's mark imprinted on the nose. The mark typically provides the name of the manufacturer or the individual planemaker. It also often provides the city in which it was made.

Metallic chariot plane: Although the chariot plane is a British invention, there were also some American makers who produced them, like the Metallic plane company, one of the most important early manufacturers of metal planes in the United States. *Collection of Max Stebelton.*

Miter plane, Lie-Nielsen: Miter planes, like the Lie-Nielsen shown here, were designed specifically for miter work with both sides machined perpendicular to the sole. This allowed the user to take accurate cuts when the plane was used while it was resting on its side, for example, on a shooting board.

Miller's patent, Stanley: The Miller's patent—like this magnificent gun metal #42—is often described as the most beautiful metal plow ever manufactured. *Collection of Max Stebelton.*

Model maker's block plane, Lie-Nielsen: The model maker's block plane is designed for detail work. The squirrel tail of this plane is designed to nestle in the palm of the user's hand with the fingertips actually controlling the plane.

Miniatures: Some collectors specialize in miniatures, like the baby smoother in the foreground of this image. These planes weren't intended to be used in normal shop routine. *Collection of Max Stebelton.*

Multiform planes: These patented planes allowed a 19th century user to purchase only one tote which could be used with any number of plane bodies. *Collection of Max Stebelton.*

Natural lapping stones: While some users prefer man-made lapping and honing stones, other users prefer nature-made stones like these Arkansas and Washita stones.

Oil stone: These mandmade oil-lubricated honing stones were the sharpening abrasives of choice during much of the 20th century.

Norris-style adjuster: After its patent in 1913, the T. Norris & Son company's adjuster gave that company a competitive edge over other makers of high-quality infill planes. This modern version of that adjuster, like the original, combines lateral adjustment and depth-of-cut adjustment in the same knob.

Panel planes: Panel planes are British style infills of intermediate size, longer than smoothers and shorter than jointers. These two examples illustrate the considerable difference in length among planes in this class.

Nosing plane: These planes were designed to create a round edge on, for example, a stair tread.

Panel raising plane: These planes—sometimes called panel planes—were designed to create the field around a panel. *Collection of Max Stebelton.*

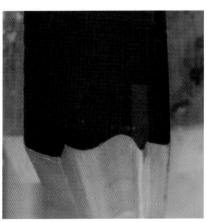

Ogee: A double curve consisting of a concave element and a convex element, the ogee is one of most important shapes in molding design. This simple form has been rendered in hundreds of variations produced by molding planes and, later, by shaper and router bits.

Pattern maker's plane: The upper body of this plane detaches from the sole, allowing that upper body to be joined with any number of soles, each with a different profile. *Collection of Max Stebelton.*

Phillips patent plow: One of the more unusual and more beautiful of the early metal planes manufactured in this country, the Phillips patent has a fence riding on a single rod, rather than the paired rods found on so many other plows. *Collection of Max Stebelton.*

Ray Iles smoother: After years of making parts for infill planes, the English tool maker Ray Iles began to manufacture infill smoothers based on the Norris A5.

Plank planes: Sold in pairs, these planes cut matching tongues and grooves in the edges of, for example, floor boards. *Collection of Max Stebelton.*

Razee-style planes: A razee plane has a tote that connects the top of the plane body with a lower step.

Plow plane, small, Veritas: Veritas offers this modern plow about the size of the Record 044. Collets inside large brass nuts lock the rods tight.

Reeding plane: Reeding planes can create two or more rows of parallel beads. *Collection of Max Stebelton.*

Rabbet plane, wooden, Clark and Williams: A simple rabbet plane is nothing more than a block of wood with a full-width iron, sometimes set on a skewed bed, designed for—among other purposes—to rough in molding shapes which will later be refined with either dedicated molders or other shaping planes. Sometimes moving filletsters are also called rabbet planes.

Routers, Lie-Nielsen, Stanley: The router on the right is a Stanley #71-1/2. The small router at the bottom is a Lie-Nielsen #271. The large router on the left is a Lie-Nielsen #71, which is an improved version of earlier manufactured routers.

Router, Millers Falls: Hand routers, like this Millers Falls example, have been manufactured by several companies. They were designed to excavate mortises for inlay work or for cleaning the bottoms of grooves. *Collection of Max Stebelton.*

Scrapers, Sargent, Stanley: Cabinet scrapers have been offered historically in many different configurations, such as two wood-bottomed scrapers you see here: a Sargent on the left and a Stanley #12-1/2 on the right. *Collection of Max Stebelton.*

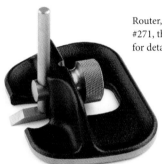

Router, small, Veritas: Like the Stanley #271, this simple small router is ideal for detail work.

Scraper, small, Veritas: Veritas makes almost a dozen different scrapers, such as the one-hander shown here.

Router, Veritas: This Veritas router is an improved version of earlier large-format routers manufactured by Stanley and Millers Falls.

Scraper, large, Veritas: This is the large scraper plane in the Veritas line, an improved version of the Stanley #112.

Routers, wood: Many early wooden routers were sawn to a D-shape with the cutter attached to the inside of the straight line of the D. These two handsome routers also have hand grips on either side. *Collection of Max Stebelton.*

Screw-arm plow: The most popular 19th century American wooden plow plane style, the screw arm plow had a fence that was locked between a threaded washer and threaded nut on each arm. It came in both toted (left) and untoted (right) configurations.

Scrub plane, Veritas, Stanley: Both the Veritas scrub plane (left) and the Stanley #40 (right) feature heavily cambered irons and wide mouths for hogging off large amounts of surface material in a short period of time.

Shoulder plane, small, Veritas: The smallest shoulder plane in the Veritas line—1/2" wide—this plane includes the Veritas adjuster.

Shooting boards: Shooting boards allow miter plane users to create joinery with a high degree of accuracy.

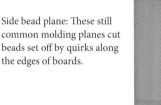

Side bead plane: These still common molding planes cut beads set off by quirks along the edges of boards.

Shoulder plane, large, Veritas: The 1-1/4" width of this shoulder plane makes it a good choice for sizing tenon cheeks. It includes the Veritas adjuster.

Skewed iron: Most planes have irons bedded at a perpendicular angle to the sides of the sole, like the plane at the bottom. The irons of some planes have irons bedded at a sharper angle to improve cutting performance.

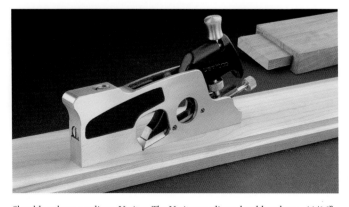

Shoulder plane, medium, Veritas: The Veritas medium shoulder plane—11/16" wide—includes the Veritas adjuster.

Snipe bills, Clark and Williams: Together with rabbet planes, as well as with hollows and rounds, snipe bills can be used to create many molding profiles.

Spill planes: These planes were designed for the singular purpose of creating tightly twisted shavings that were once used to transfer flame from one place in the home to another. *Collection of Max Stebelton.*

Thumb plane, Norris: Among the smallest offerings in the Norris catalog, these planes were identified as #31 (with lever cap) and #32 (with wedge). *Collection of Joel Moskowitz. Joel Moskowitz photo.*

Spring lines: These etched lines—extensions of a molding plane's fence and depth stop—establish the correct vertical and horizontal alignment of that plane in use.

Tongue and groove planes: Like the plank planes, these planes were made to cut the two mating parts of the tongue-and-groove joint, often used in the 19th century for flooring and siding.

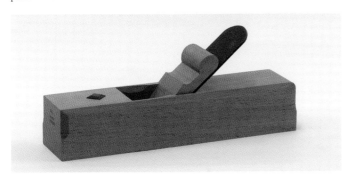

Strike block, Clark and Williams: The bevel-down iron in this miter plane is bedded at 40 degrees. This is a plane designed specifically to be used with a shooting board.

Toothing planes: These planes have irons bedded in a nearly vertical configuration. The backs of these irons are scored by narrow grooves. These grooves produce a scored surface on the work, ideal for the substrate under veneer. These planes can also be used to level wild grain with minimal tearout. The grain would then be cleaned up with a card scraper. *Collection of Max Stebelton.*

Table planes: Paired planes designed to create the male and female halves of the joints that meet between table leaves and the central panel of the table.

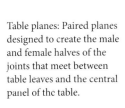

Totes: The grips for the plane users' push hand come in two basic styles: the open tote is essentially a hand-sized grip rising from the plane body (left) and the closed tote which surrounds the hand with a wood ring (right).

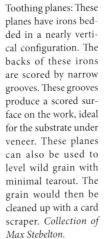

Transitional planes: These planes have wood bodies into which a metal frame is inserted. That frame includes a partial frog and an adjuster.

Try plane, wooden, Clark and Williams: This is the plane an 18th century craftsman would have reached for after the fore plane, when the craftsman was ready to do the final truing up of a board or panel.

Victor plane: This little (3-1/8" x 1-1/4") is one of Leonard Bailey's most intriguing designs. It's now being reproduced by Veritas. This, however, is the Bailey original.

Violin plane, Norris: T. Norris and Sons was an early manufacturer of tiny violin planes, which were identified in the company's catalog as numbers 1, 2, and 3. Number 1 was also—perhaps oddly—the designation for the company's largest plane, its jointer. *Joel Moskowitz photo. Collection of Joel Moskowitz.*

Waterstone: This water-lubricated honing stone became popular in this country in the closing decades of the 20th century.

Wedge-arm plow: This fence arms of this English plow plane are secured with tapering wedges fit into tapering slots cut into the plane body adjacent to the fence arm mortises.

Wedges: The irons in traditional wooden planes were secured with tapered wedges which fit into tapered wedge slots (or mortises) in the plane's body. The large wedges fit bench planes. The smaller wedges fit molding and joinery planes.

Wooden bench planes: Any 19th century American woodshop would have included in its tool inventory a group of wooden bench planes, among which would have been at least one smoother (the two planes on the right), a jack (the third plane from the right), perhaps a try or fore plane (the fourth plane from the right), and a jointer (the plane on the extreme left).

Yankee plow: This early New England plow plane style is characterized by sliding fence arms anchored in place with boxwood thumbscrews. The bottoms of the fence arms are typically mounted in shallow dadoes.

Chapter 13
Troubleshooting Your Planes

A well tuned group of hand planes can constitute the difference between failure and success in the woodshop.

The following list of problems and solutions may help you find solutions to some of the more common problems faced by hand plane users.

Bench Planes

PROBLEM #1: *No matter how far I turn my depth-of-cut adjuster on my Bailey-style plane, I can't get the cutting edge to penetrate the sole (or conversely to take a light enough cut).*

SOLUTION: You probably need to change the relationship of the iron/cap iron, either moving the cap iron slightly up or slightly down from its position on the back of the iron. Remember that the yoke on the adjuster can only move about 1/4", so if you have the lip of the cap iron set a distance from the iron's cutting edge that is outside that narrow range of movement, the cutting edge can't be positioned where you want it.

PROBLEM #2: *I have a sharp iron in my smoother, but it won't cut.*

SOLUTION #1: You might have a mouth closed too tight to pass a shaving as thick as the shaving you're taking. Raise the iron all the way into the plane. Then lower it incrementally. At some point, you should see a shaving curling up in the plane's throat.

SOLUTION #2: The bevel grind on your iron might be too steep. Lay a straightedge along the length of the sole with the cutting edge exposed. If the heel of the iron's ground bevel touches the straightedge before the cutting edge touches the straightedge, you need to regrind the bevel so that the angle is shallow enough to allow the cutting edge to strike the work before the heel of the bevel. This problem is fairly common with American miter planes which combine a low bedding angle and bevel-down configuration.

SOLUTION #3: You might have a bowed sole. If, for example, there is an upward arc in the sole measuring 1/16" in the middle of its length and the cutting edge protrudes only half that distance from the sole, you never will be able to take a shaving. Check the sole with a straightedge. If you see an arc, flatten the sole on a lapping plate.

PROBLEM #3: *My smoother is leaving behind patches of torn out wood.*

187

SOLUTION #1: The shaving you're taking might be too thick. Reduce the depth of cut.

SOLUTION #2: You might be planing in the wrong direction. Try working one of those bad patches in the other direction.

SOLUTION #3: Your mouth might be set too wide. Tighten it up.

SOLUTION #4: Try skewing the plane as you push it forward.

PROBLEM #4: *My plane takes a heavy shaving on one side and nothing on the other.*

SOLUTION #1: The problem is in the plane's lateral (side to side) adjustment. If the plane is a Bailey/Stanley type, there should be a lateral adjustment lever rising from the top of the frog just underneath the iron. Rack that lever from side to side until you can see or feel a consistent amount of exposure across the full width of the iron. If your metal plane doesn't have a lateral adjustment lever, move the top of the iron from side to side with your fingertips. (You may need to first reduce the tension on the lever cap by backing off the lever cap screw.) If you're having this problem with a wooden plane, tap the edges of the iron at the top with a wood mallet until you've achieved consistent cutting-edge exposure.

SOLUTION #2: The cutting edge might not be perpendicular to the sides of the plane. If the error is large enough, there is no lateral adjustment you can make that will achieve the correct cutting edge exposure all across your plane. The only SOLUTION in such a case is to regrind the bevel.

PROBLEM #5: *I ground a new bevel on the iron in my infill smoother (panel plane, jointer) that is perfectly perpendicular to the sides of the iron, but when I put the iron in the plane, one side of the cutting edge sticks out while the other side is still up inside the throat. And there's not enough room in the plane's metal shell to rack the iron into alignment.*

SOLUTION: This is a problem I've seen a couple of times with infill planes. In fact, I now have a Spiers panel plane with the same problem. Sometimes the dovetailed sides of the sole are not quite perpendicular to the sole, so somebody at some time in the past has ground a bevel that is not perpendicular to the sides of the iron in order to fit this particular off-kilter plane. With a square, check the perpendicularity of plane sides and sole. If you see an error, the only SOLUTION is to grind the bevel to match the slouch in your plane shell.

PROBLEM #6: *When I moved the frog of my transitional plane forward to close up an expanding mouth, I found the iron no longer rests on the wooden bed.*

SOLUTION: This is a problem Stanley recognized, and they recommended shims on the wooden bed. That's one SOLUTION. The SOLUTION I use is to treat that transitional like a wooden plane and use a patch to close the mouth, keeping the frog in its original position. However, I'm not sure that the use of shims is a bad idea. A friend of mine who had an opportunity to use a plane that James Krenov had made for his own use told me the bed of that plane was shimmed to keep the iron in the right alignment.

PROBLEM #7: *My lateral adjuster doesn't go far enough to square up the cutting edge.*

SOLUTION: The ground bevel across the bottom of the iron may have been ground at a non-perpendicular angle. Check the cutting edge with a square from both sides. If you see an error, regrind the bevel.

PROBLEM #8: *I can't get my lateral adjustment lever to work.*

SOLUTION: If you're using a metal plane, reduce the lever-cap pressure by backing off the lever cap screw. If that doesn't allow the lateral adjustment lever to move, remove the iron/cap iron assembly and try the adjuster without any pressure. If it still can't be racked, there may be rust on the bottom of the lever. Spray the base of the lever with WD-40; then let it sit for a few minutes. Try the lever again. It will probably move this time. If so, work it back and forth until you get the WD-40 to penetrate farther into the joint. You may need to spray the base of the lever a second time to get the lever working smoothly.

PROBLEM #9: *I can't turn my depth-of-cut adjuster.*

SOLUTION: When this problem occurs with a Bailey/Stanley metal plane, there usually is rust on the threaded rod on which the adjustment wheel is mounted. (I always check this before buying a plane.) Spray some WD-40 onto the threaded rod on both sides of the wheel. Let it sit a few minutes. Try turning the wheel. If it still won't turn, give it another shot of WD-40.

I would use pliers or channel locks on this wheel only as a last resort, and then I would use it cautiously with the plier's jaws wrapped in tape because most of these wheels are made from soft brass.

PROBLEM #10: *I removed the iron from my plane so I could sharpen it, and I can't get the iron and cap iron back in—at least in far enough to get the cutting edge through the mouth.*

SOLUTION: Check the iron/cap iron synchronicity. Sometimes the sides of these two parts don't match up as well as they should, with some of the cap iron's width extending past one edge of the iron, particularly if the cap iron isn't installed squarely. If you reset the cap iron until its perimeter matches the perimeter of the iron, this will likely solve the problem.

PROBLEM #11: *No matter how much I turn the tote screw, I can't get the tote to snug up.*

SOLUTION: Because of its grain alignment, over time the tote can shrink in height. If it shrinks enough, the main tote screw rod needs to be shortened in order for it to be able to draw the tote down against the plane body. The SOLUTION is to grind off a bit of length from the threaded rod that penetrates the tote.

PROBLEM #12: *Chips are getting stuck between the lip of the cap iron and the back of the iron on my Stanley bench plane.*

SOLUTION #1: Tighten the cap-iron screw in order to bring those two surfaces more tightly together.

SOLUTION #2: Check the fit of the cap iron against the back of the iron by releasing the pressure on the cap iron screw. If you see one side of the cap iron lifted away from the iron, you can correct the problem in one of two ways. First, you can abrade material from the tightly fit side of the cap iron lip. Second, if the cap iron is twisted, you may be able to straighten it with well placed blow of a hammer while the cap iron is on a solid surface, for example the ground table of your tablesaw.

Joinery Planes

PROBLEM #13: *My moving filletster (rabbet plane) leaves a slanted, stepped shoulder.*

SOLUTION: The right edge of the iron (the one adjacent to the shoulder) isn't positioned far enough to the right. Reposition the iron so that the right edge just barely peeks out from the right side of the plane. (You can clean up the slanted shoulder with a shoulder plane laying on its side on the bottom of the rabbet.)

PROBLEM #14: *I bought some loose irons for my wooden plow plane, and I can't get them to fit my plane.*

SOLUTION: Although you might think they should, not all plow plane irons will fit all plows. One way you can be sure that potential irons will fit your plow is to buy only irons stamped with the name of the planemaking firm which made your plow. Unfortunately, not every planemaking firm stamped their irons. Some of the big companies like Ohio Tool and Sandusky Tool did, but few smaller firms did. More often, the irons aren't stamped at all, or—if they are stamped—they're stamped with the name of the firm that made irons, not the firm that made the plow. The only other method is to try them in your plow before you've purchased them. But I know that's often difficult to arrange.

Molding Planes

PROBLEM #15: *The wedge in my molding plane won't come out.*

SOLUTION: Clamp the wedge in a vise. Then use a wooden mallet on the heel of the plane to drive the plane off of the wedge.

PROBLEM #16: *Whenever I use my molding plane, shavings jam up in the mouth.*

SOLUTION #1: You may have too much iron exposed. Retract it slightly.
SOLUTION #2: Be sure to clear the throat after each pass. If one loose shaving remains in the throat when you take a second pass, the two shavings together may become impacted.
SOLUTION #3: Some molding planes seem more disposed to this problem than others. If I'm using such a plane, after each pass I pull out any impacted shavings with a pair of tweezers.

PROBLEM #17: *When the depth stop on my molding plane bottoms out, half the profile is still uncut.*

SOLUTION: The profile of the iron's cutting edge doesn't match the profile of the sole. Sometimes this can be a result of an improperly aligned iron. Check to see that the iron can be aligned so that its cutting edge mirrors the sole of the plane. If it can be positioned in this way, wedge it in that position. If it can't, you're going to have to re-shape the profile so that it matches the sole.

PROBLEM #18: *My side bead only cuts a partial quirk.*

SOLUTION: Antique side bead planes often show evidence of heavy wear because there are so many applications for this profile. As a result of many re-sharpenings, that portion of the iron which is supposed to cut the quirk is worn down to a nub. The quirk boxing may also be badly worn. The only SOLUTION is to buy a different side bead.

PROBLEM #19: *I can't keep my complex molder from jumping its fence and digging into the profile.*

SOLUTION: The fences on most molding planes are incredibly low, sometimes 1/8" or less. I've found—particularly when I'm working a hardwood—some complex molders want to jump. My SOLUTION is to install a fence extension of an extra 1/4" or more. This is a modification I've seen on some antique planes when they arrive in my shop, which means an earlier user had trouble with that particular plane. Of course, if the plane has either rarity and/or financial value, you might not want to modify it in this way.

Scrapers

PROBLEM #20: *I've got a nice burr on the iron in my Stanley (Lie-Nielsen) #112, but I can't get it to cut, even though the edge projects below the sole of the scraper.*

SOLUTION: Not all burrs are alike. You have to adjust the angle of the iron holder to match the cutting angle of each burr. In cross section, each burr resembles a fish hook. In some alignments, the bottom of that hook rides on the surface, making it impossible to take a shaving, but if you tilt the hook forward far enough, the sharp point will begin to cut.

Any Plane

PROBLEM #21: *My metal bench plane/block plane/joinery plane/ scraper leaves scratches on the work surface.*

SOLUTION: You probably have a metal burr on the sole of your plane. These are most common around the outside of the sole or around the mouth. Run your fingers over these areas. If you find a burr, remove it with a bit of sandpaper. I use 320 grit.

PROBLEM #22: *The irons in my Veritas planes seem to be stuck in place.*

SOLUTION: Maybe nobody else is dense enough to be confounded by this problem, but I was—the first few times I re-sharpened the irons in my Veritas planes. Unlike other planemakers, Veritas has installed a pair or two of set screws on each side of each plane shell. These set screws bottom out on the edges of the plane's iron in order to hold it in the correct position. Because they were features to which I was unaccustomed, I had forgotten about them the first three or four times I tried to pull the irons. The SOLUTION, of course, is to get out an Allen wrench and back off these set screws.

PROBLEM #23: *I've oiled and waxed my metal planes, but I'm still getting rust spots.*

SOLUTION: There aren't any easy SOLUTIONs. The same thing is happening to my planes. I've used the camellia oil Lie-Nielsen recommends, and it hasn't eliminated rust spots. The only sure way to beat this problem is to keep the planes in boxes or plane socks. I've also had pretty good luck with planes stored in cabinets. At least in my shop, the problem seems to be exposure of plane irons and steels to the open air.

Bibliography

Biographical Record of Fairfield County, Ohio. New York and Chicago: The S. J. Clarke Publishing Company, 1902.

(Website) Clark, Joshua. *The Stanley Bench Plane Page*. www.hyperkitten.com/tools/stanley_bench_plane

Correspondence and notes compiled by Max Stebelton of Lancaster, Ohio, about the lives of John and George Strode

Dunbar, Michael. *Restoring, Tuning & Using Classic Woodworking Tools*. New York: Sterling Publishing, Inc., 1989.

Fisher, Dennis & Rosebrook, Donald. *Wooden Plow Planes: A Celebration of the Planemaker's Art*. Mendham NJ: The Astragal Press, 2003.

Hack, Garret. *The Hand Plane Book*. Newtown CT: The Taunton Press, 1999.

Illustrated Catalog and Invoice Price List of Wooden Bench Planes, Moulding Tools etc. Manufactured by the Greenfield Tool Company (1872). Fitzwilliam N. H.: Ken Roberts Publishing Company, 1978.

Krause, John Thorvald. *TATHS (Tool and Trades History Society) Newsletter. Winter 2004*.

Leach, Patrick. *The Superior Works: Patrick's Blood and Gore* (website). www.supertool.com/StanleyBG/stan0.htm

Lee, Leonard. *The Complete Guide to Sharpening*. Newtown Ct.: The Taunton Press, 1995.

McConnell, Don. *Traditional Molding Techniques: The Basics* (DVD). Warren ME:Lie-Nielsen Toolworks, Inc., No date.

Moskowitz, Joel. *Norris Metal Planes*. Mendham NJ: The Astragal Press, 2002.

Moxon, Joseph. *Mechanik Exercises or the Doctrine of Handy-Works*. London: J. Moxon, 1678.

Pollack, Emil & Martyl. *A Guide to the Makers of American Wooden Planes. 4th Edition*. Mendham NJ: The Astragal Pres, 2001.

Rees, Jane and Mark. *Christopher Gabriel and the Tool Trade in 18th Century London*. Mendham NJ: The Astragal Press, 1997.

Rees, Mark. *TATHS Newsletter*. Summer 1999.

Roberts, Kenneth D. *Scottish & English Planes by Spiers and Norris*. Fitzwillian NH: Ken Roberts Publishing Co., 1991.

Roberts, Kenneth D. *Wooden Planes in the 19th Century: Supplement to First Edition*. Fitzwillian NH: Ken   Roberts Publishing Co., 1978.

Roberts, Kenneth D. *Wooden Planes in the 19th Century: Volume 2*. Fitzwillian NH: Ken Roberts Publishing Co., 1983.

The Sandusky Tool Company Catalog No. 25. Mendham NJ: The Astragal Press, No year.

Saalman, R. A. *Dictionary of Woodworking Tools*. Newton CT: The Taunton Press, 1989.

Sellens, Alvin. *The Stanley Plane: A History and Descriptive Inventory*. Early American Industries Association, 1975.

Taylor, Vic. *Woodworker's Dictionary*. Pownal VT: Storey Publishing, 1990.

Whelan, John. *The Wooden Plane: Its History, Form, and Function*. Mendham NJ: The Astragal Press, 1993.

Wood, Jack P. *Stanley Tools: A Price Guide*. Gas City IN: L-W Book Sales, No Year.

Index